ETHER

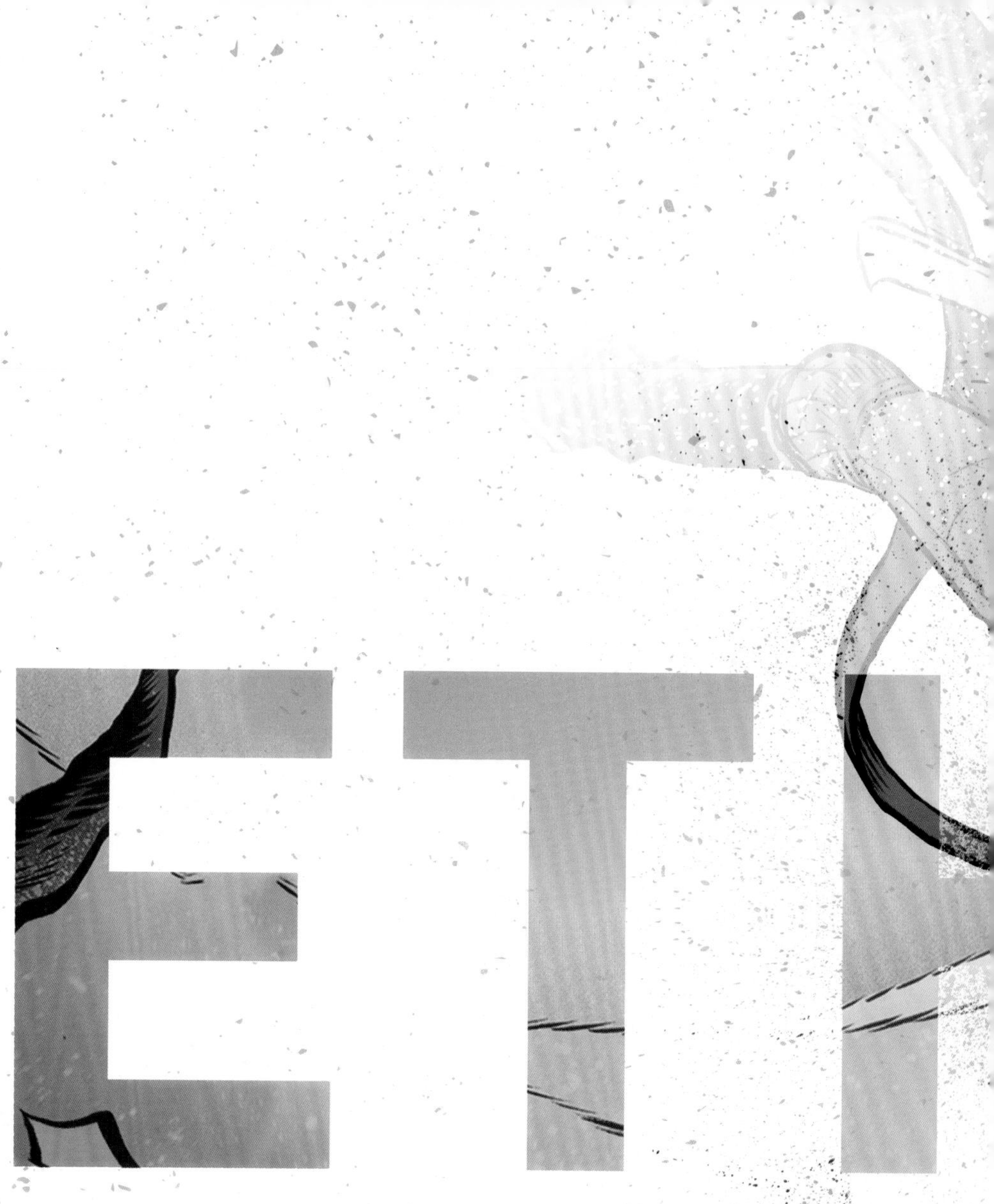

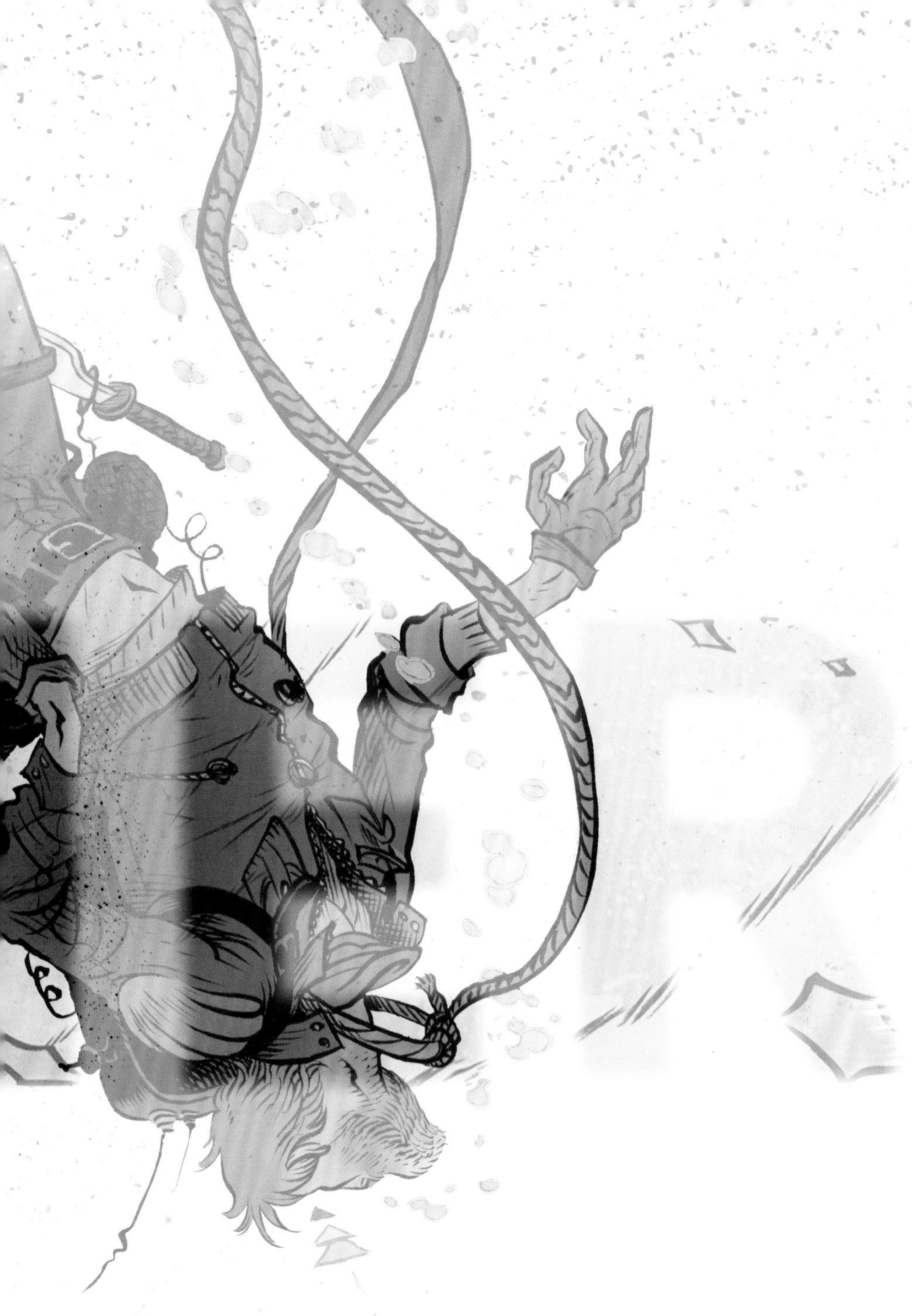

DEATH OF THE LAST GOLDEN BLAZE

script by **MATT KINDT**
art by **DAVID RUBÍN**

DARK HORSE BOOKS

president and publisher **MIKE RICHARDSON**

editor **DANIEL CHABON**

assistant editor **CARDNER CLARK**

designer **ANITA MAGAÑA**

digital art technician **MELISSA MARTIN**

This volume collects issues #1–#5 of the Dark Horse Comics series *Ether*.

Names: Kindt, Matt, author. | Rubín, David, 1977- artist.
Title: Ether. Volume 1, Death of the last golden blaze / script by Matt Kindt
 ; art by David Rubín.
Other titles: Death of the last golden blaze
Description: First edition. | Milwaukie, OR : Dark Horse Books, 2017. | "This
 volume collects issues #1-#5 of the Dark Horse Comics series Ether"
Identifiers: LCCN 2017003067 | ISBN 9781506701745 (paperback)
Subjects: LCSH: Comic books, strips, etc. | BISAC: COMICS & GRAPHIC NOVELS /
 Fantasy. | COMICS & GRAPHIC NOVELS / Crime & Mystery. | COMICS & GRAPHIC
 NOVELS / Science Fiction.
Classification: LCC PN6728.E85 K56 2017 | DDC 741.5/973--dc23
LC record available at https://lccn.loc.gov/2017003067

Published by
Dark Horse Books
A division of Dark Horse Comics LLC
10956 SE Main Street
Milwaukie, OR 97222

DarkHorse.com

To find a comics shop in your area, visit comicshoplocator.com.
International Licensing: (503) 905-2377

First edition: July 2017
ISBN 978-1-50670-174-5

3 5 7 9 10 8 6 4 2
Printed in China

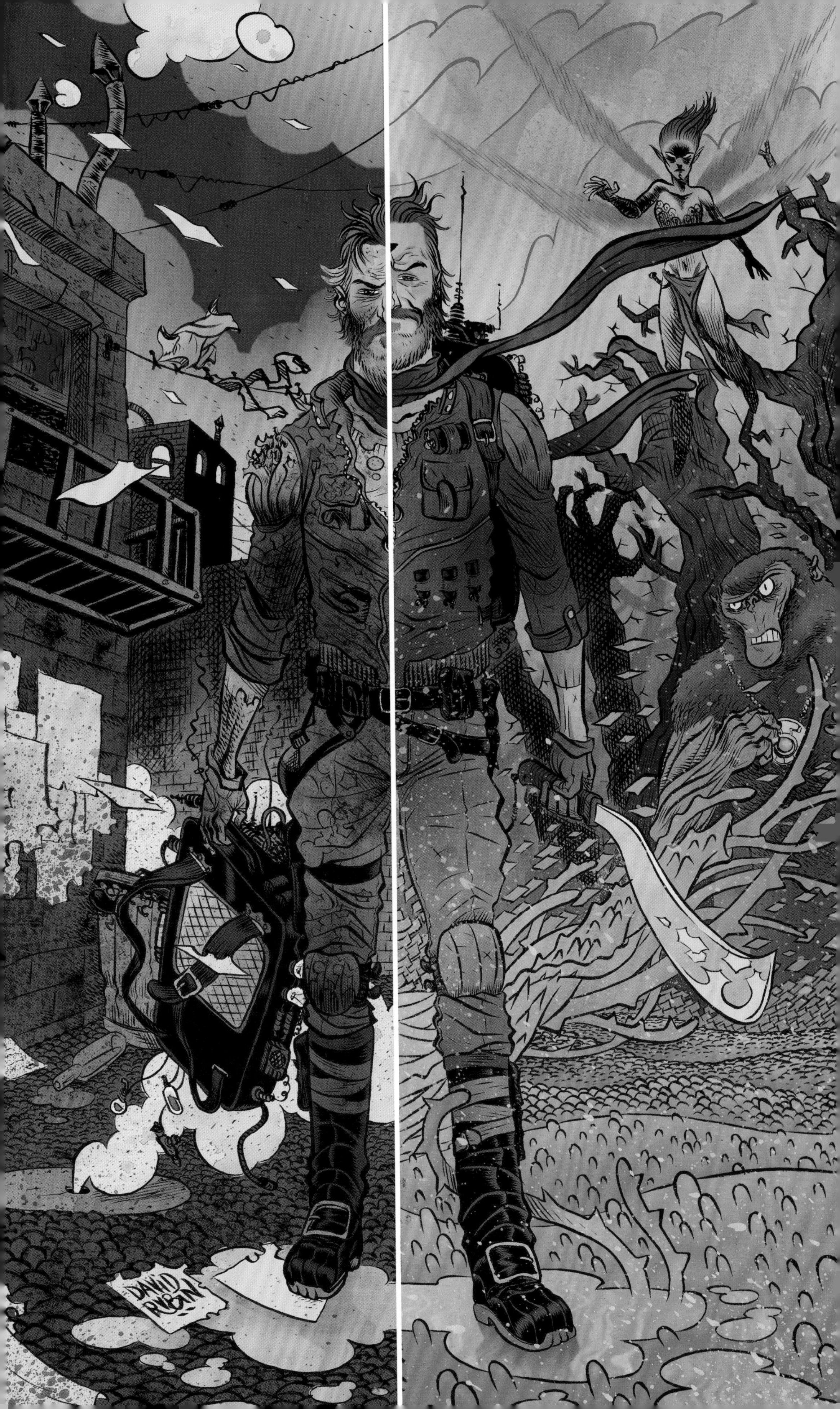
DAVID RUBIN

1

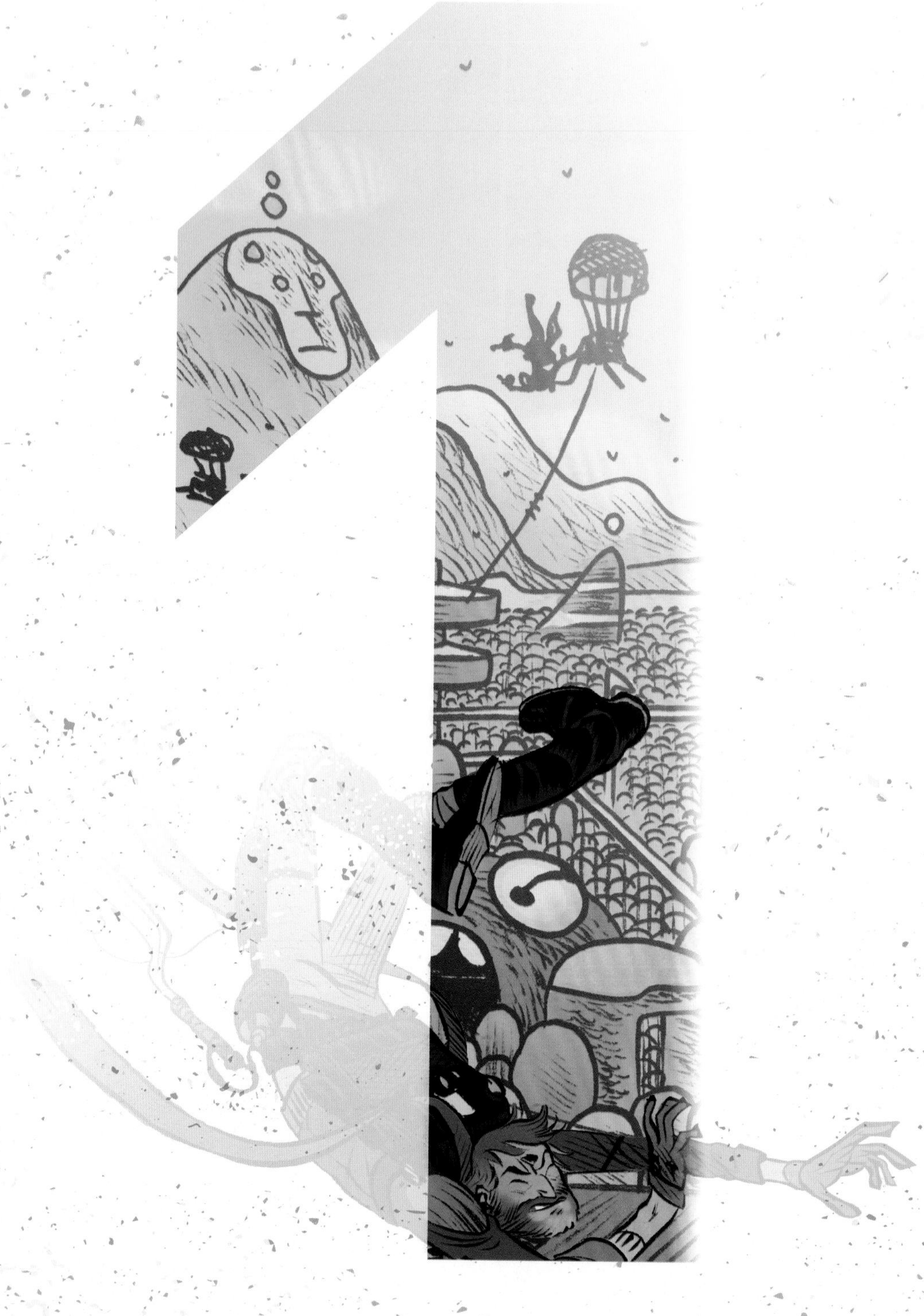

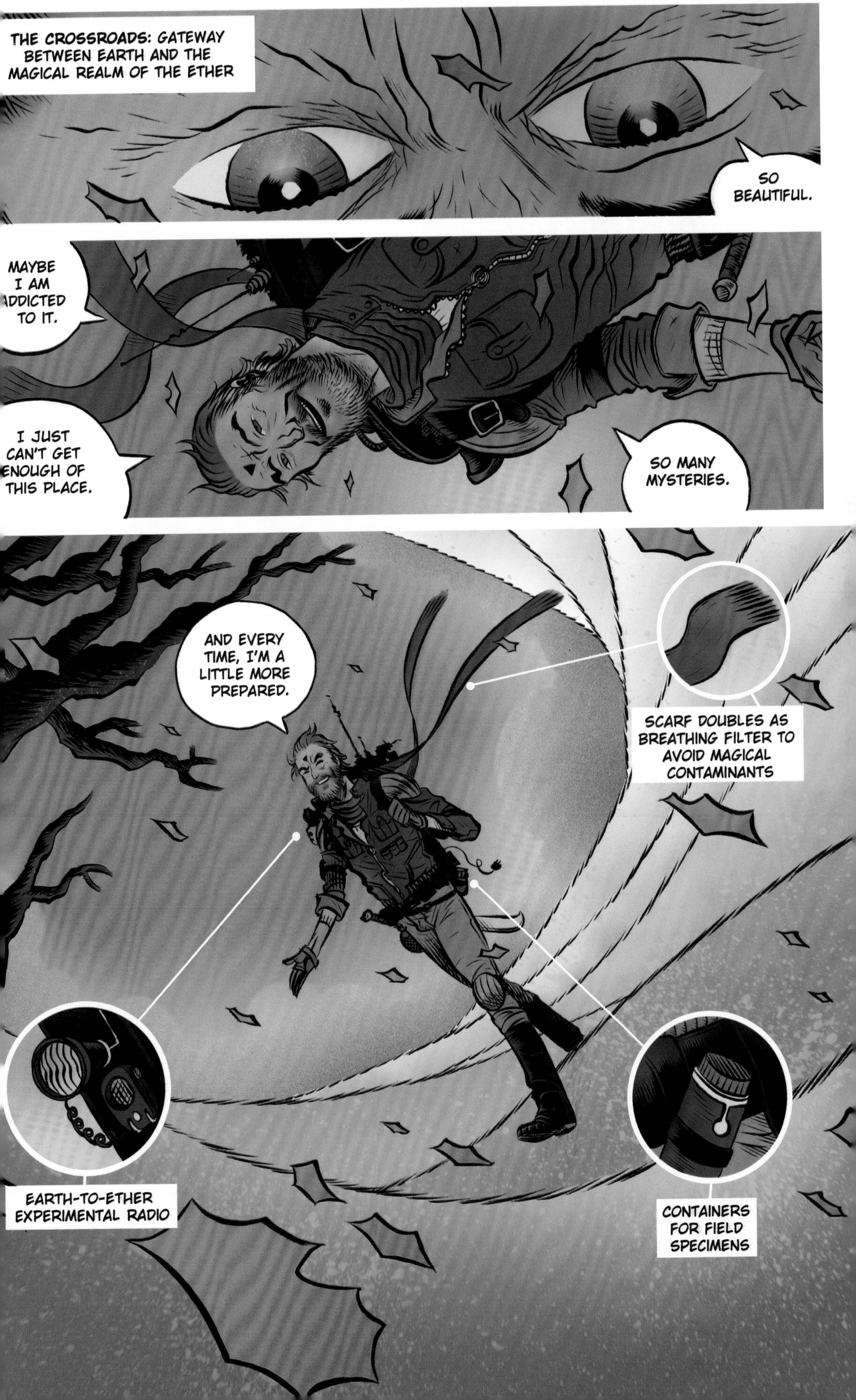
THE CROSSROADS: GATEWAY BETWEEN EARTH AND THE MAGICAL REALM OF THE ETHER
SO BEAUTIFUL.
MAYBE I AM ADDICTED TO IT.
I JUST CAN'T GET ENOUGH OF THIS PLACE.
SO MANY MYSTERIES.
AND EVERY TIME, I'M A LITTLE MORE PREPARED.
SCARF DOUBLES AS BREATHING FILTER TO AVOID MAGICAL CONTAMINANTS
EARTH-TO-ETHER EXPERIMENTAL RADIO
CONTAINERS FOR FIELD SPECIMENS

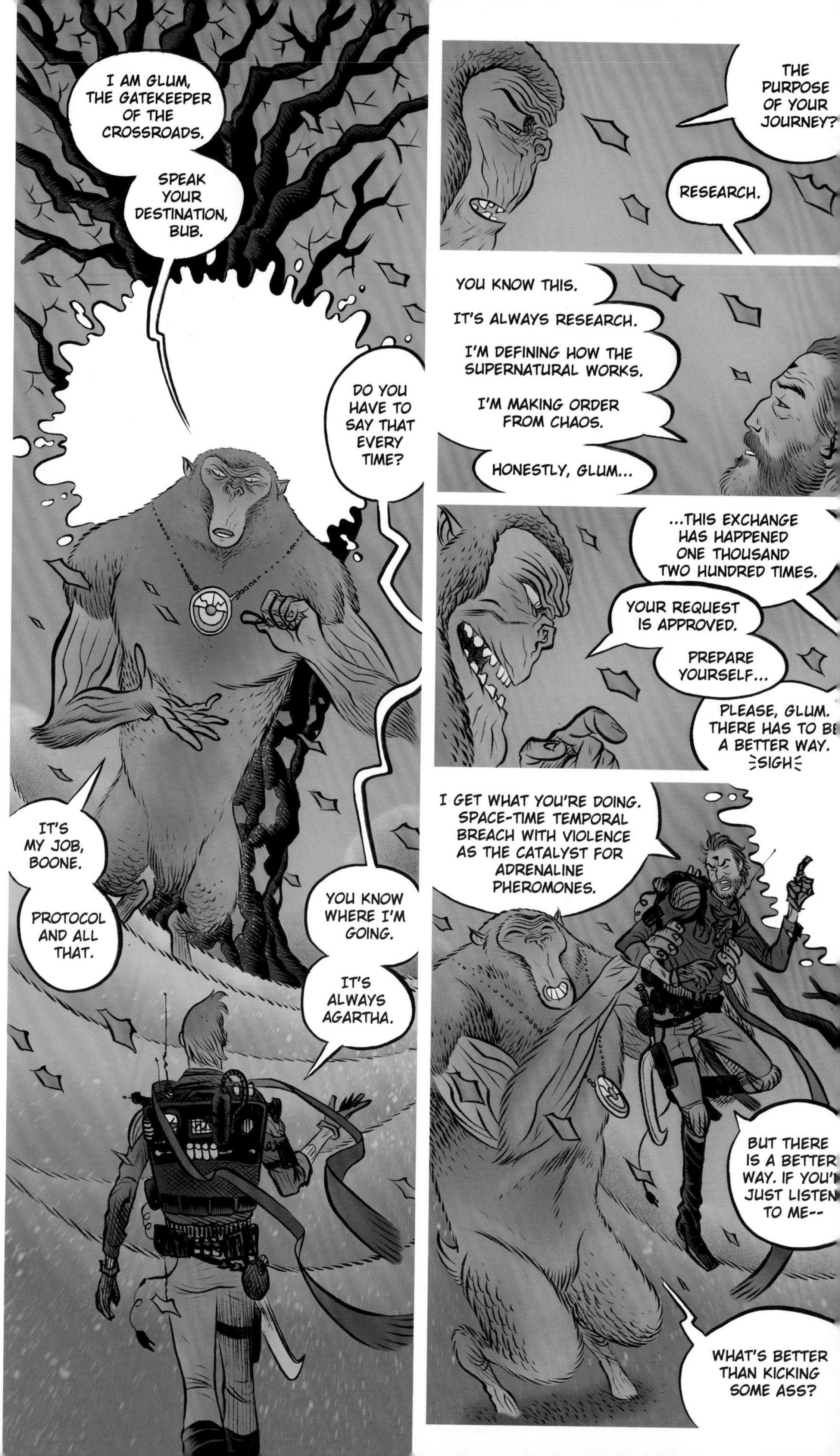

I AM GLUM, THE GATEKEEPER OF THE CROSSROADS.
SPEAK YOUR DESTINATION, BUB.
DO YOU HAVE TO SAY THAT EVERY TIME?
IT'S MY JOB, BOONE.
PROTOCOL AND ALL THAT.
YOU KNOW WHERE I'M GOING.
IT'S ALWAYS AGARTHA.
THE PURPOSE OF YOUR JOURNEY?
RESEARCH.
YOU KNOW THIS.
IT'S ALWAYS RESEARCH.
I'M DEFINING HOW THE SUPERNATURAL WORKS.
I'M MAKING ORDER FROM CHAOS.
HONESTLY, GLUM...
...THIS EXCHANGE HAS HAPPENED ONE THOUSAND TWO HUNDRED TIMES.
YOUR REQUEST IS APPROVED.
PREPARE YOURSELF...
PLEASE, GLUM. THERE HAS TO BE A BETTER WAY. SIGH
I GET WHAT YOU'RE DOING. SPACE-TIME TEMPORAL BREACH WITH VIOLENCE AS THE CATALYST FOR ADRENALINE PHEROMONES.
BUT THERE IS A BETTER WAY. IF YOU'D JUST LISTEN TO ME--
WHAT'S BETTER THAN KICKING SOME ASS?

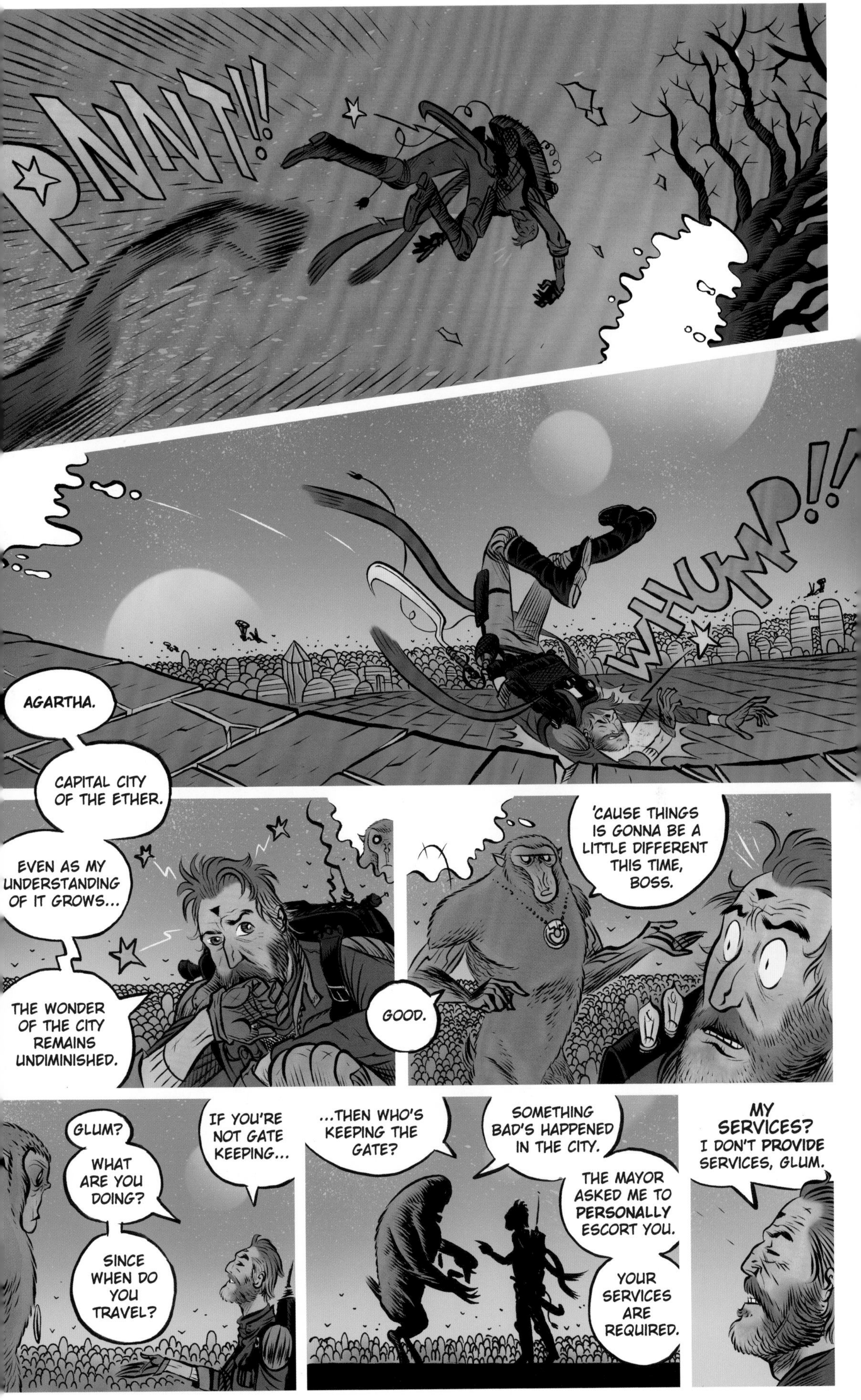
PWANT!!
WHUMP!!
AGARTHA.
CAPITAL CITY OF THE ETHER.
EVEN AS MY UNDERSTANDING OF IT GROWS...
THE WONDER OF THE CITY REMAINS UNDIMINISHED.
GOOD.
'CAUSE THINGS IS GONNA BE A LITTLE DIFFERENT THIS TIME, BOSS.
GLUM?
WHAT ARE YOU DOING?
SINCE WHEN DO YOU TRAVEL?
IF YOU'RE NOT GATE KEEPING...
...THEN WHO'S KEEPING THE GATE?
SOMETHING BAD'S HAPPENED IN THE CITY.
THE MAYOR ASKED ME TO PERSONALLY ESCORT YOU.
YOUR SERVICES ARE REQUIRED.
MY SERVICES? I DON'T PROVIDE SERVICES, GLUM.

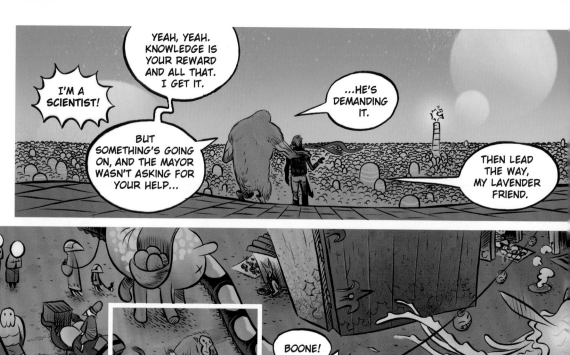

I'M A SCIENTIST!

YEAH, YEAH. KNOWLEDGE IS YOUR REWARD AND ALL THAT. I GET IT.

...HE'S DEMANDING IT.

BUT SOMETHING'S GOING ON, AND THE MAYOR WASN'T ASKING FOR YOUR HELP...

THEN LEAD THE WAY, MY LAVENDER FRIEND.

BOONE!

BOONE DIAS!

TIPO? HOW ARE YOU?

DO YOU HAVE SOMETHING FOR ME TODAY?

YES, YES!

A VERY RARE ITEM!

PLEASE, EXAMINE!

FAP!

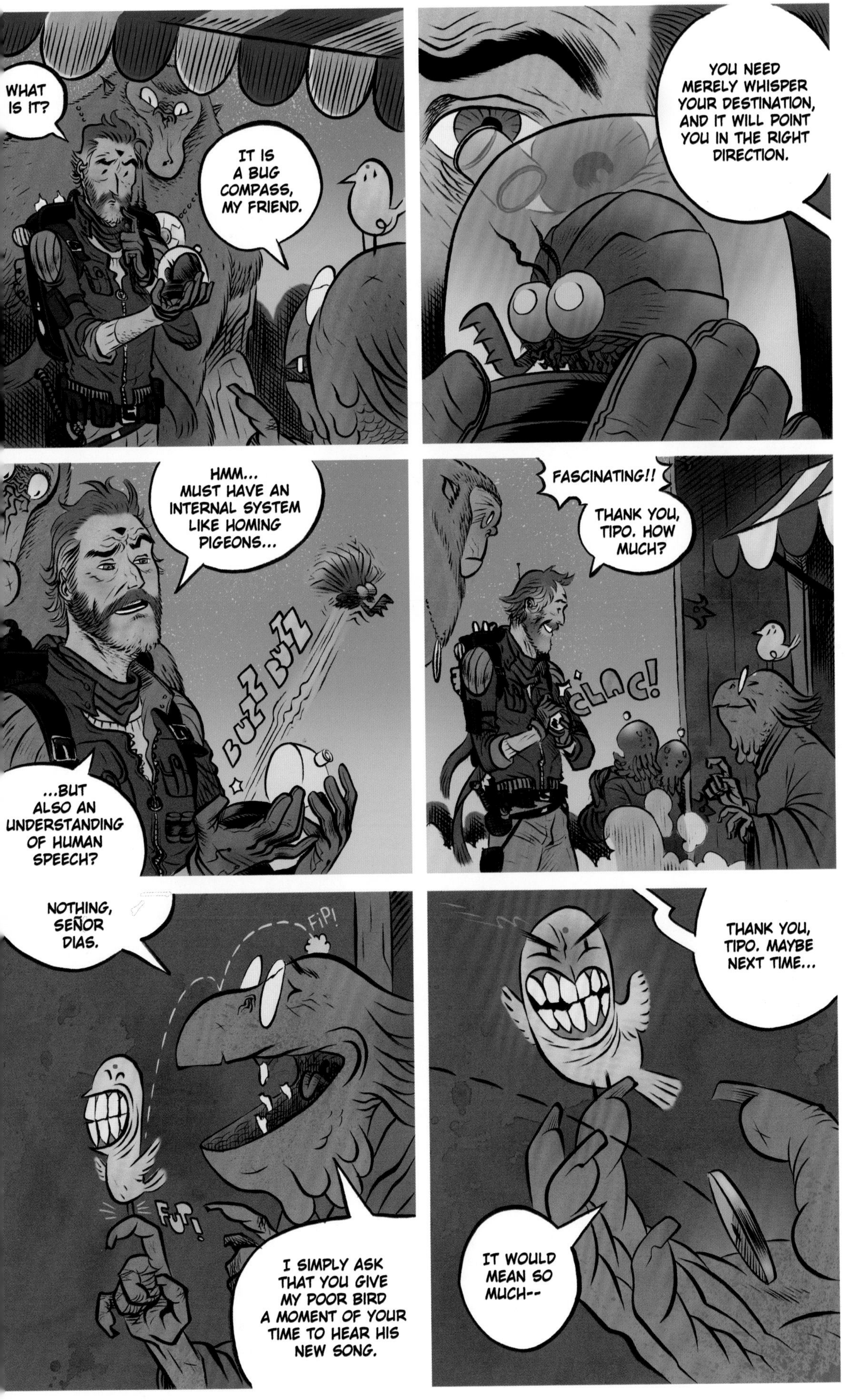
WHAT IS IT?
IT IS A BUG COMPASS, MY FRIEND.
YOU NEED MERELY WHISPER YOUR DESTINATION, AND IT WILL POINT YOU IN THE RIGHT DIRECTION.
HMM... MUST HAVE AN INTERNAL SYSTEM LIKE HOMING PIGEONS...
BUZZ BUZZ
...BUT ALSO AN UNDERSTANDING OF HUMAN SPEECH?
FASCINATING!!
THANK YOU, TIPO. HOW MUCH?
CLAC!
NOTHING, SEÑOR DIAS.
FIP!
FUP!
I SIMPLY ASK THAT YOU GIVE MY POOR BIRD A MOMENT OF YOUR TIME TO HEAR HIS NEW SONG.
THANK YOU, TIPO. MAYBE NEXT TIME...
IT WOULD MEAN SO MUCH--

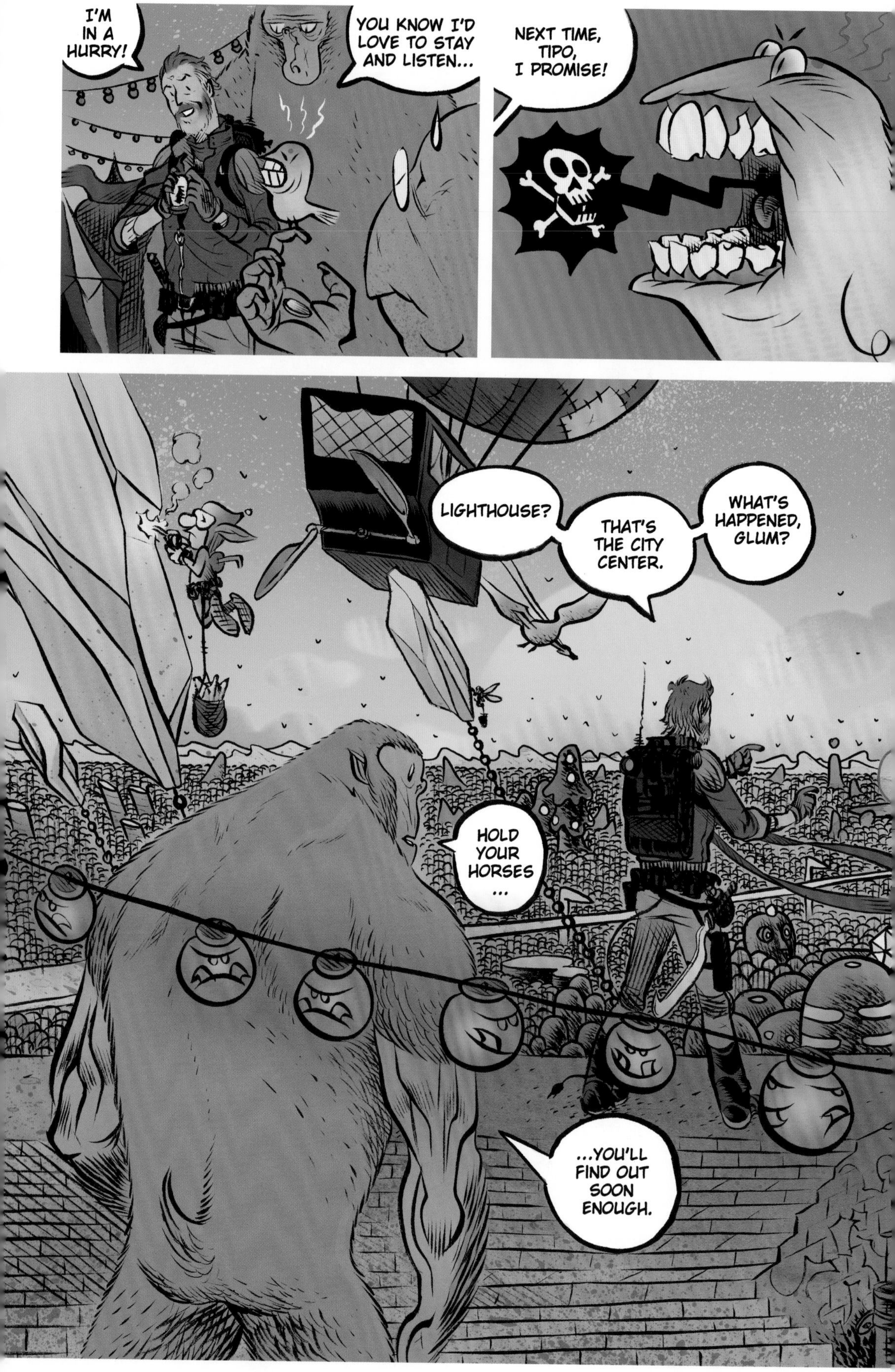
I'M IN A HURRY!
YOU KNOW I'D LOVE TO STAY AND LISTEN...
NEXT TIME, TIPO, I PROMISE!
LIGHTHOUSE?
THAT'S THE CITY CENTER.
WHAT'S HAPPENED, GLUM?
HOLD YOUR HORSES ...
...YOU'LL FIND OUT SOON ENOUGH.

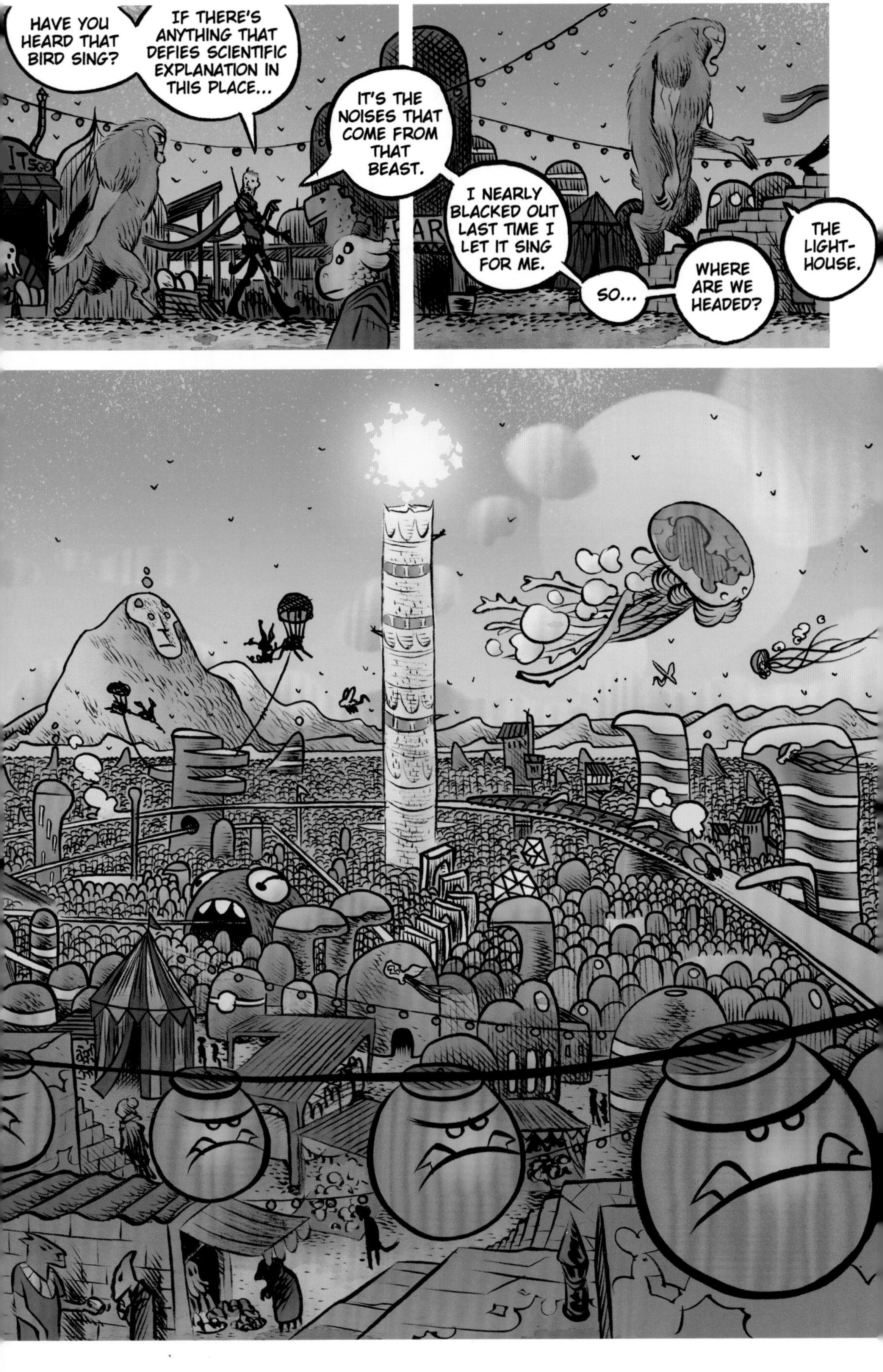
HAVE YOU HEARD THAT BIRD SING?
IF THERE'S ANYTHING THAT DEFIES SCIENTIFIC EXPLANATION IN THIS PLACE...
IT'S THE NOISES THAT COME FROM THAT BEAST.
I NEARLY BLACKED OUT LAST TIME I LET IT SING FOR ME.
SO...
WHERE ARE WE HEADED?
THE LIGHT-HOUSE.

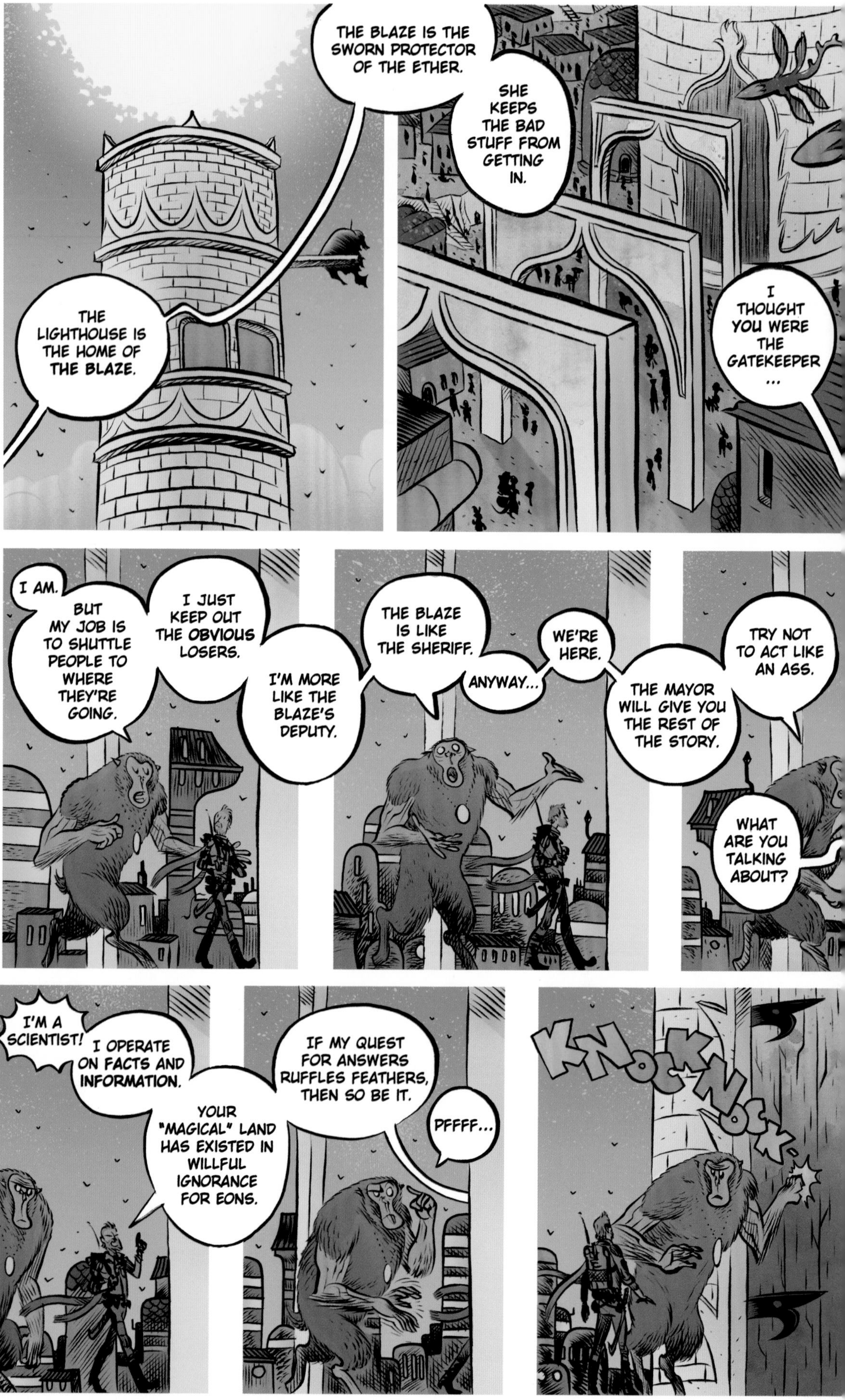
THE BLAZE IS THE SWORN PROTECTOR OF THE ETHER.
THE LIGHTHOUSE IS THE HOME OF THE BLAZE.
SHE KEEPS THE BAD STUFF FROM GETTING IN.
I THOUGHT YOU WERE THE GATEKEEPER ...
I AM.
BUT MY JOB IS TO SHUTTLE PEOPLE TO WHERE THEY'RE GOING.
I JUST KEEP OUT THE OBVIOUS LOSERS.
I'M MORE LIKE THE BLAZE'S DEPUTY.
THE BLAZE IS LIKE THE SHERIFF.
ANYWAY...
WE'RE HERE.
THE MAYOR WILL GIVE YOU THE REST OF THE STORY.
TRY NOT TO ACT LIKE AN ASS.
WHAT ARE YOU TALKING ABOUT?
I'M A SCIENTIST!
I OPERATE ON FACTS AND INFORMATION.
YOUR "MAGICAL" LAND HAS EXISTED IN WILLFUL IGNORANCE FOR EONS.
IF MY QUEST FOR ANSWERS RUFFLES FEATHERS, THEN SO BE IT.
PFFFF...
KNOCK KNOCK

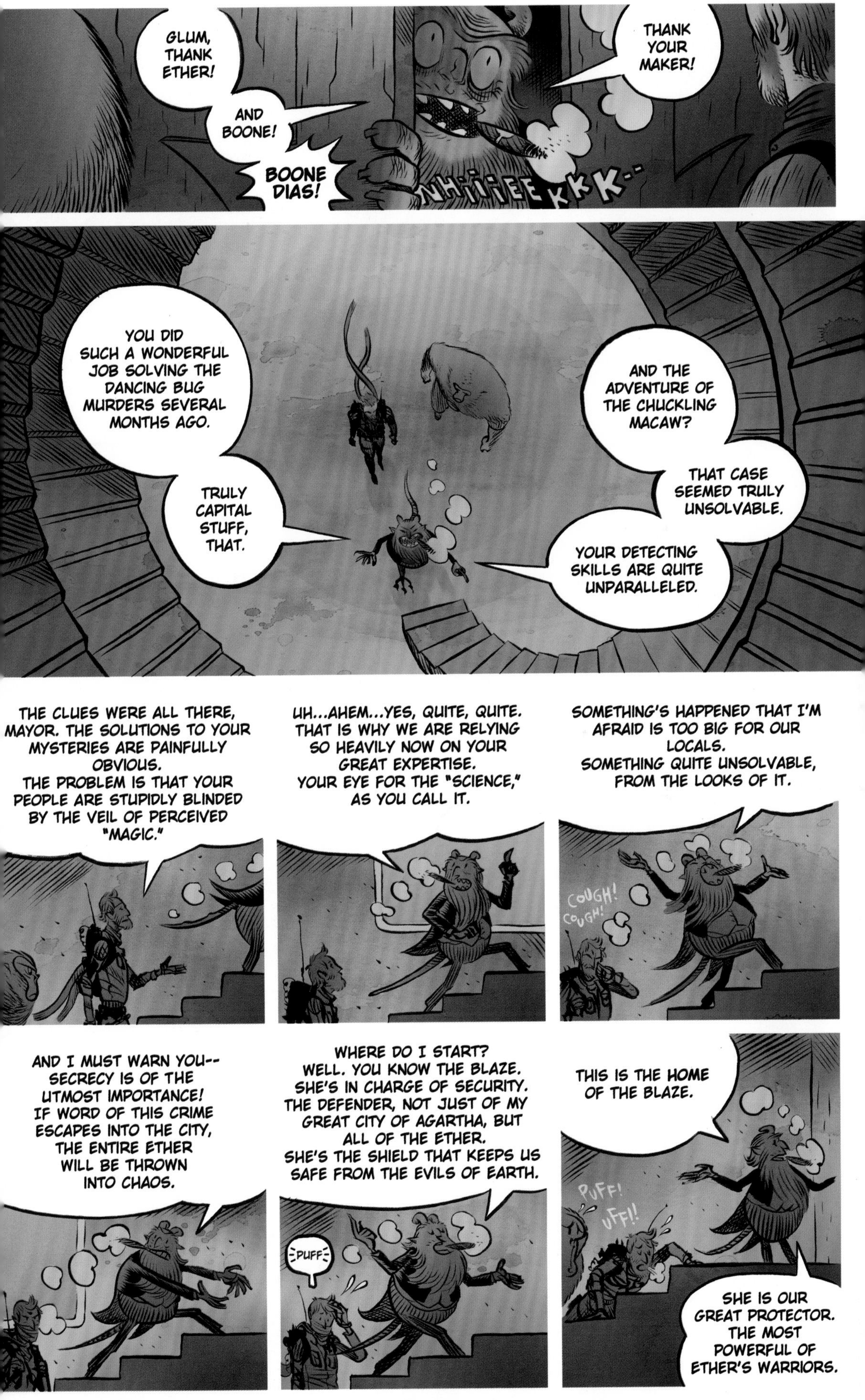
GLUM, THANK ETHER!
AND BOONE!
BOONE DIAS!
THANK YOUR MAKER!
NHIIIEEKKK--
YOU DID SUCH A WONDERFUL JOB SOLVING THE DANCING BUG MURDERS SEVERAL MONTHS AGO.
TRULY CAPITAL STUFF, THAT.
AND THE ADVENTURE OF THE CHUCKLING MACAW?
THAT CASE SEEMED TRULY UNSOLVABLE.
YOUR DETECTING SKILLS ARE QUITE UNPARALLELED.
THE CLUES WERE ALL THERE, MAYOR. THE SOLUTIONS TO YOUR MYSTERIES ARE PAINFULLY OBVIOUS. THE PROBLEM IS THAT YOUR PEOPLE ARE STUPIDLY BLINDED BY THE VEIL OF PERCEIVED "MAGIC."
UH...AHEM...YES, QUITE, QUITE. THAT IS WHY WE ARE RELYING SO HEAVILY NOW ON YOUR GREAT EXPERTISE. YOUR EYE FOR THE "SCIENCE," AS YOU CALL IT.
SOMETHING'S HAPPENED THAT I'M AFRAID IS TOO BIG FOR OUR LOCALS. SOMETHING QUITE UNSOLVABLE, FROM THE LOOKS OF IT.
COUGH! COUGH!
AND I MUST WARN YOU-- SECRECY IS OF THE UTMOST IMPORTANCE! IF WORD OF THIS CRIME ESCAPES INTO THE CITY, THE ENTIRE ETHER WILL BE THROWN INTO CHAOS.
WHERE DO I START? WELL. YOU KNOW THE BLAZE. SHE'S IN CHARGE OF SECURITY. THE DEFENDER, NOT JUST OF MY GREAT CITY OF AGARTHA, BUT ALL OF THE ETHER. SHE'S THE SHIELD THAT KEEPS US SAFE FROM THE EVILS OF EARTH.
PUFF
THIS IS THE HOME OF THE BLAZE.
PUFF! UFF!!
SHE IS OUR GREAT PROTECTOR. THE MOST POWERFUL OF ETHER'S WARRIORS.

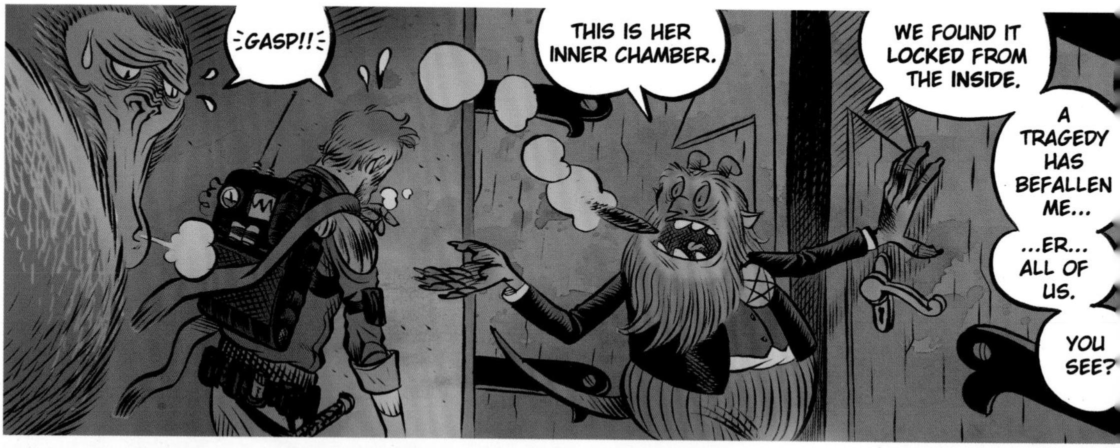
GASP!!
THIS IS HER INNER CHAMBER.
WE FOUND IT LOCKED FROM THE INSIDE.
A TRAGEDY HAS BEFALLEN ME...
...ER... ALL OF US.
YOU SEE?

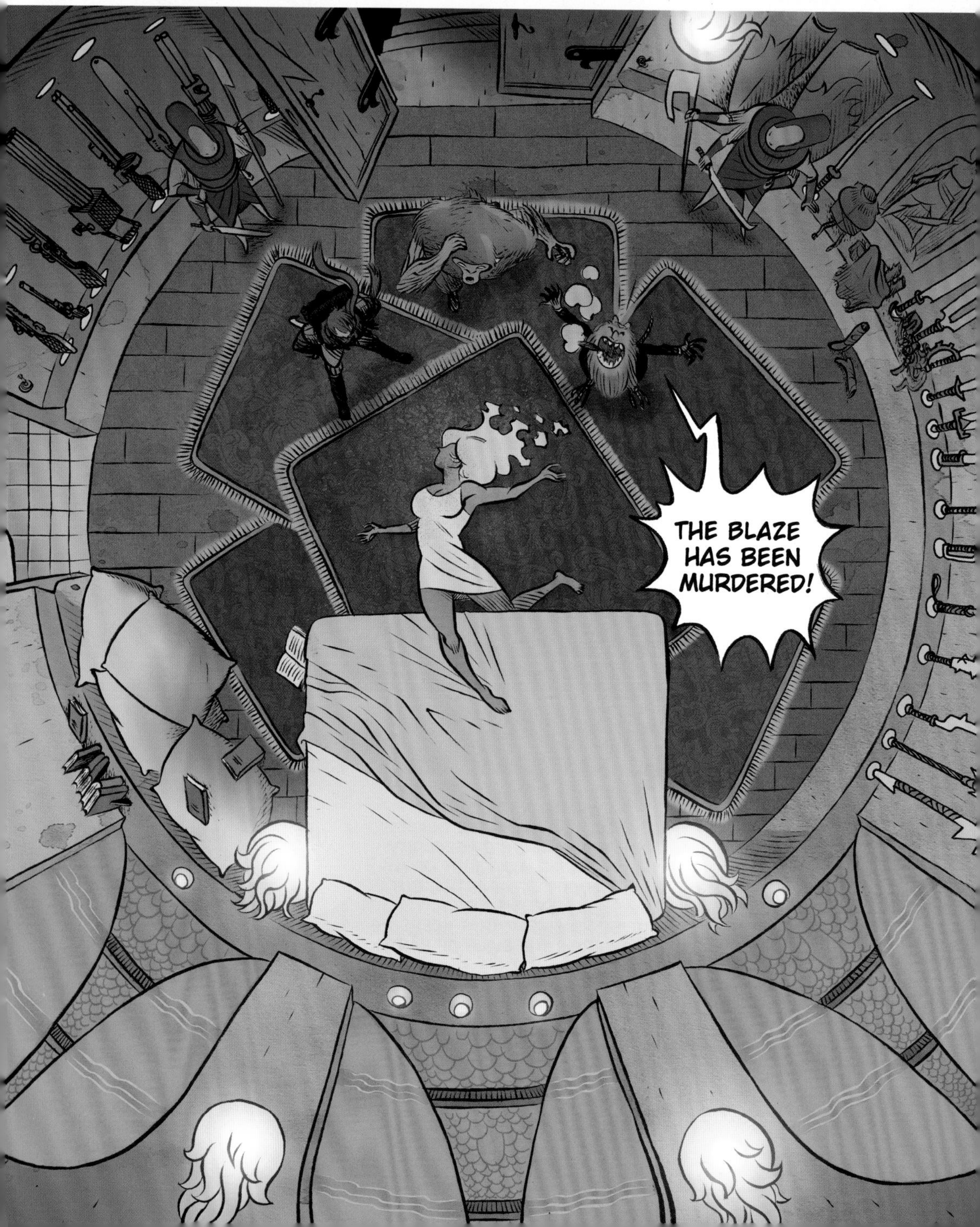
THE BLAZE HAS BEEN MURDERED!

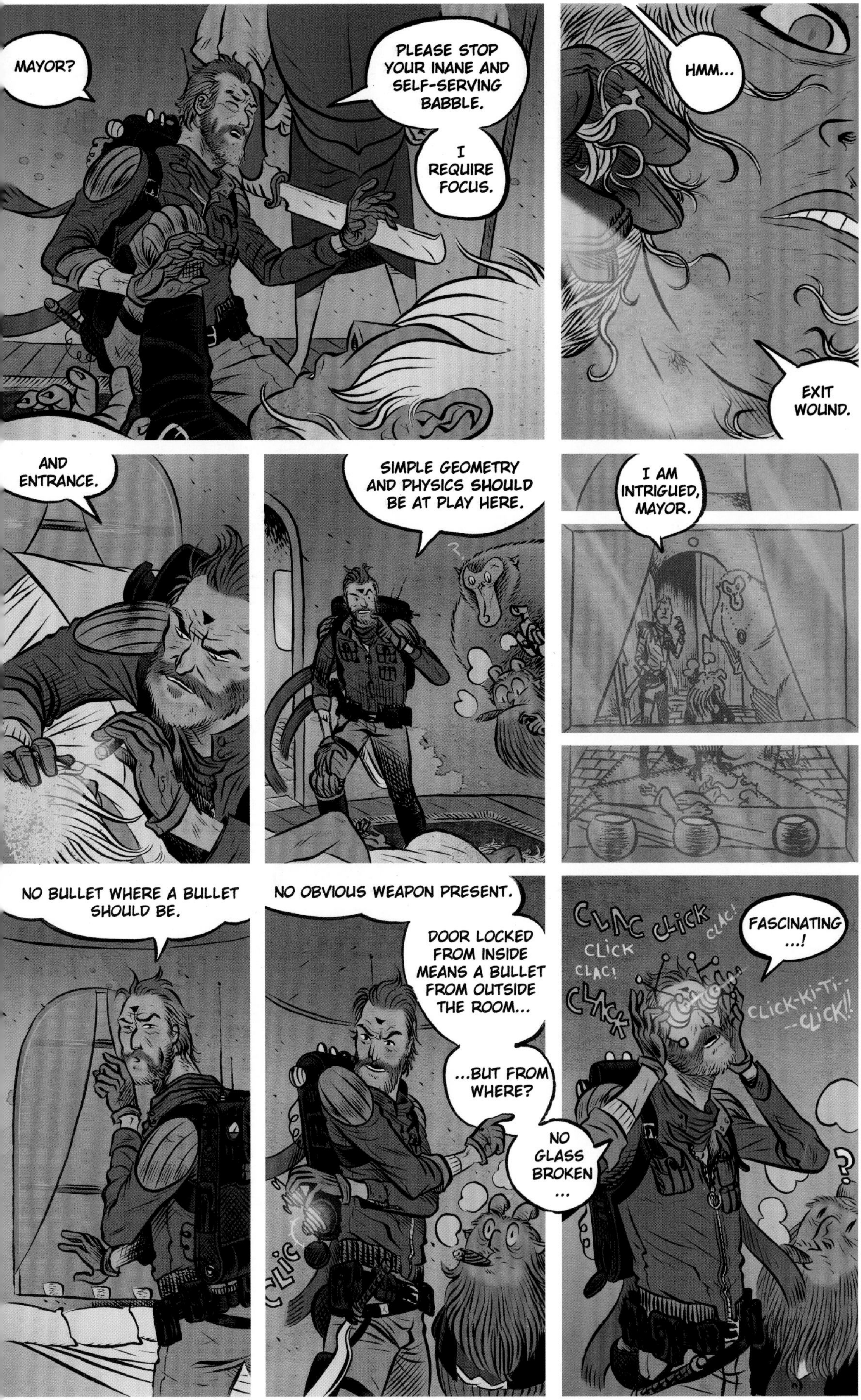
MAYOR?
PLEASE STOP YOUR INANE AND SELF-SERVING BABBLE.
I REQUIRE FOCUS.
HMM...
EXIT WOUND.
AND ENTRANCE.
SIMPLE GEOMETRY AND PHYSICS SHOULD BE AT PLAY HERE.
?
I AM INTRIGUED, MAYOR.
NO BULLET WHERE A BULLET SHOULD BE.
NO OBVIOUS WEAPON PRESENT.
DOOR LOCKED FROM INSIDE MEANS A BULLET FROM OUTSIDE THE ROOM...
...BUT FROM WHERE?
NO GLASS BROKEN ...
CLIC
CLAC CLICK CLAC!
CLICK
CLAC!
CLACK
FASCINATING ...!
CLICK-KI-TI- --CLICK!!
?

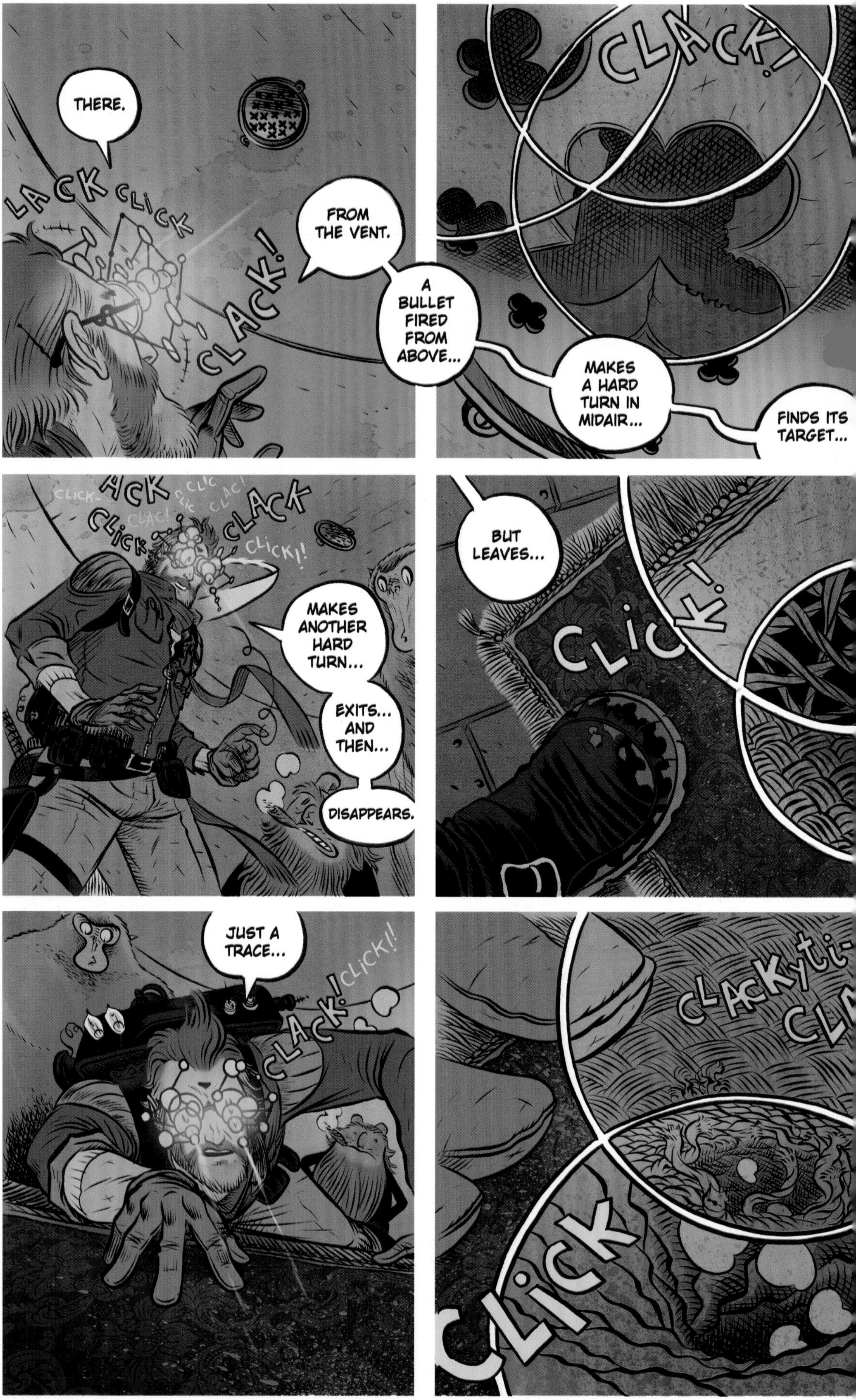
THERE.
LACK CLICK
CLACK!
FROM THE VENT.
A BULLET FIRED FROM ABOVE...
CLACK!
MAKES A HARD TURN IN MIDAIR...
FINDS ITS TARGET...
ACK CLICK CLACK
CLICK-
CLICK!
MAKES ANOTHER HARD TURN...
EXITS... AND THEN...
DISAPPEARS.
BUT LEAVES...
CLICK!
JUST A TRACE...
CLACK! CLICK!
CLACKyti-
CLICK

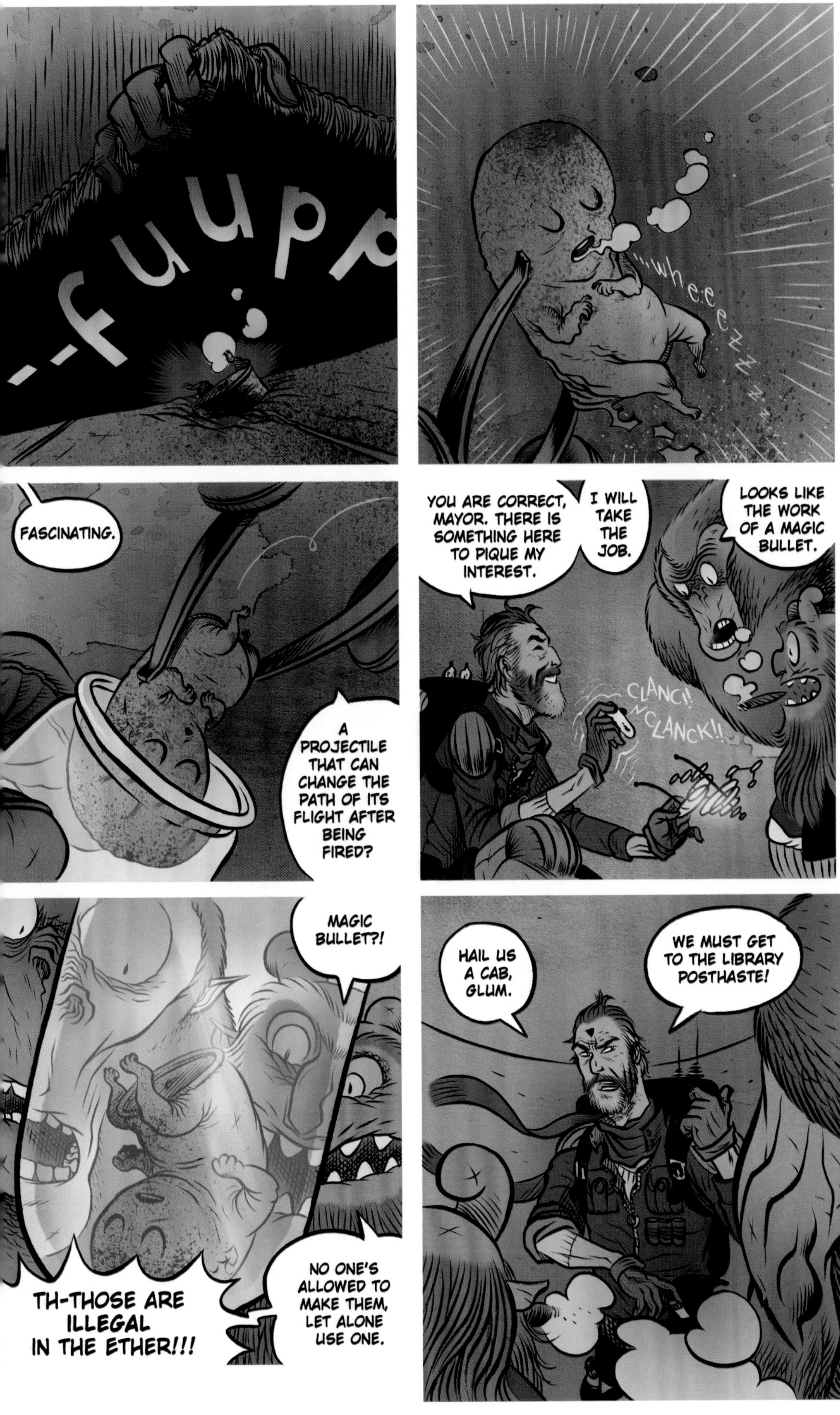
--fuupp
wheeezzz
FASCINATING.
A PROJECTILE THAT CAN CHANGE THE PATH OF ITS FLIGHT AFTER BEING FIRED?
YOU ARE CORRECT, MAYOR. THERE IS SOMETHING HERE TO PIQUE MY INTEREST.
I WILL TAKE THE JOB.
LOOKS LIKE THE WORK OF A MAGIC BULLET.
CLANC!!
CLANCK!!
MAGIC BULLET?!
TH-THOSE ARE ILLEGAL IN THE ETHER!!!
NO ONE'S ALLOWED TO MAKE THEM, LET ALONE USE ONE.
HAIL US A CAB, GLUM.
WE MUST GET TO THE LIBRARY POSTHASTE!

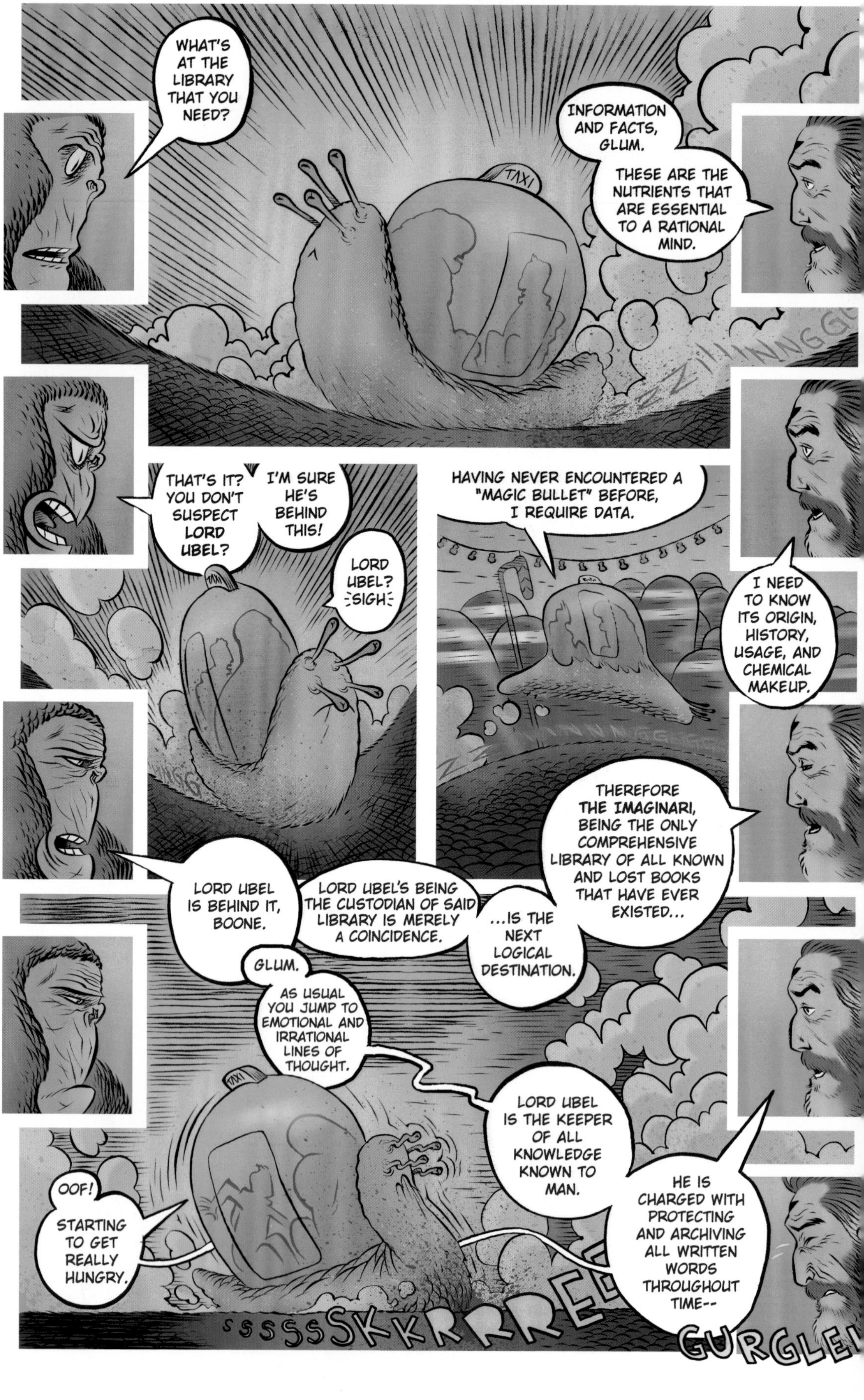

WHAT'S AT THE LIBRARY THAT YOU NEED?
INFORMATION AND FACTS, GLUM.
THESE ARE THE NUTRIENTS THAT ARE ESSENTIAL TO A RATIONAL MIND.
TAXI
ZZZIIIINNGG
THAT'S IT? YOU DON'T SUSPECT LORD UBEL?
I'M SURE HE'S BEHIND THIS!
LORD UBEL? SIGH
HAVING NEVER ENCOUNTERED A "MAGIC BULLET" BEFORE, I REQUIRE DATA.
I NEED TO KNOW ITS ORIGIN, HISTORY, USAGE, AND CHEMICAL MAKEUP.
THEREFORE THE IMAGINARI, BEING THE ONLY COMPREHENSIVE LIBRARY OF ALL KNOWN AND LOST BOOKS THAT HAVE EVER EXISTED...
LORD UBEL IS BEHIND IT, BOONE.
LORD UBEL'S BEING THE CUSTODIAN OF SAID LIBRARY IS MERELY A COINCIDENCE.
...IS THE NEXT LOGICAL DESTINATION.
GLUM.
AS USUAL YOU JUMP TO EMOTIONAL AND IRRATIONAL LINES OF THOUGHT.
LORD UBEL IS THE KEEPER OF ALL KNOWLEDGE KNOWN TO MAN.
HE IS CHARGED WITH PROTECTING AND ARCHIVING ALL WRITTEN WORDS THROUGHOUT TIME--
OOF!
STARTING TO GET REALLY HUNGRY.
sssssSKKRRREE
GURGLE

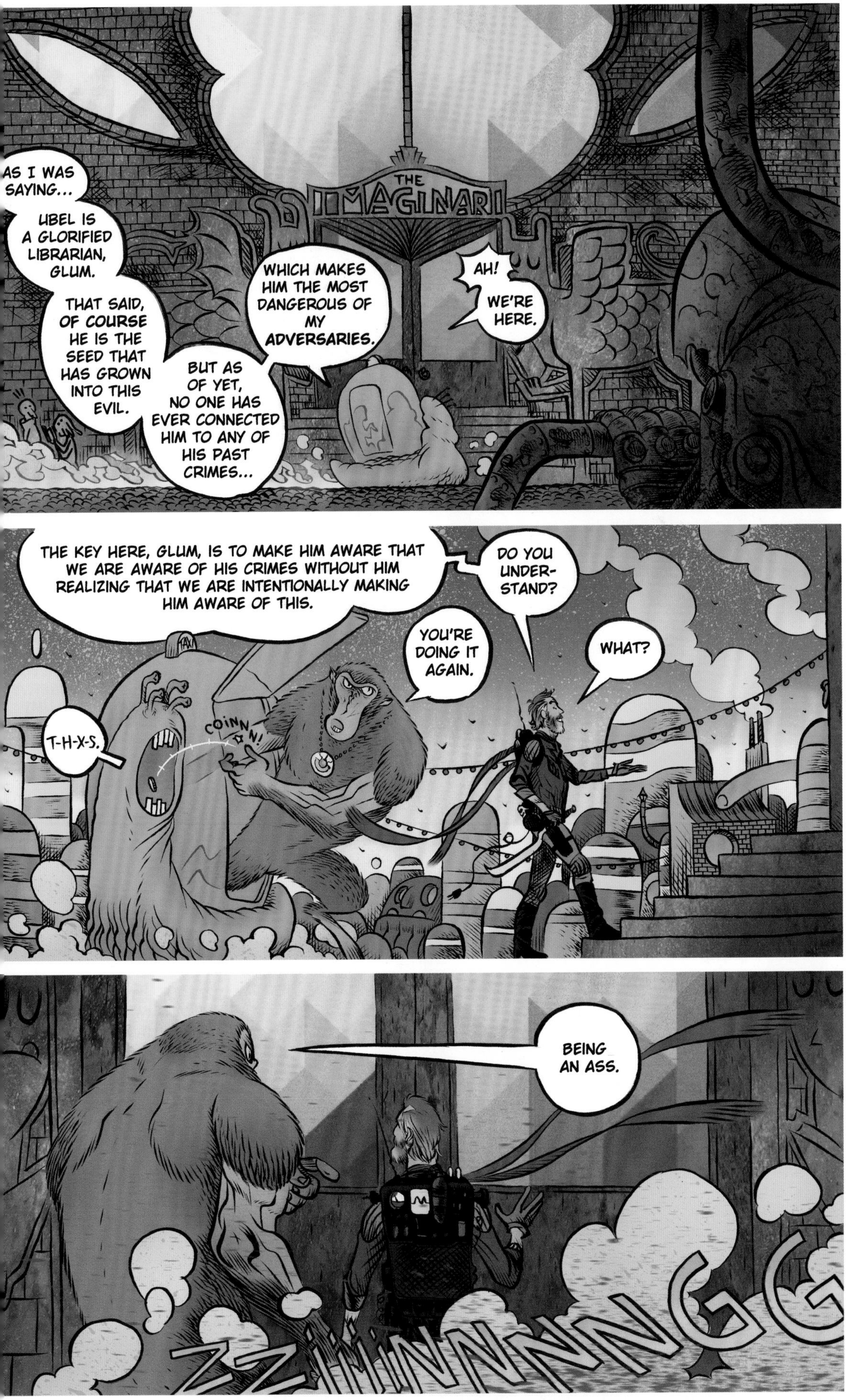
THE
IMAGINARI
AS I WAS SAYING...
UBEL IS A GLORIFIED LIBRARIAN, GLUM.
THAT SAID, OF COURSE HE IS THE SEED THAT HAS GROWN INTO THIS EVIL.
BUT AS OF YET, NO ONE HAS EVER CONNECTED HIM TO ANY OF HIS PAST CRIMES...
WHICH MAKES HIM THE MOST DANGEROUS OF MY ADVERSARIES.
AH!
WE'RE HERE.
THE KEY HERE, GLUM, IS TO MAKE HIM AWARE THAT WE ARE AWARE OF HIS CRIMES WITHOUT HIM REALIZING THAT WE ARE INTENTIONALLY MAKING HIM AWARE OF THIS.
DO YOU UNDER-STAND?
TAXI
T-H-X-S.
COINNN!
YOU'RE DOING IT AGAIN.
WHAT?
BEING AN ASS.
ZZHIINNNNNGG

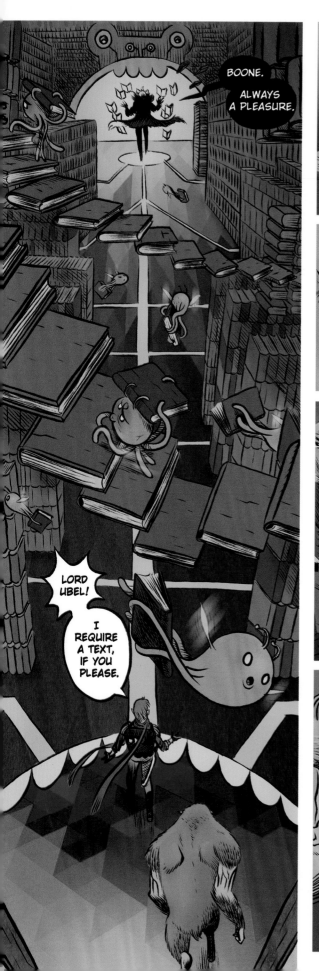

BOONE.

ALWAYS A PLEASURE.

LORD UBEL!

I REQUIRE A TEXT, IF YOU PLEASE.

WELCOME, ONCE AGAIN, WITHIN MY HALLOWED HALLS.

I HAVE ALWAYS ADMIRED YOUR QUEST FOR ABSOLUTE TRUTH.

I JUST HAVE ONE REQUEST...

...PLEASE ASK YOUR TRAINED APE TO KEEP HIS DISTANCE.

HRM...

OF COURSE. SANITATION STANDARDS IN REGARDS TO YOUR VAST WEALTH OF KNOWLEDGE MUST ALWAYS BE OBSERVED, GLUM?

I REQUIRE TWO VOLUMES, IF YOU WOULD DO ME THE HONOR.

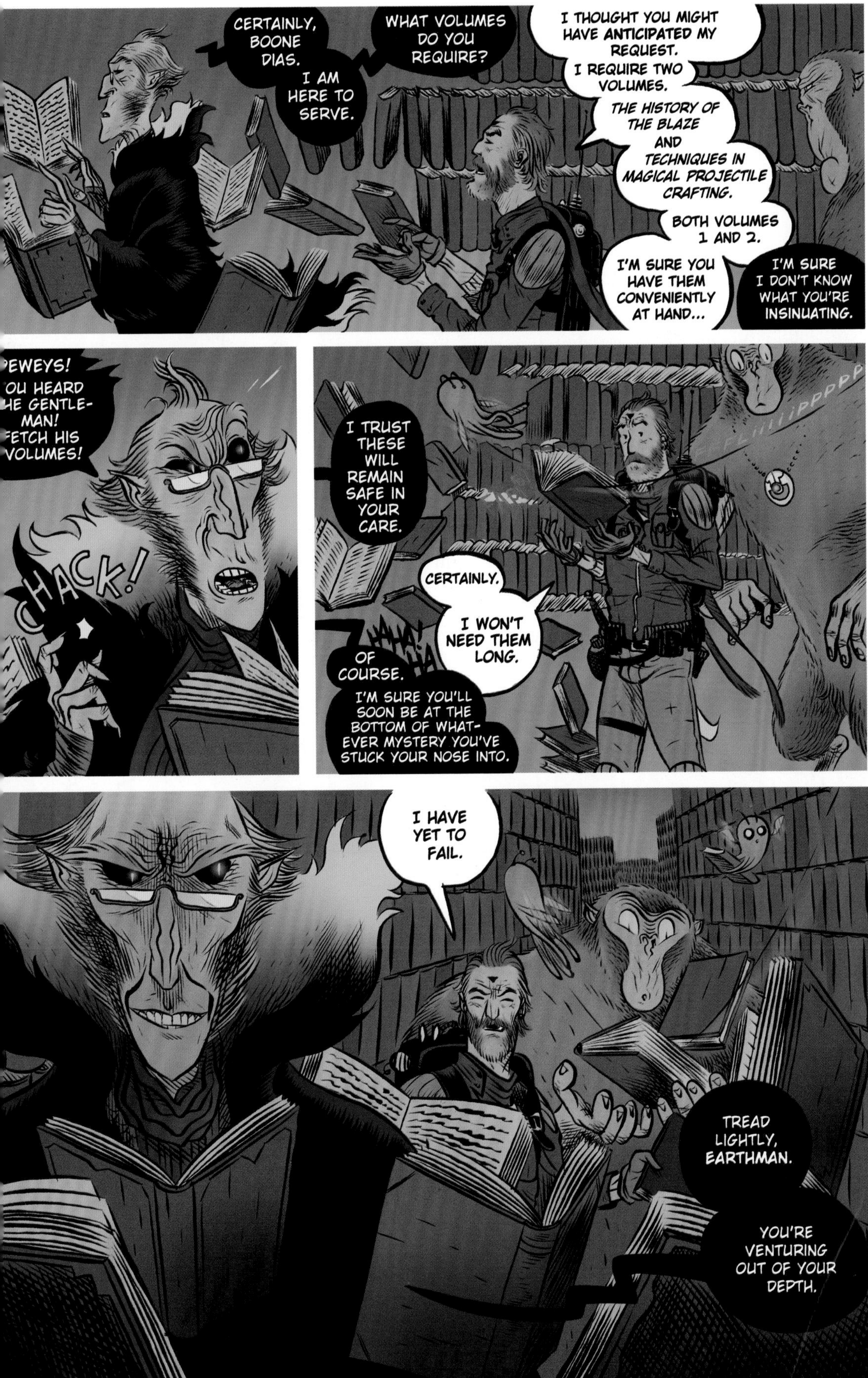
CERTAINLY, BOONE DIAS.
I AM HERE TO SERVE.
WHAT VOLUMES DO YOU REQUIRE?
I THOUGHT YOU MIGHT HAVE ANTICIPATED MY REQUEST.
I REQUIRE TWO VOLUMES.
THE HISTORY OF THE BLAZE
AND
TECHNIQUES IN MAGICAL PROJECTILE CRAFTING.
BOTH VOLUMES 1 AND 2.
I'M SURE YOU HAVE THEM CONVENIENTLY AT HAND...
I'M SURE I DON'T KNOW WHAT YOU'RE INSINUATING.
EWEYS! OU HEARD HE GENTLE-MAN! FETCH HIS VOLUMES!
CHACK!
I TRUST THESE WILL REMAIN SAFE IN YOUR CARE.
FFFLIIIIIPPPPP
CERTAINLY.
I WON'T NEED THEM LONG.
HAHA! HA
OF COURSE.
I'M SURE YOU'LL SOON BE AT THE BOTTOM OF WHAT-EVER MYSTERY YOU'VE STUCK YOUR NOSE INTO.
I HAVE YET TO FAIL.
TREAD LIGHTLY, EARTHMAN.
YOU'RE VENTURING OUT OF YOUR DEPTH.

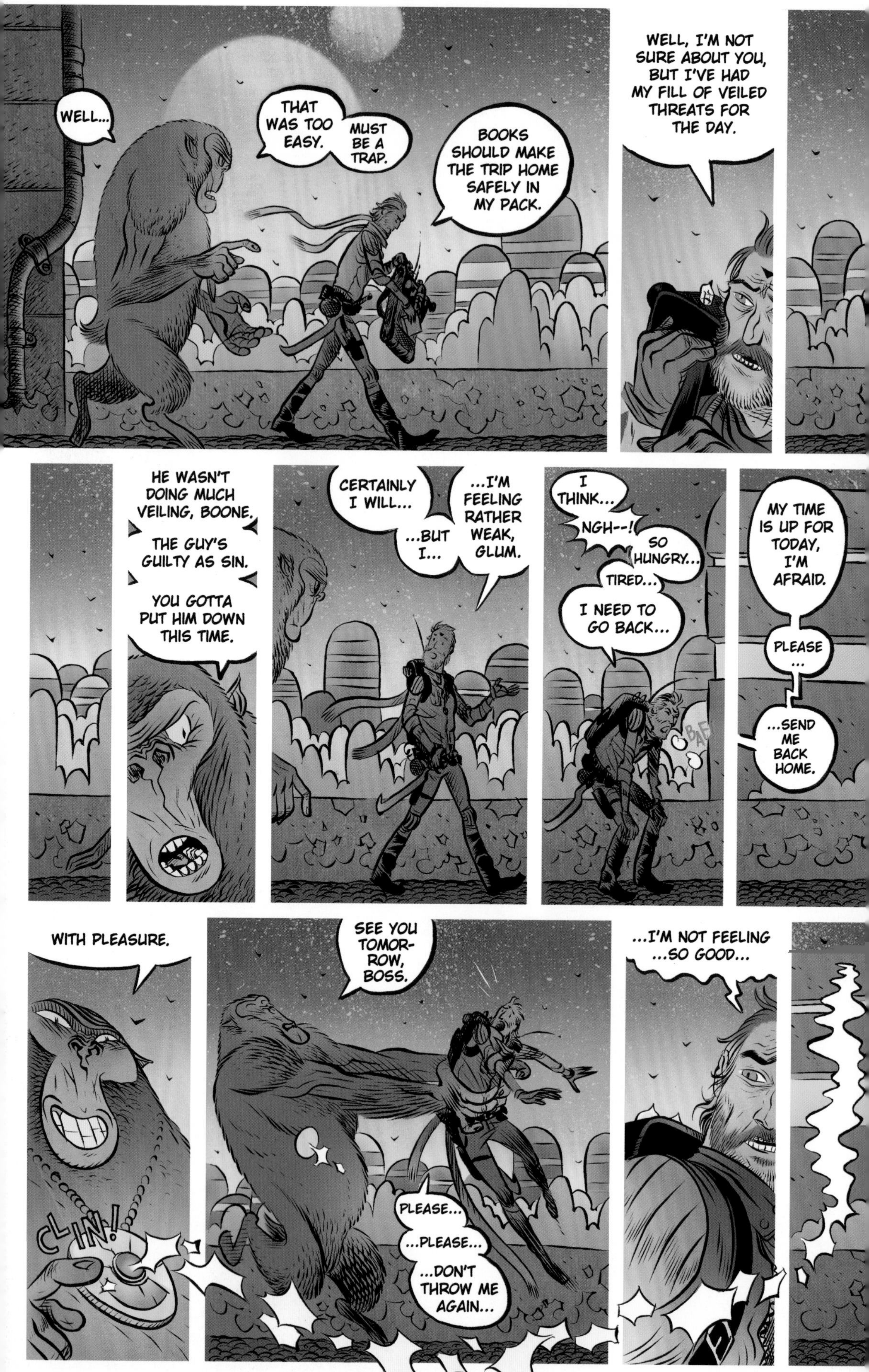
WELL...
THAT WAS TOO EASY.
MUST BE A TRAP.
BOOKS SHOULD MAKE THE TRIP HOME SAFELY IN MY PACK.
WELL, I'M NOT SURE ABOUT YOU, BUT I'VE HAD MY FILL OF VEILED THREATS FOR THE DAY.
HE WASN'T DOING MUCH VEILING, BOONE.
THE GUY'S GUILTY AS SIN.
YOU GOTTA PUT HIM DOWN THIS TIME.
CERTAINLY I WILL...
...BUT I...
...I'M FEELING RATHER WEAK, GLUM.
I THINK...
NGH--!
SO HUNGRY...
TIRED...
I NEED TO GO BACK...
BAF
MY TIME IS UP FOR TODAY, I'M AFRAID.
PLEASE...
...SEND ME BACK HOME.
WITH PLEASURE.
CLIN!
SEE YOU TOMOR-ROW, BOSS.
PLEASE...
...PLEASE...
...DON'T THROW ME AGAIN...
...I'M NOT FEELING ...SO GOOD...

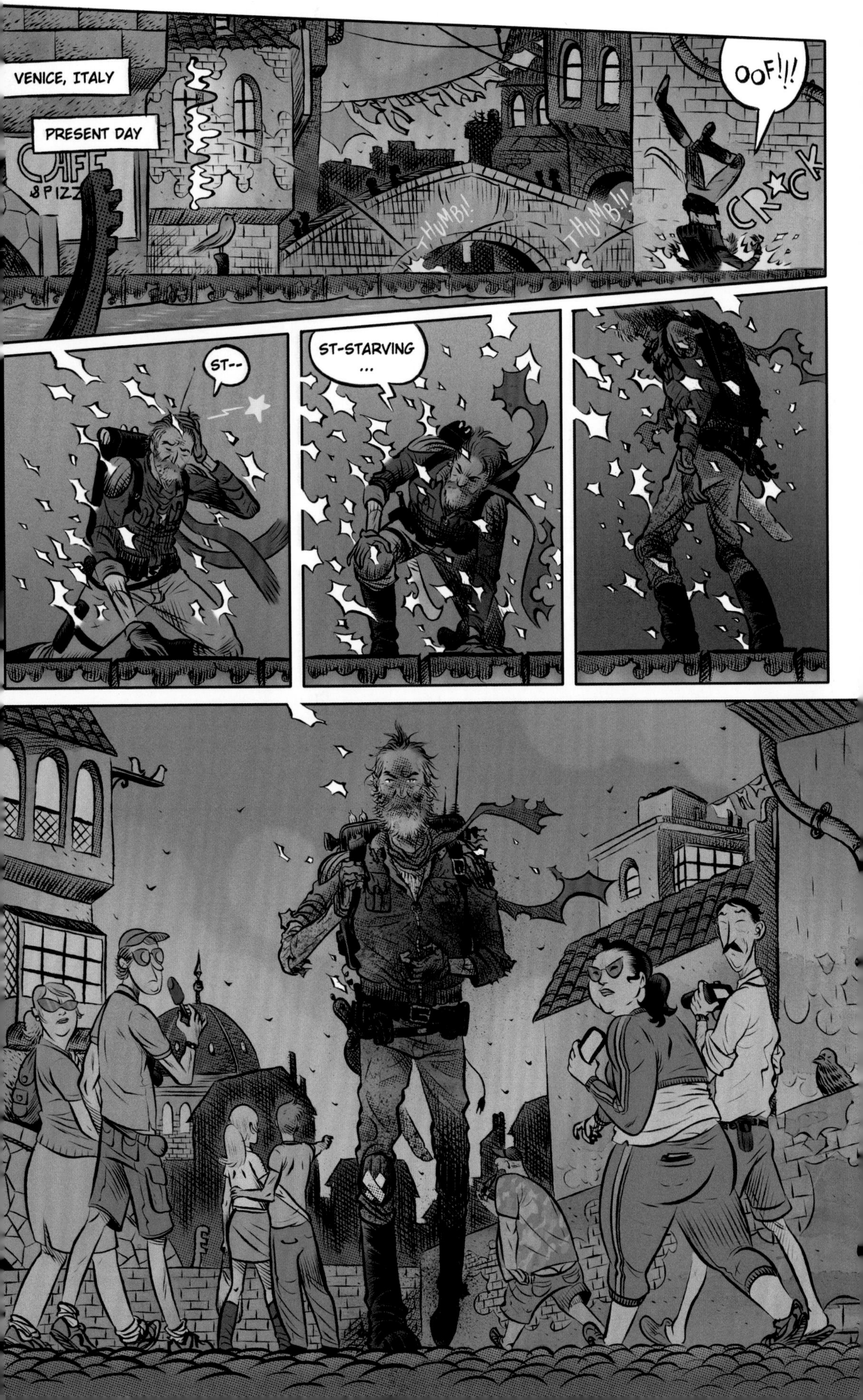
VENICE, ITALY
PRESENT DAY
CAFE
& PIZZ
THUMB!
THUMB!!!
OOF!!!
CRACK
ST--
ST-STARVING
...

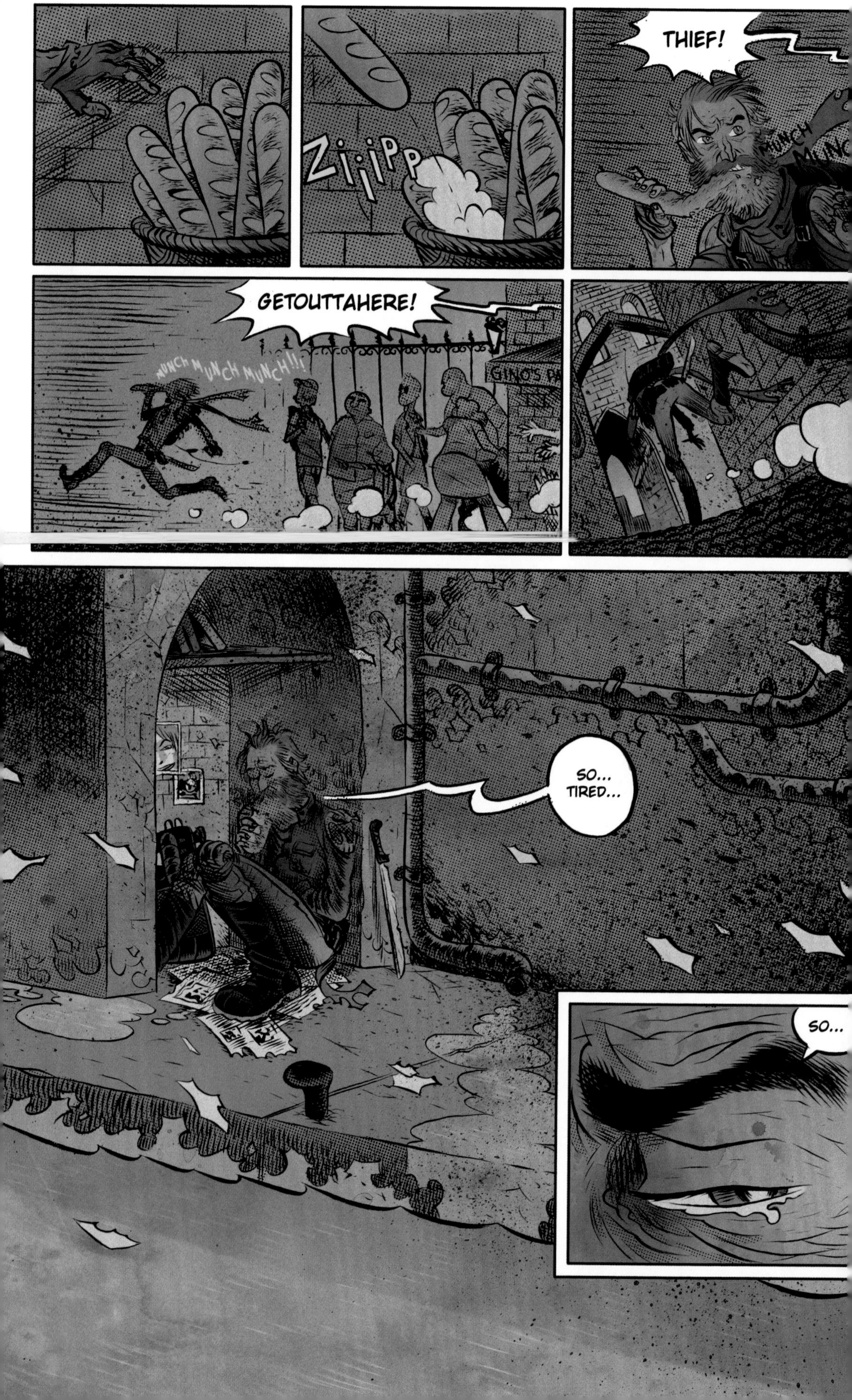

ZIIIPP
THIEF!
MUNCH MUNCH
GETOUTTAHERE!
MUNCH MUNCH MUNCH!!!
GINO'S
SO... TIRED...
SO...

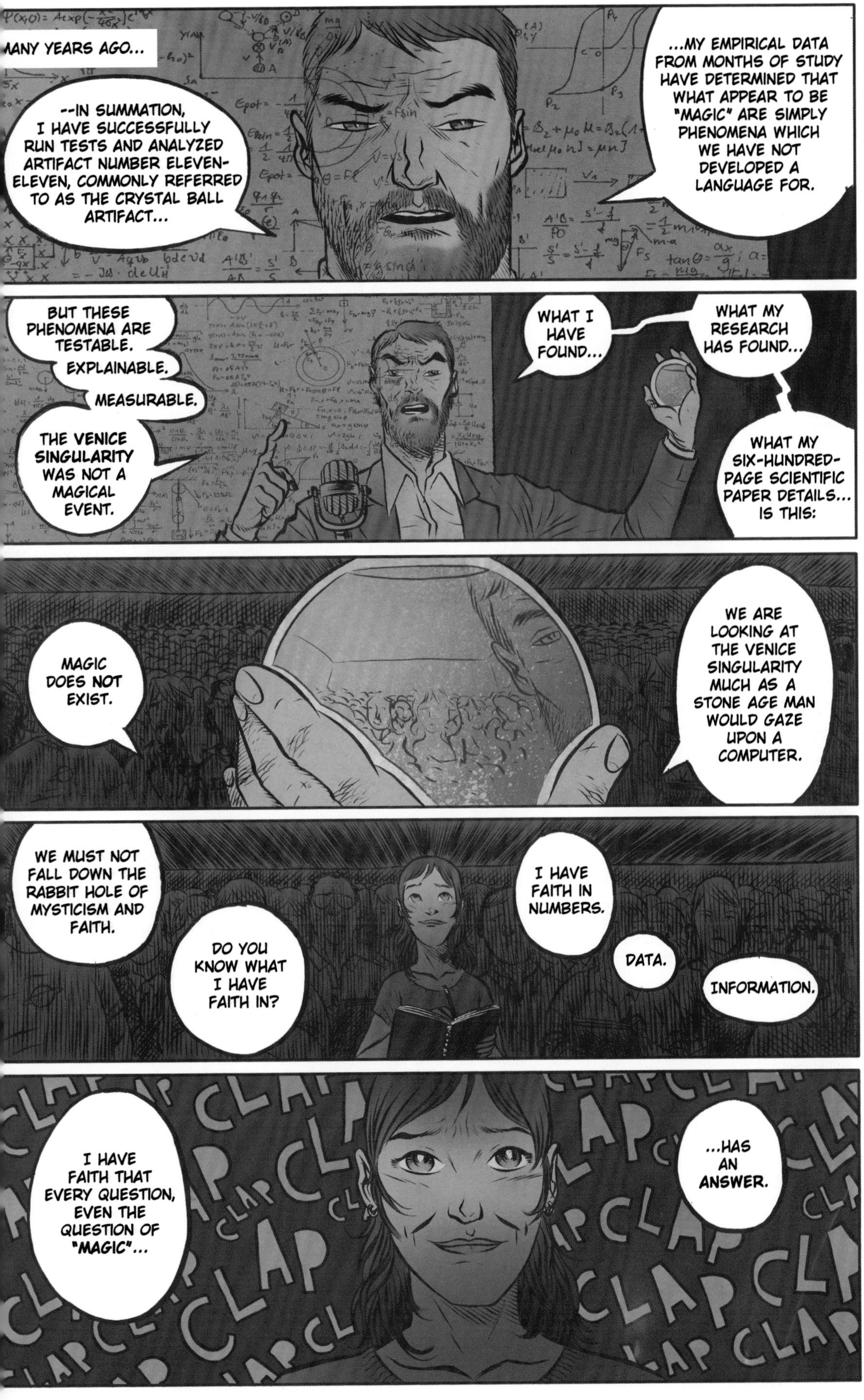

MANY YEARS AGO...
--IN SUMMATION, I HAVE SUCCESSFULLY RUN TESTS AND ANALYZED ARTIFACT NUMBER ELEVEN-ELEVEN, COMMONLY REFERRED TO AS THE CRYSTAL BALL ARTIFACT...
...MY EMPIRICAL DATA FROM MONTHS OF STUDY HAVE DETERMINED THAT WHAT APPEAR TO BE "MAGIC" ARE SIMPLY PHENOMENA WHICH WE HAVE NOT DEVELOPED A LANGUAGE FOR.
BUT THESE PHENOMENA ARE TESTABLE.
EXPLAINABLE.
MEASURABLE.
THE VENICE SINGULARITY WAS NOT A MAGICAL EVENT.
WHAT I HAVE FOUND...
WHAT MY RESEARCH HAS FOUND...
WHAT MY SIX-HUNDRED-PAGE SCIENTIFIC PAPER DETAILS... IS THIS:
MAGIC DOES NOT EXIST.
WE ARE LOOKING AT THE VENICE SINGULARITY MUCH AS A STONE AGE MAN WOULD GAZE UPON A COMPUTER.
WE MUST NOT FALL DOWN THE RABBIT HOLE OF MYSTICISM AND FAITH.
DO YOU KNOW WHAT I HAVE FAITH IN?
I HAVE FAITH IN NUMBERS.
DATA.
INFORMATION.
I HAVE FAITH THAT EVERY QUESTION, EVEN THE QUESTION OF "MAGIC"...
...HAS AN ANSWER.
CLAP CLAP CLAP

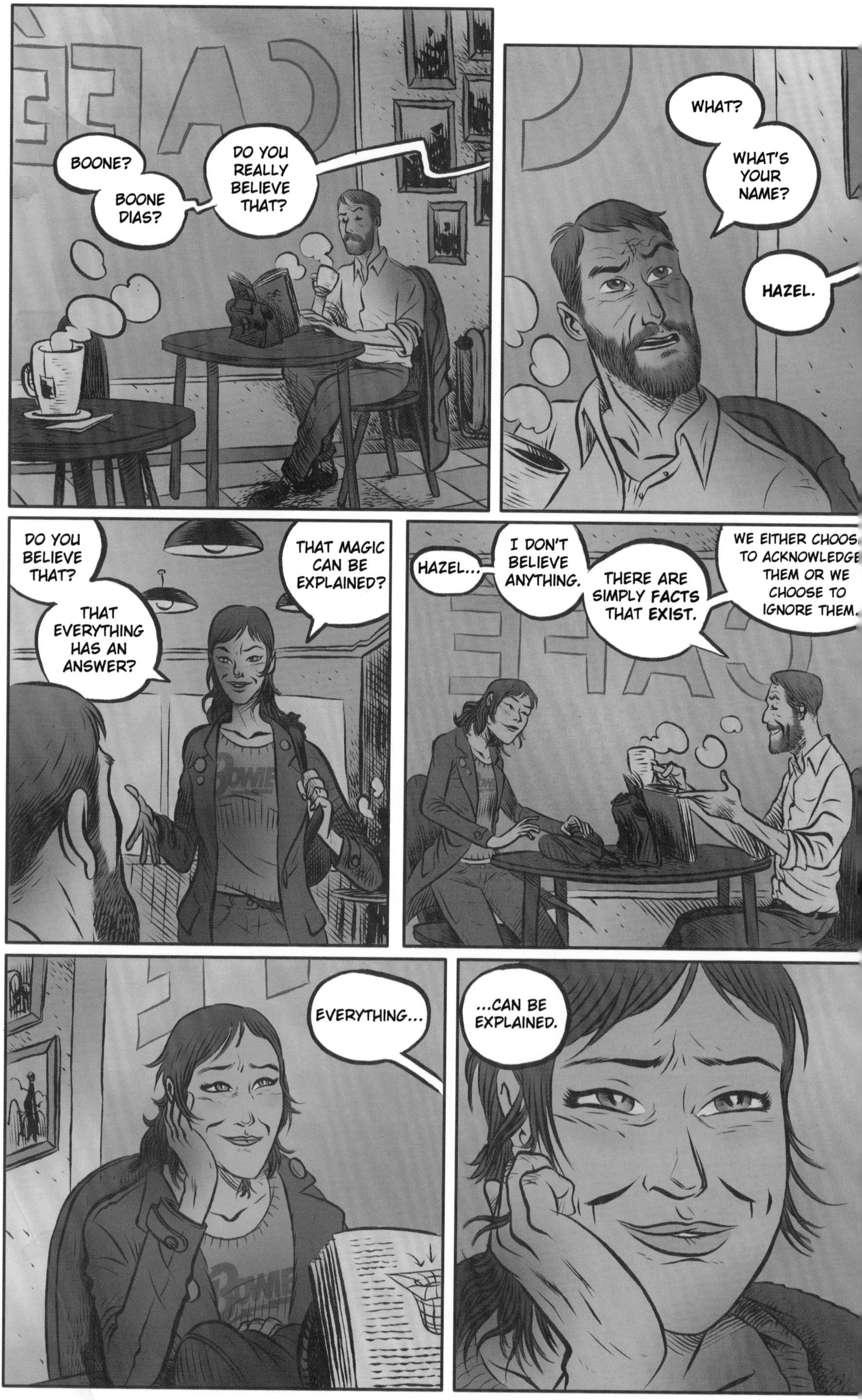
BOONE?
BOONE DIAS?
DO YOU REALLY BELIEVE THAT?
WHAT?
WHAT'S YOUR NAME?
HAZEL.
DO YOU BELIEVE THAT?
THAT EVERYTHING HAS AN ANSWER?
THAT MAGIC CAN BE EXPLAINED?
HAZEL...
I DON'T BELIEVE ANYTHING.
THERE ARE SIMPLY FACTS THAT EXIST.
WE EITHER CHOOS TO ACKNOWLEDGE THEM OR WE CHOOSE TO IGNORE THEM.
EVERYTHING...
...CAN BE EXPLAINED.

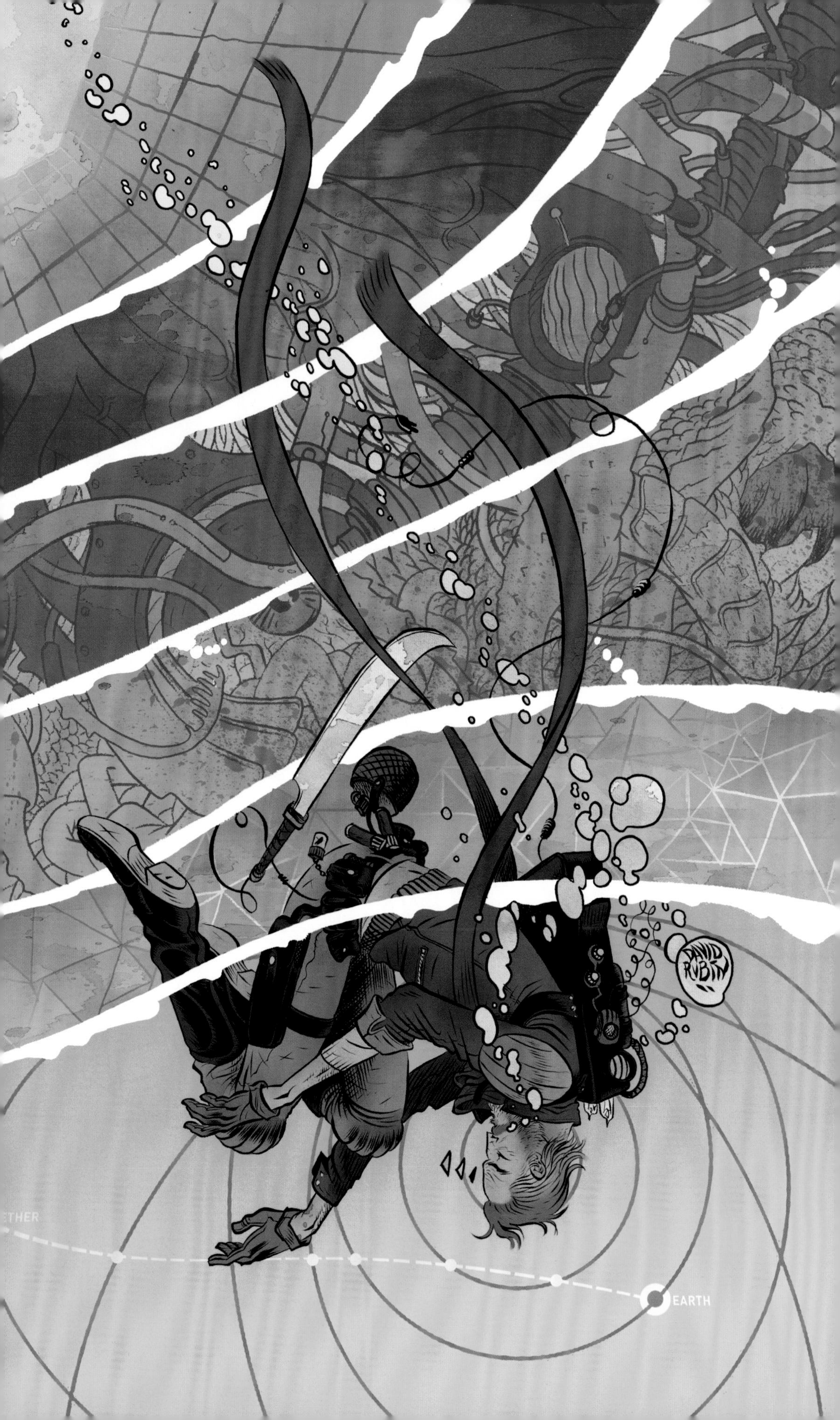
DAVID RUBIN
ETHER
EARTH

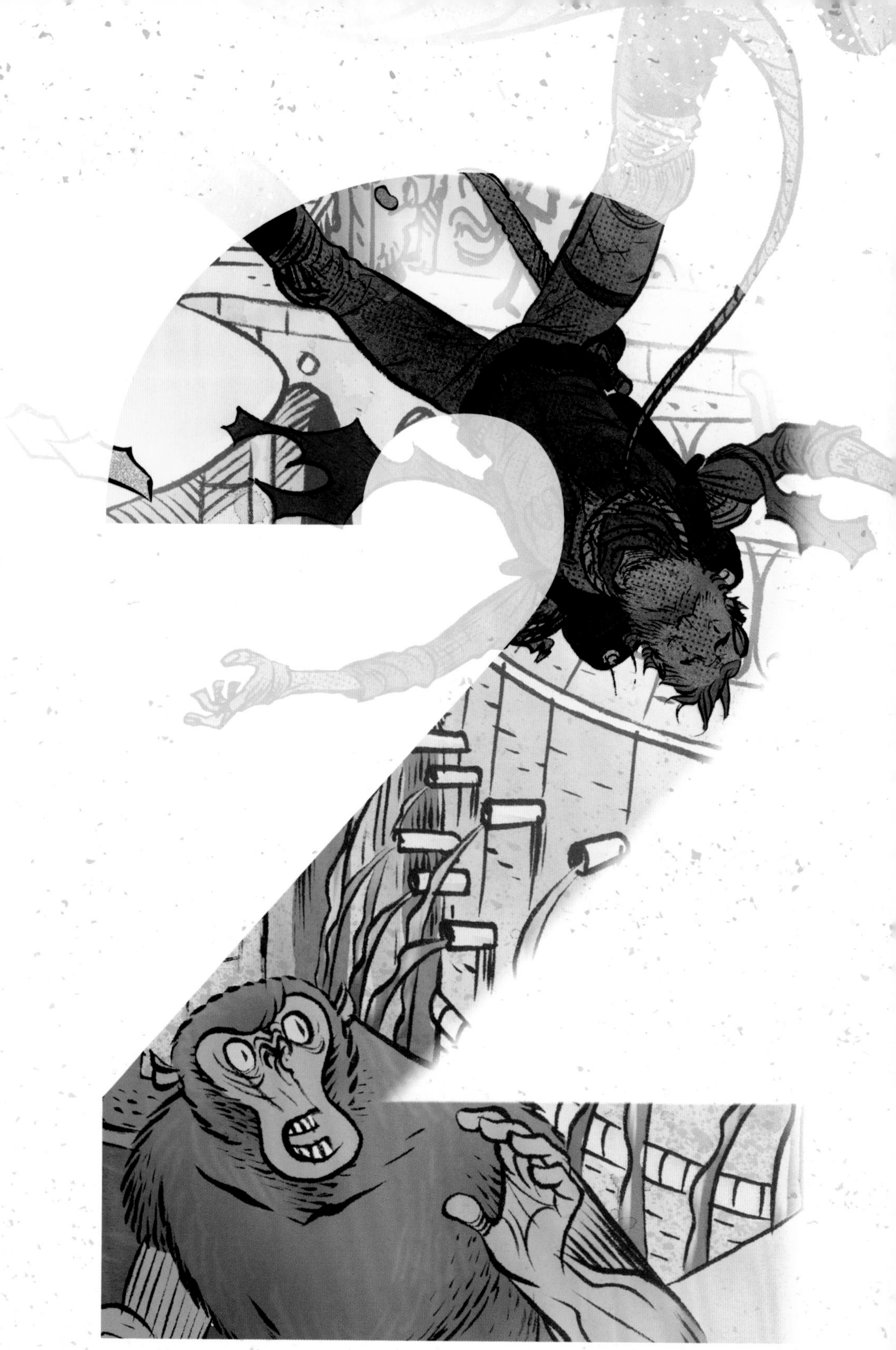

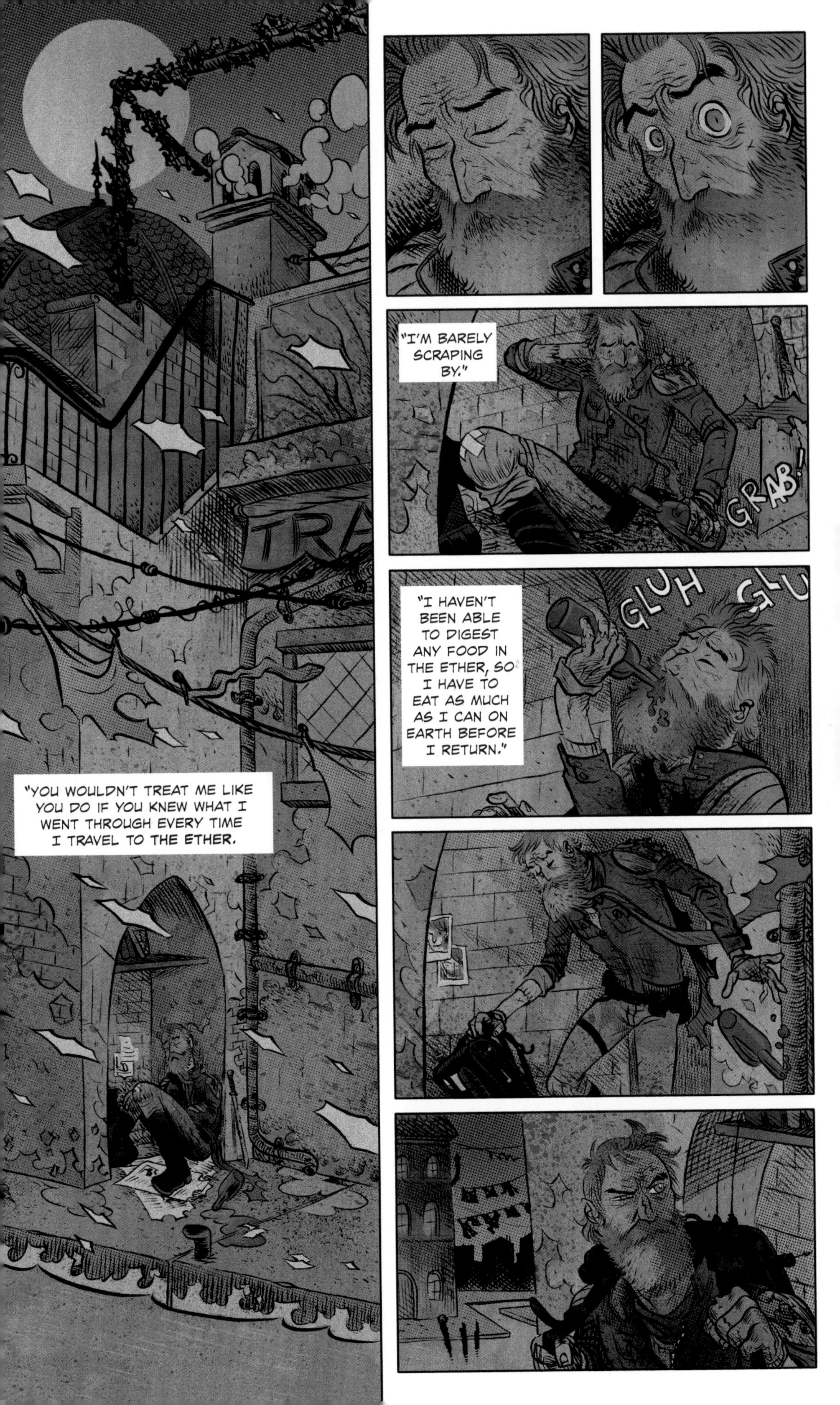

TRA
"YOU WOULDN'T TREAT ME LIKE YOU DO IF YOU KNEW WHAT I WENT THROUGH EVERY TIME I TRAVEL TO THE ETHER.
"I'M BARELY SCRAPING BY."
GRAB!
"I HAVEN'T BEEN ABLE TO DIGEST ANY FOOD IN THE ETHER, SO I HAVE TO EAT AS MUCH AS I CAN ON EARTH BEFORE I RETURN."
GLUH GLU

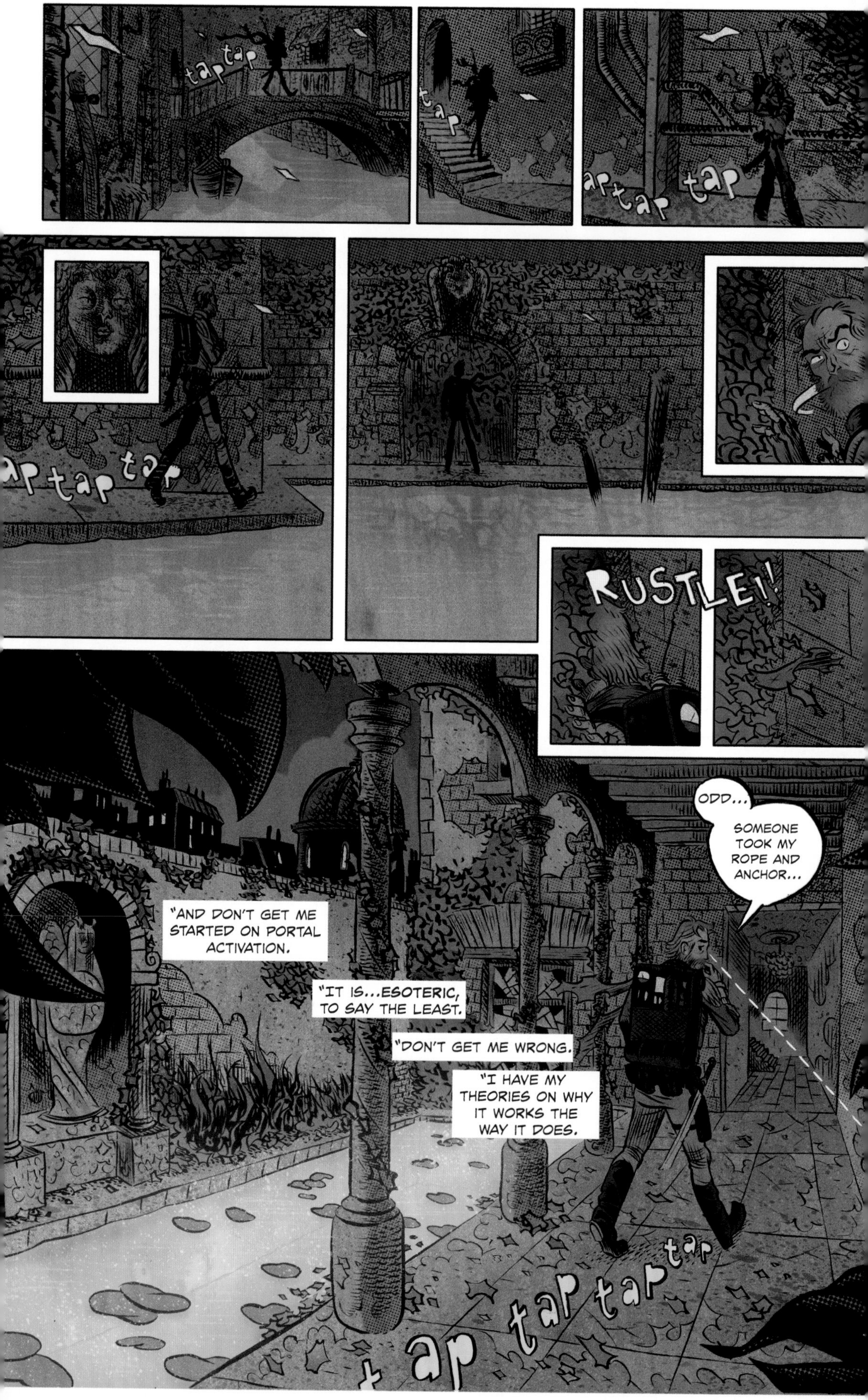
tap tap
tap
tap tap tap
tap tap tap
RUSTLE!
ODD...
SOMEONE TOOK MY ROPE AND ANCHOR...
"AND DON'T GET ME STARTED ON PORTAL ACTIVATION.
"IT IS...ESOTERIC, TO SAY THE LEAST.
"DON'T GET ME WRONG.
"I HAVE MY THEORIES ON WHY IT WORKS THE WAY IT DOES.
tap tap tap tap

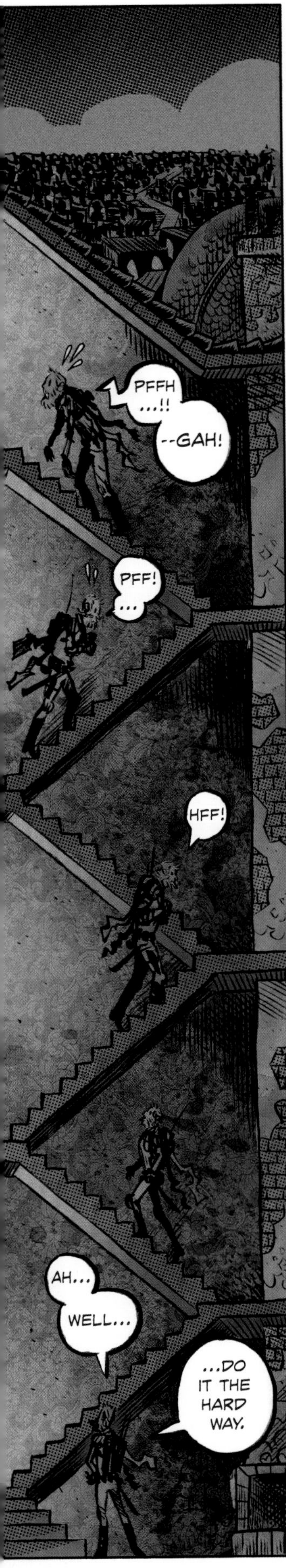
PFFH ...!!
--GAH!
PFF! ...
HFF!
AH...
WELL...
...DO IT THE HARD WAY.
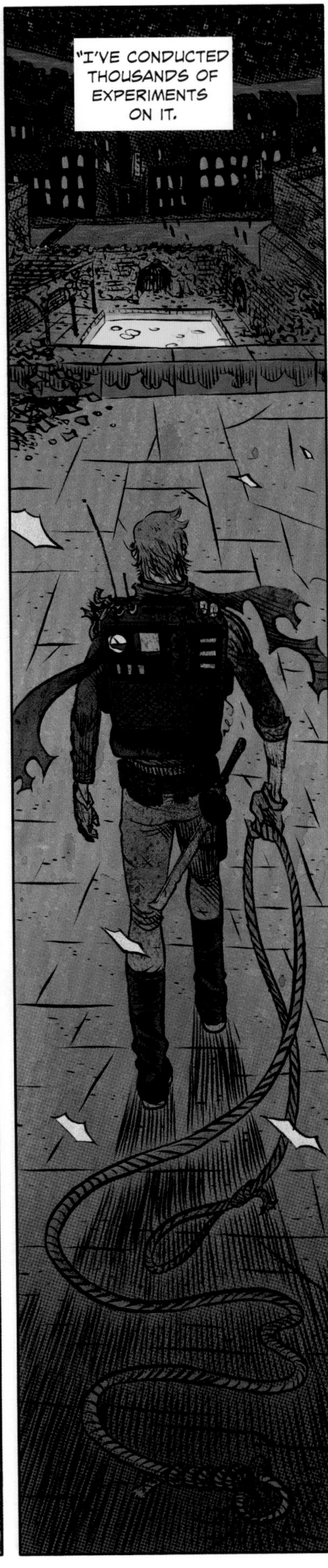
"I'VE CONDUCTED THOUSANDS OF EXPERIMENTS ON IT.
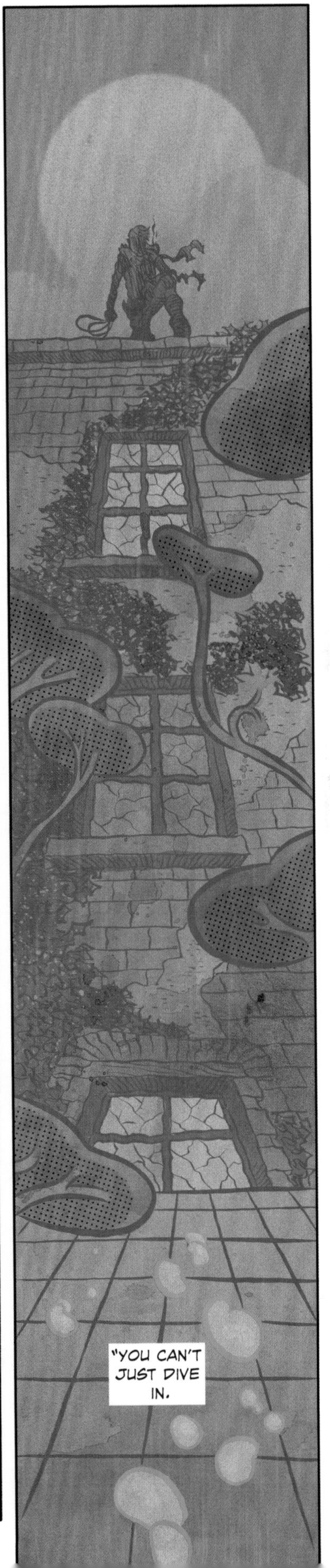
"YOU CAN'T JUST DIVE IN.

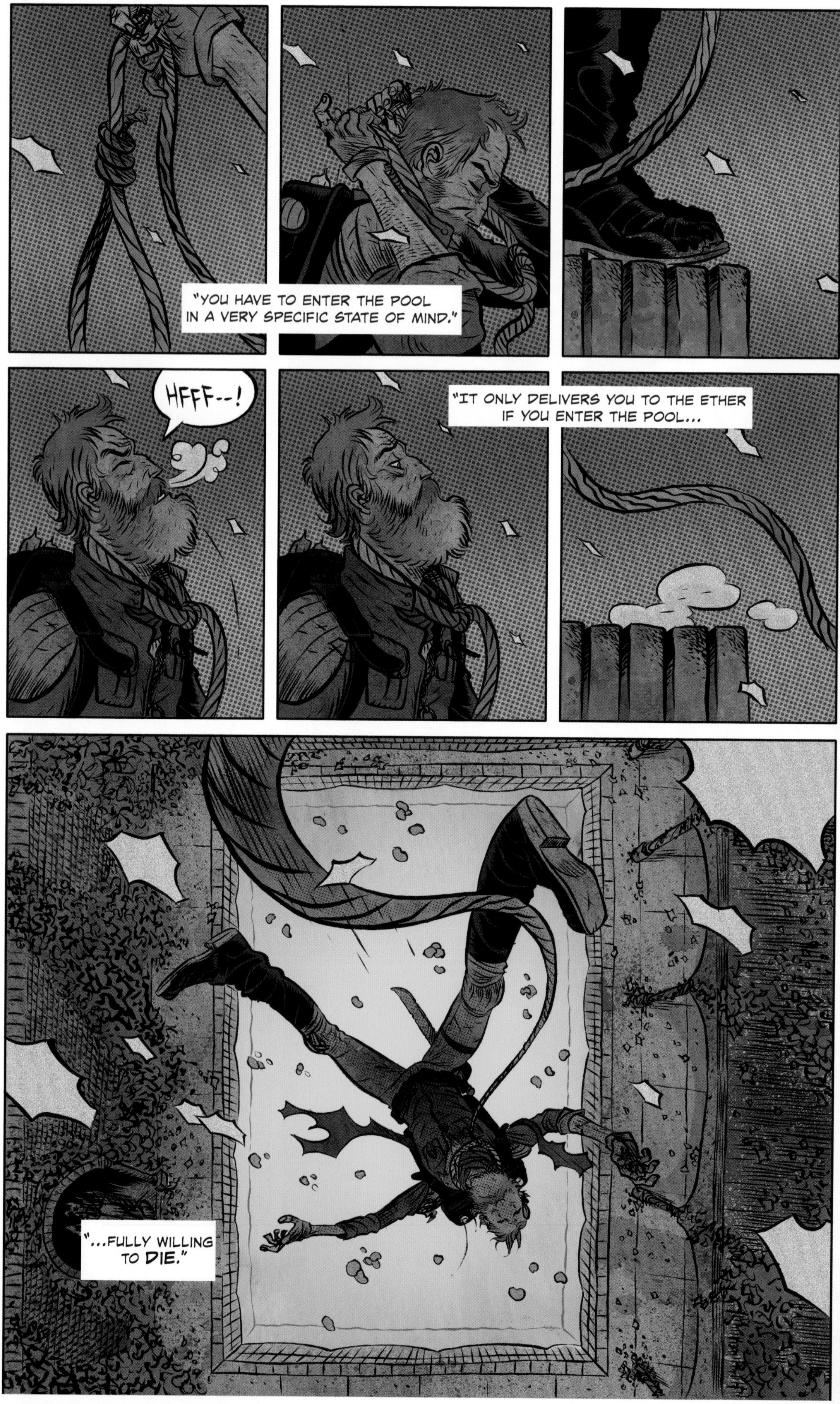
"YOU HAVE TO ENTER THE POOL
IN A VERY SPECIFIC STATE OF MIND."
HFFF--!
"IT ONLY DELIVERS YOU TO THE ETHER
IF YOU ENTER THE POOL...
"...FULLY WILLING
TO DIE."

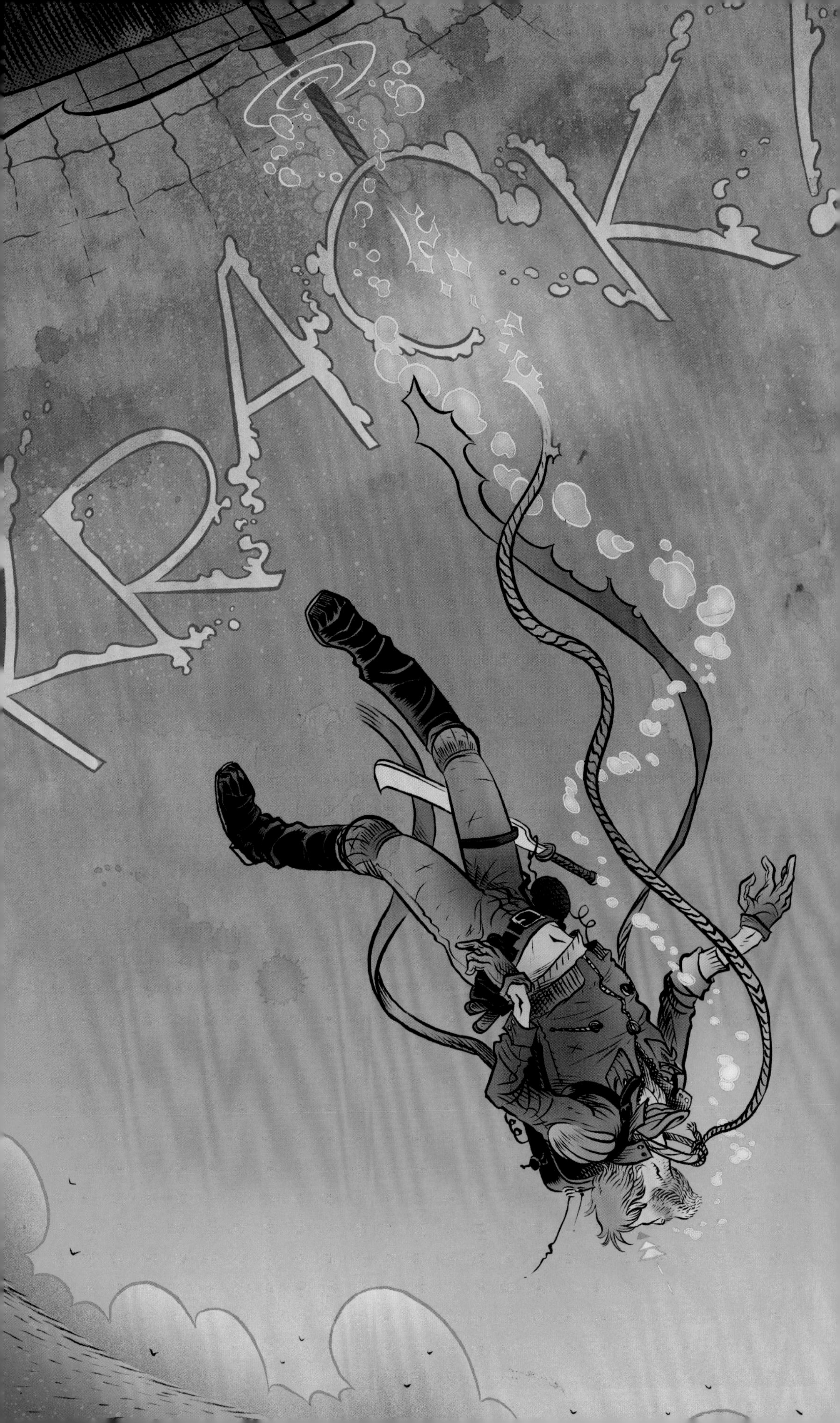
RACK!

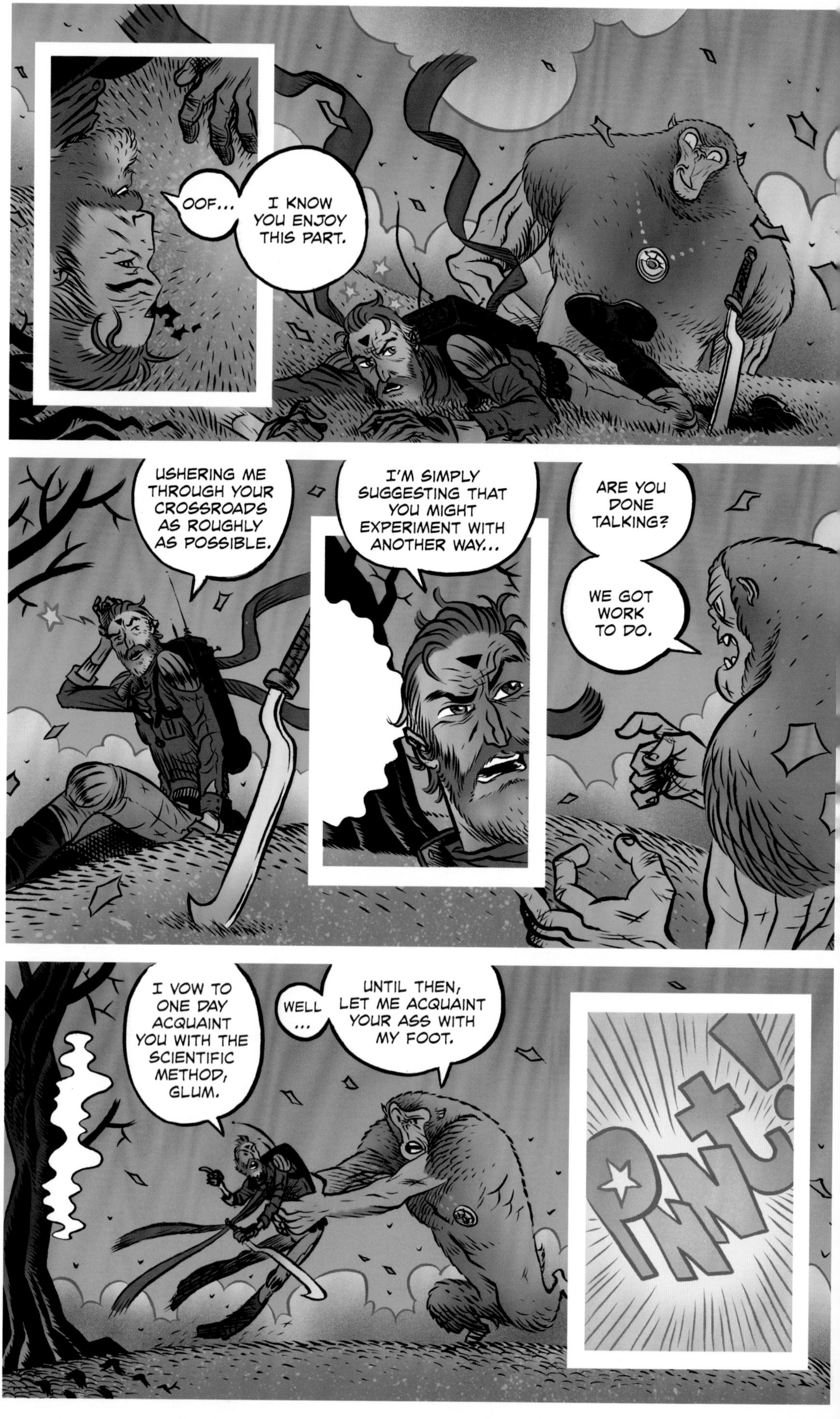
OOF...
I KNOW YOU ENJOY THIS PART.
USHERING ME THROUGH YOUR CROSSROADS AS ROUGHLY AS POSSIBLE.
I'M SIMPLY SUGGESTING THAT YOU MIGHT EXPERIMENT WITH ANOTHER WAY...
ARE YOU DONE TALKING?
WE GOT WORK TO DO.
I VOW TO ONE DAY ACQUAINT YOU WITH THE SCIENTIFIC METHOD, GLUM.
WELL ...
UNTIL THEN, LET ME ACQUAINT YOUR ASS WITH MY FOOT.
PWNT!

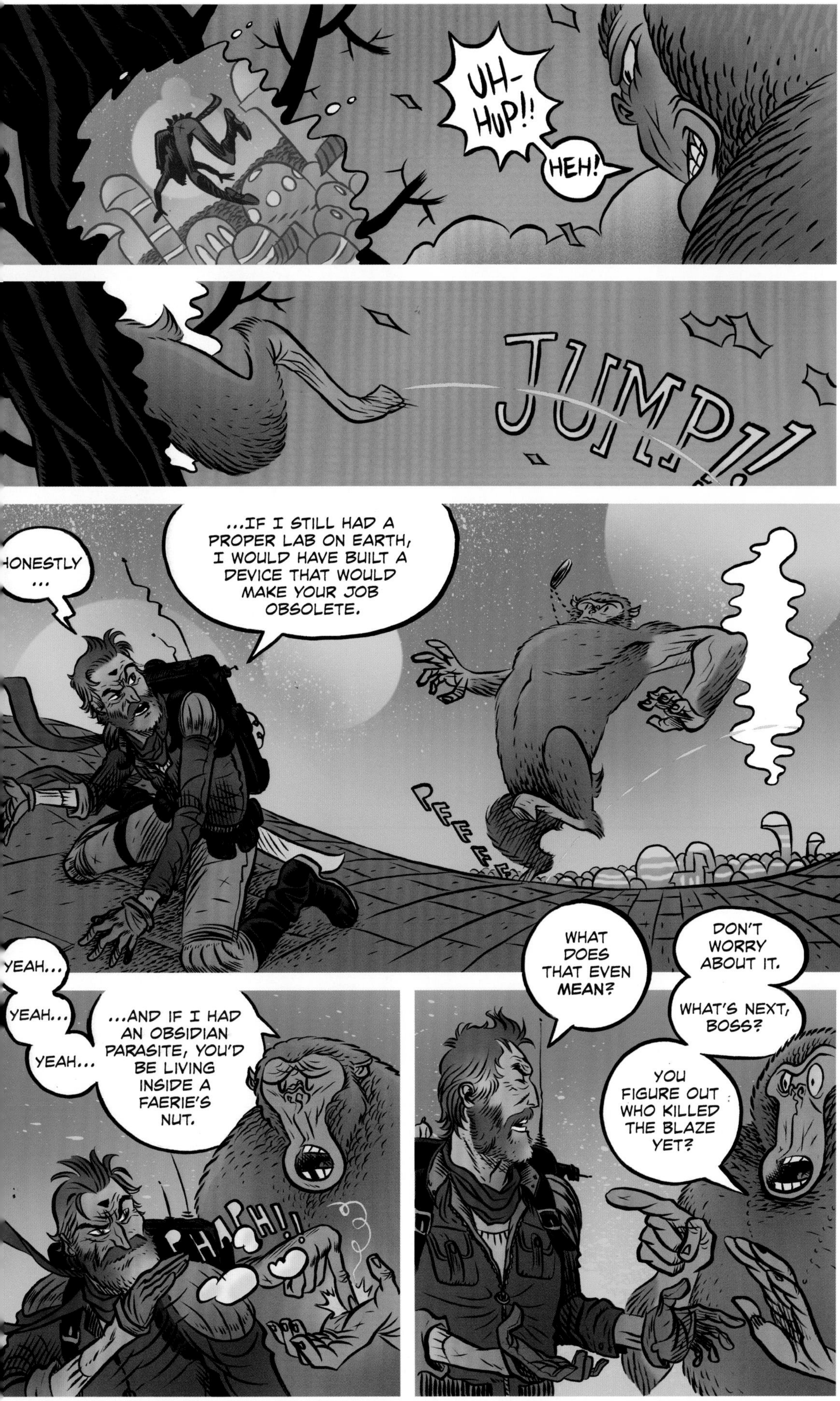
UH-HUP!!
HEH!
JUMP!!
HONESTLY...
...IF I STILL HAD A PROPER LAB ON EARTH, I WOULD HAVE BUILT A DEVICE THAT WOULD MAKE YOUR JOB OBSOLETE.
YEAH...
YEAH...
YEAH...
...AND IF I HAD AN OBSIDIAN PARASITE, YOU'D BE LIVING INSIDE A FAERIE'S NUT.
PHAH!!
WHAT DOES THAT EVEN MEAN?
DON'T WORRY ABOUT IT.
WHAT'S NEXT, BOSS?
YOU FIGURE OUT WHO KILLED THE BLAZE YET?

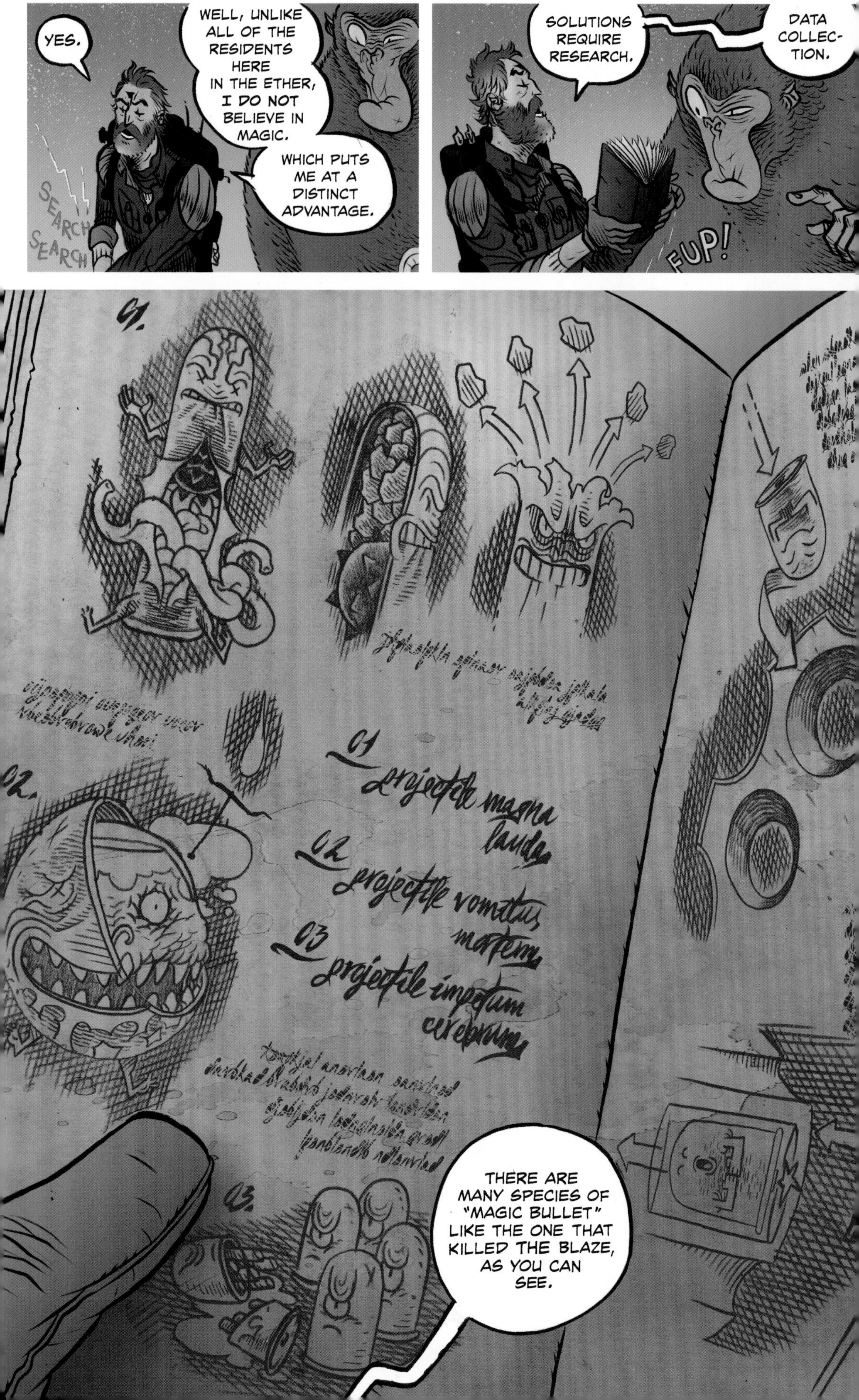
YES.
WELL, UNLIKE ALL OF THE RESIDENTS HERE IN THE ETHER, I DO NOT BELIEVE IN MAGIC.
WHICH PUTS ME AT A DISTINCT ADVANTAGE.
SEARCH SEARCH
SOLUTIONS REQUIRE RESEARCH.
DATA COLLECTION.
FUP!
01.
02.
03.
01 projectile magna laude
02 projectile vomitus mortem
03 projectile impetum cerebrum
THERE ARE MANY SPECIES OF "MAGIC BULLET" LIKE THE ONE THAT KILLED THE BLAZE, AS YOU CAN SEE.

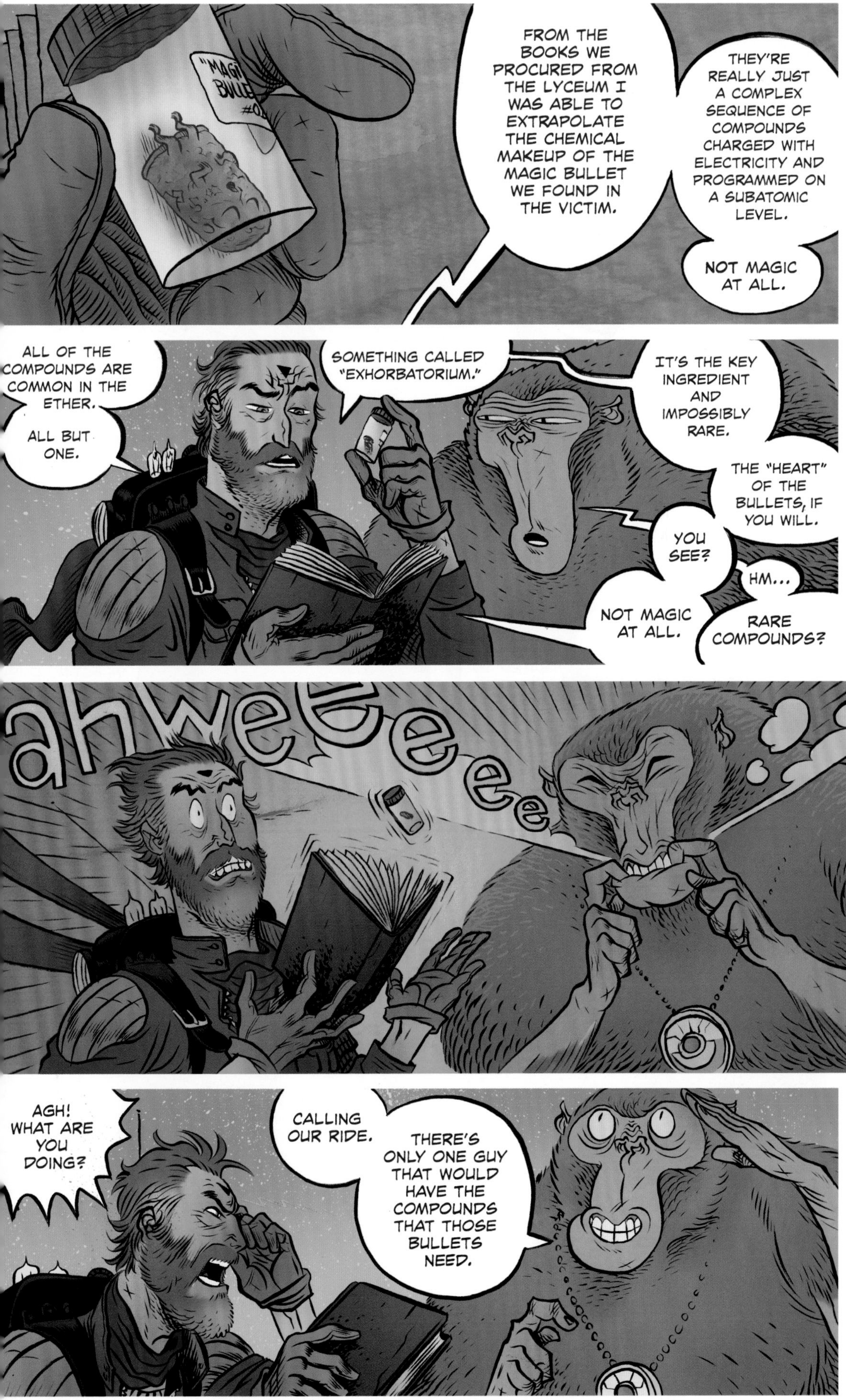
"MAGIC BULLET" #0
FROM THE BOOKS WE PROCURED FROM THE LYCEUM I WAS ABLE TO EXTRAPOLATE THE CHEMICAL MAKEUP OF THE MAGIC BULLET WE FOUND IN THE VICTIM.
THEY'RE REALLY JUST A COMPLEX SEQUENCE OF COMPOUNDS CHARGED WITH ELECTRICITY AND PROGRAMMED ON A SUBATOMIC LEVEL.
NOT MAGIC AT ALL.
ALL OF THE COMPOUNDS ARE COMMON IN THE ETHER.
ALL BUT ONE.
SOMETHING CALLED "EXHORBATORIUM."
IT'S THE KEY INGREDIENT AND IMPOSSIBLY RARE.
THE "HEART" OF THE BULLETS, IF YOU WILL.
YOU SEE?
NOT MAGIC AT ALL.
HM...
RARE COMPOUNDS?
ahwEEeeee
AGH! WHAT ARE YOU DOING?
CALLING OUR RIDE.
THERE'S ONLY ONE GUY THAT WOULD HAVE THE COMPOUNDS THAT THOSE BULLETS NEED.

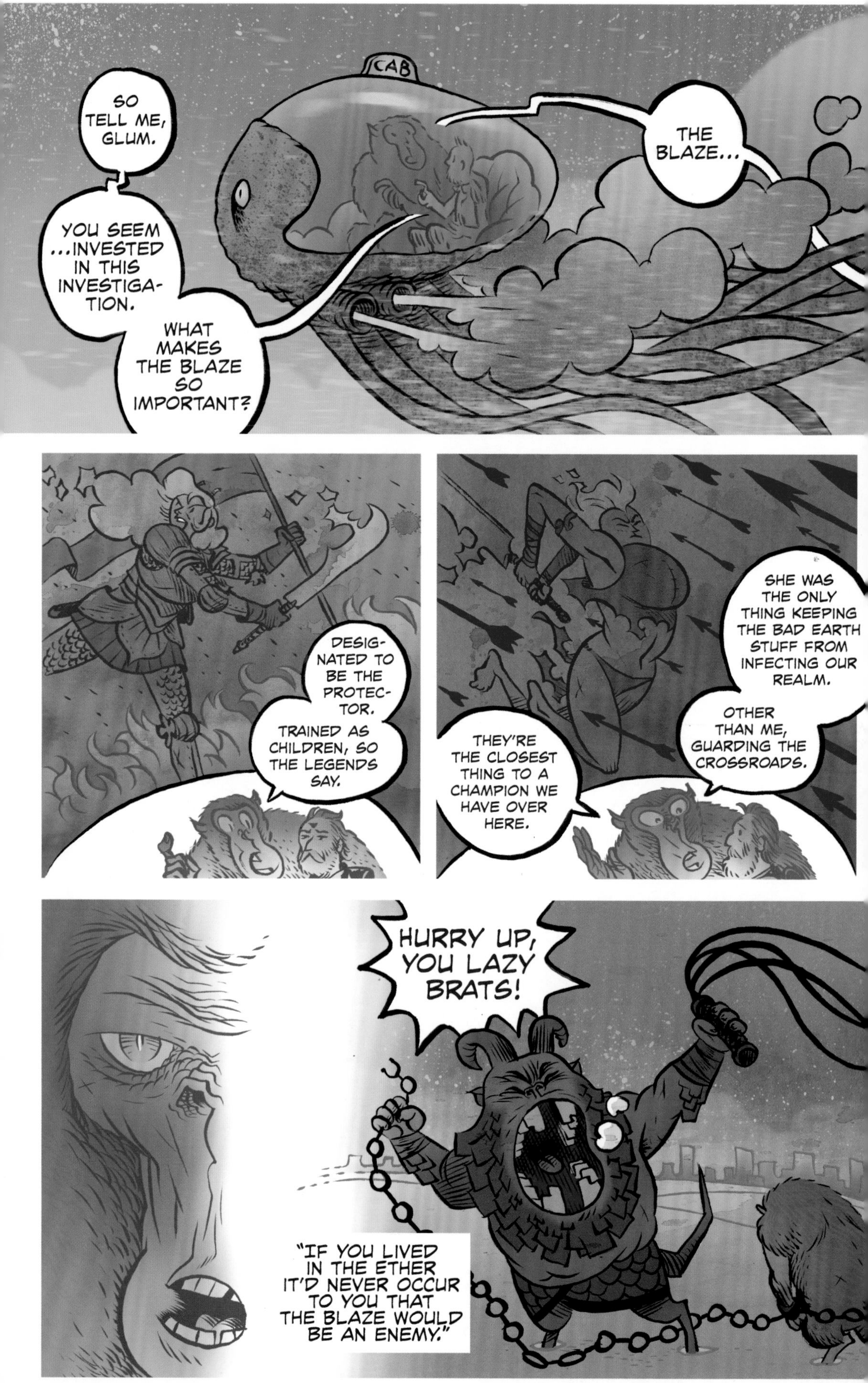
CAB
SO TELL ME, GLUM.
YOU SEEM ...INVESTED IN THIS INVESTIGA-TION.
WHAT MAKES THE BLAZE SO IMPORTANT?
THE BLAZE...
DESIG-NATED TO BE THE PROTEC-TOR.
TRAINED AS CHILDREN, SO THE LEGENDS SAY.
THEY'RE THE CLOSEST THING TO A CHAMPION WE HAVE OVER HERE.
SHE WAS THE ONLY THING KEEPING THE BAD EARTH STUFF FROM INFECTING OUR REALM.
OTHER THAN ME, GUARDING THE CROSSROADS.
HURRY UP, YOU LAZY BRATS!
"IF YOU LIVED IN THE ETHER IT'D NEVER OCCUR TO YOU THAT THE BLAZE WOULD BE AN ENEMY."

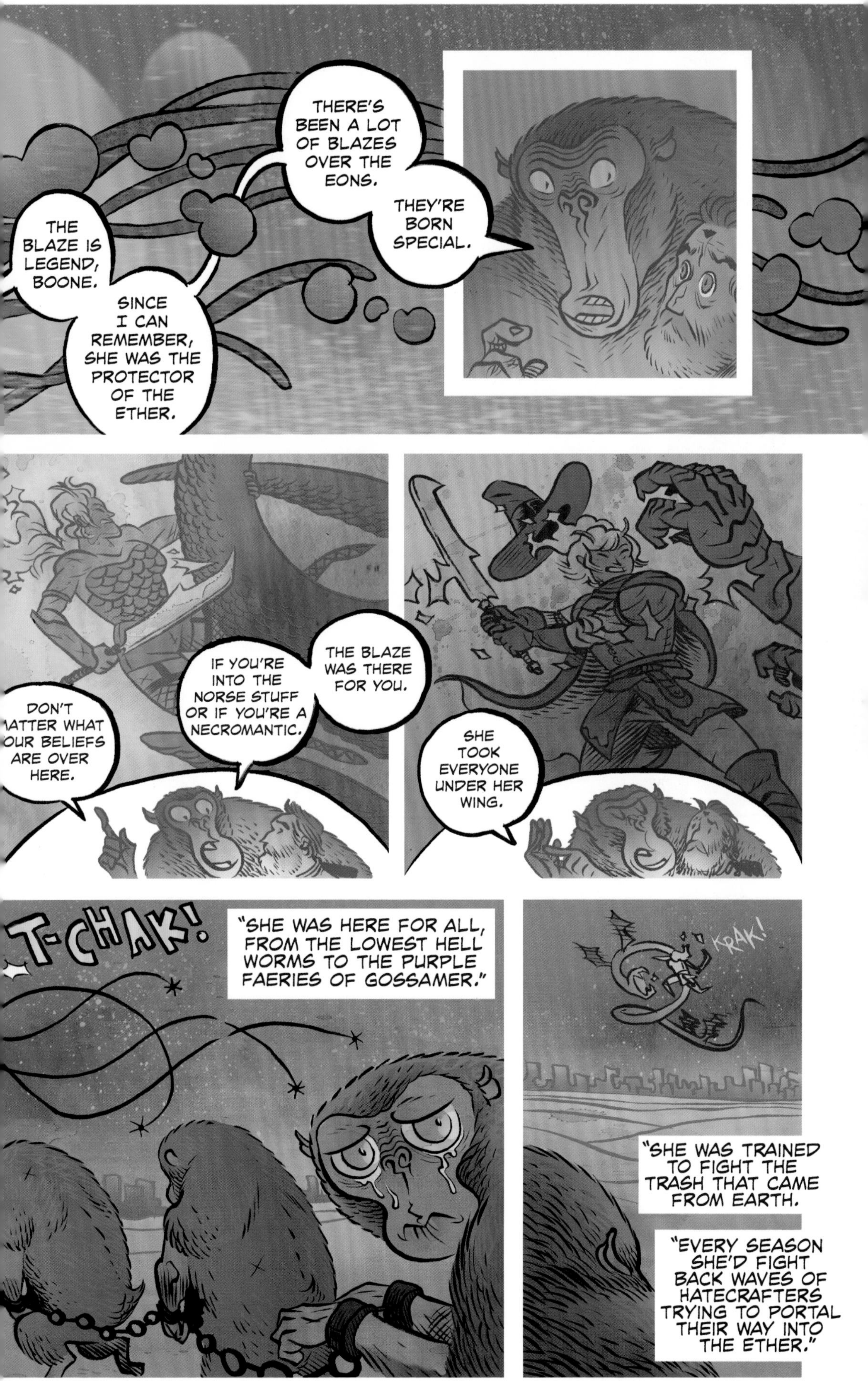
THE BLAZE IS LEGEND, BOONE.
SINCE I CAN REMEMBER, SHE WAS THE PROTECTOR OF THE ETHER.
THERE'S BEEN A LOT OF BLAZES OVER THE EONS.
THEY'RE BORN SPECIAL.
DON'T MATTER WHAT OUR BELIEFS ARE OVER HERE.
IF YOU'RE INTO THE NORSE STUFF OR IF YOU'RE A NECROMANTIC.
THE BLAZE WAS THERE FOR YOU.
SHE TOOK EVERYONE UNDER HER WING.
T-CHAK!
"SHE WAS HERE FOR ALL, FROM THE LOWEST HELL WORMS TO THE PURPLE FAERIES OF GOSSAMER."
KRAK!
"SHE WAS TRAINED TO FIGHT THE TRASH THAT CAME FROM EARTH.
"EVERY SEASON SHE'D FIGHT BACK WAVES OF HATECRAFTERS TRYING TO PORTAL THEIR WAY INTO THE ETHER."

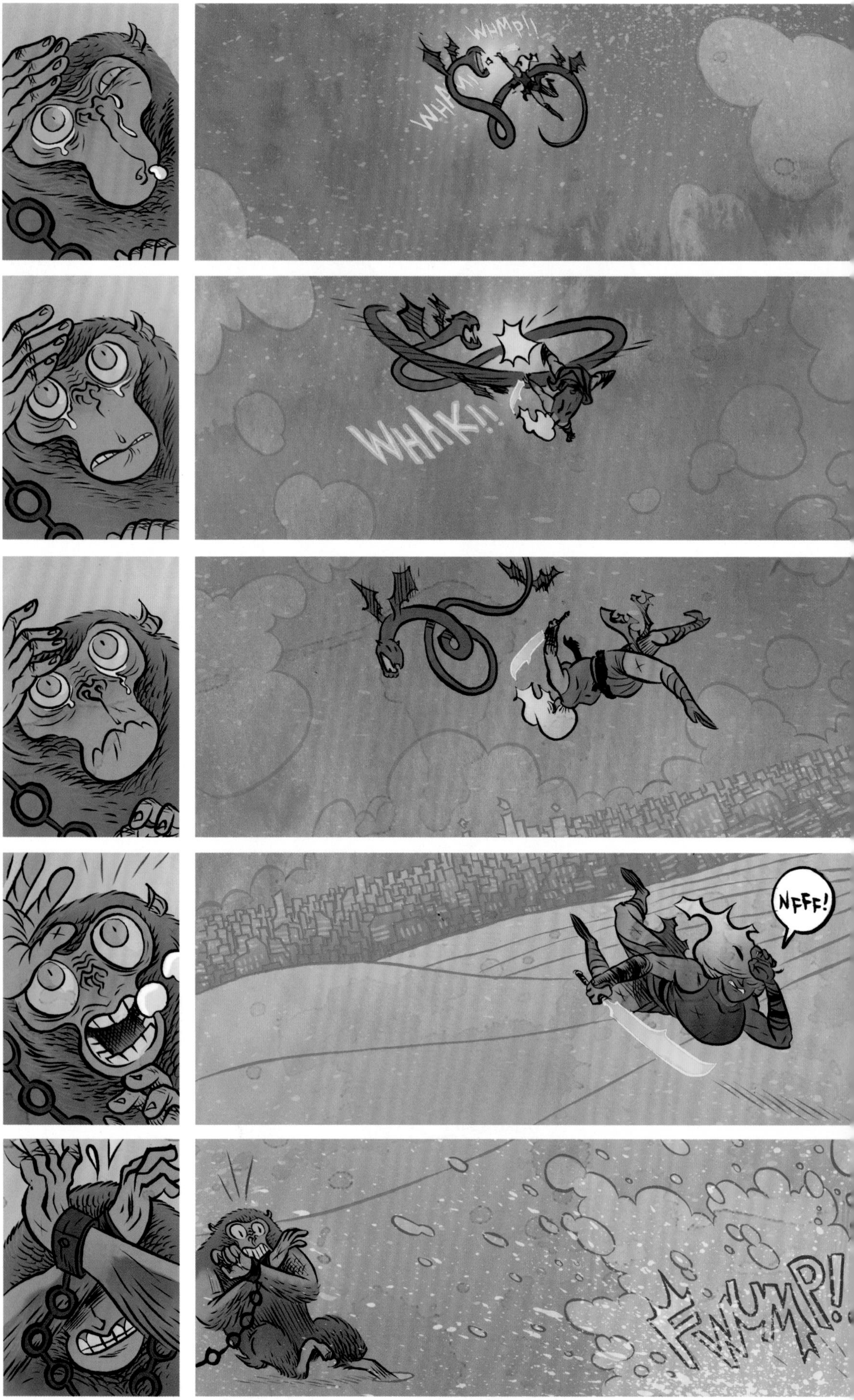
WHMP!!
WHMP!!
WHAK!!
NFFF!
FWUMP!

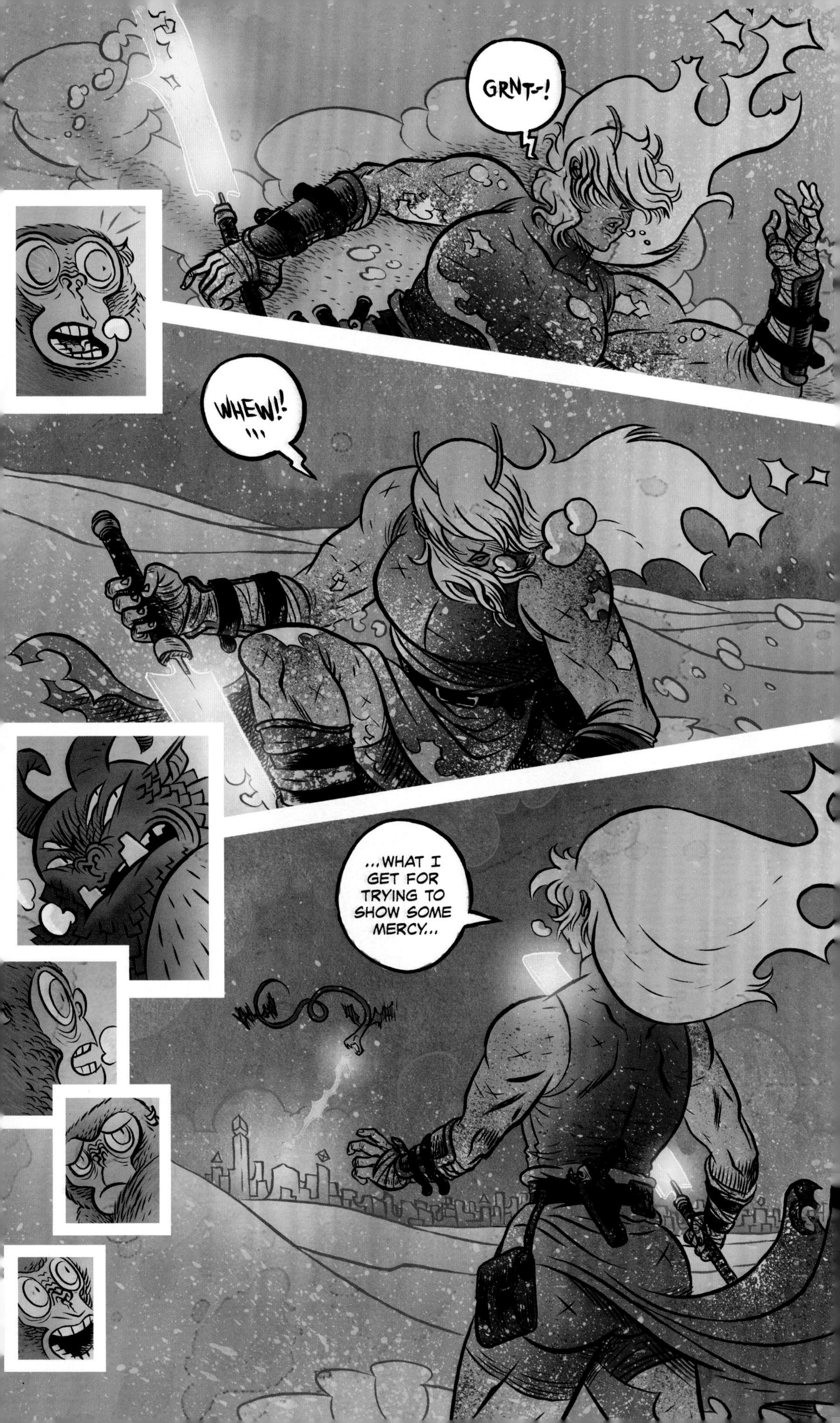
GRNT-!
WHEW!!
...WHAT I
GET FOR
TRYING TO
SHOW SOME
MERCY...

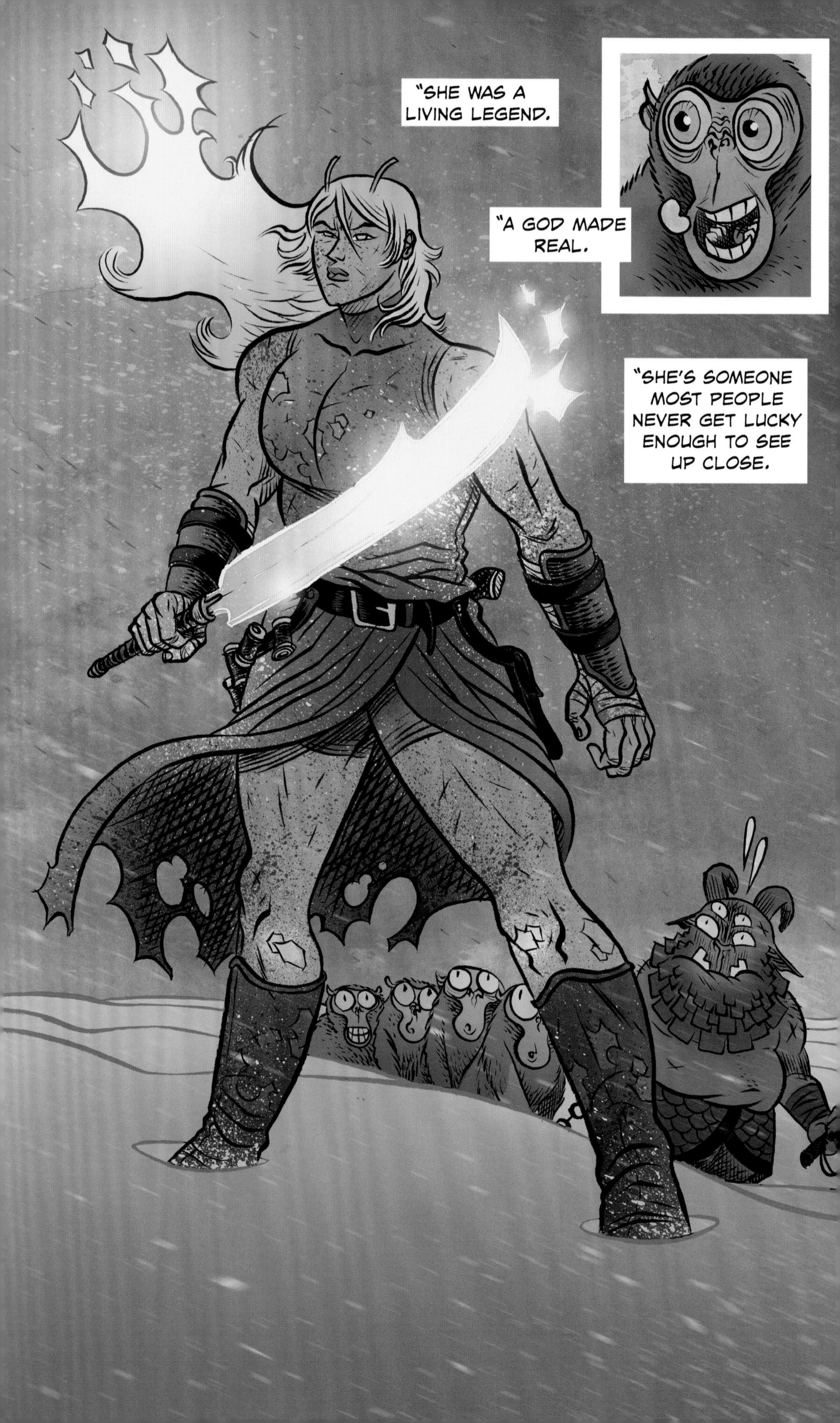

"SHE WAS A LIVING LEGEND.
"A GOD MADE REAL.
"SHE'S SOMEONE MOST PEOPLE NEVER GET LUCKY ENOUGH TO SEE UP CLOSE.

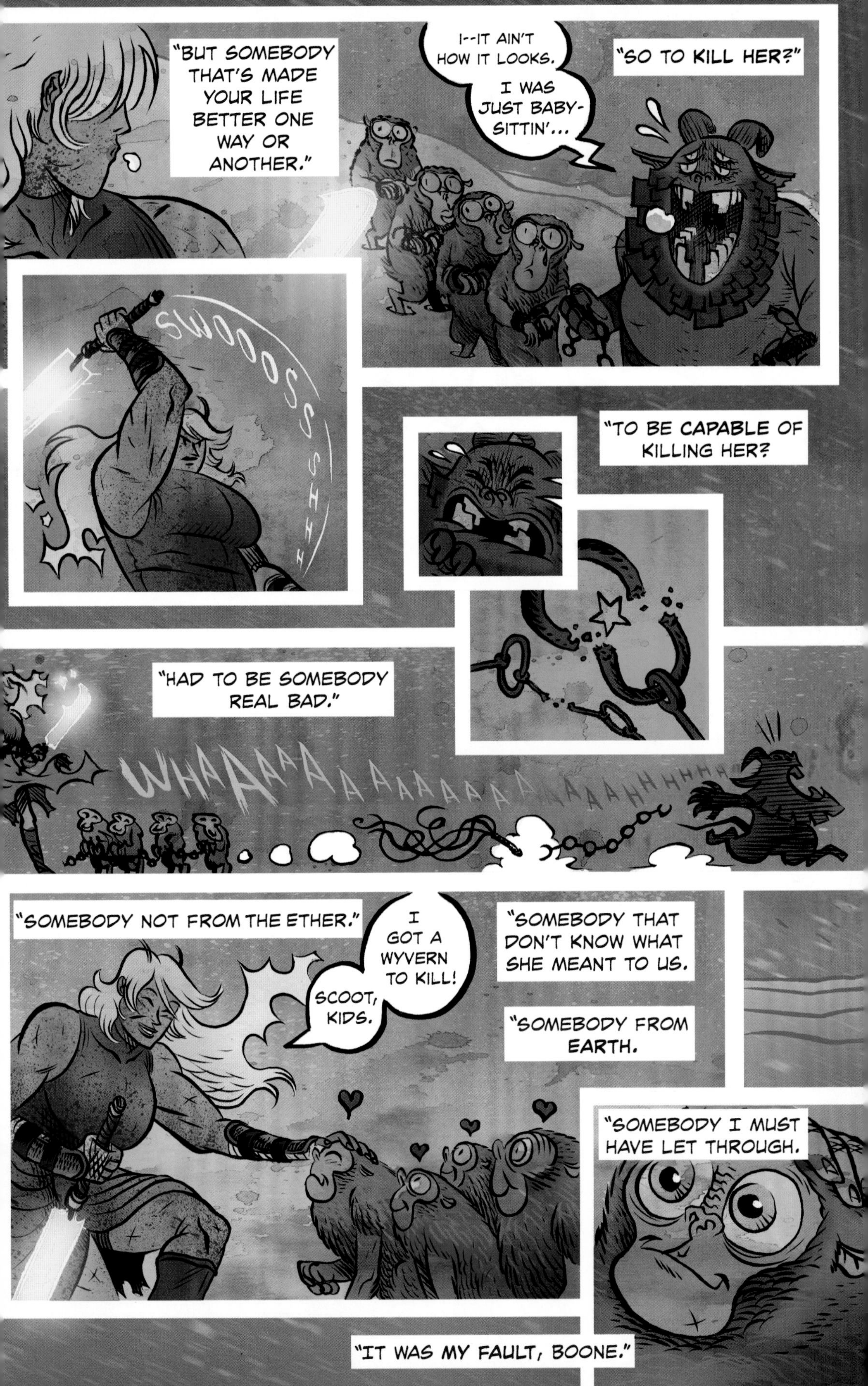
"BUT SOMEBODY THAT'S MADE YOUR LIFE BETTER ONE WAY OR ANOTHER."
I--IT AIN'T HOW IT LOOKS.
I WAS JUST BABY-SITTIN'...
"SO TO KILL HER?"
SWOOOSSSHHH
"TO BE CAPABLE OF KILLING HER?
"HAD TO BE SOMEBODY REAL BAD."
WHAAAAAAAAAAAAAAAAAHHHHHH
"SOMEBODY NOT FROM THE ETHER."
I GOT A WYVERN TO KILL!
SCOOT, KIDS.
"SOMEBODY THAT DON'T KNOW WHAT SHE MEANT TO US.
"SOMEBODY FROM EARTH.
"SOMEBODY I MUST HAVE LET THROUGH.
"IT WAS MY FAULT, BOONE."

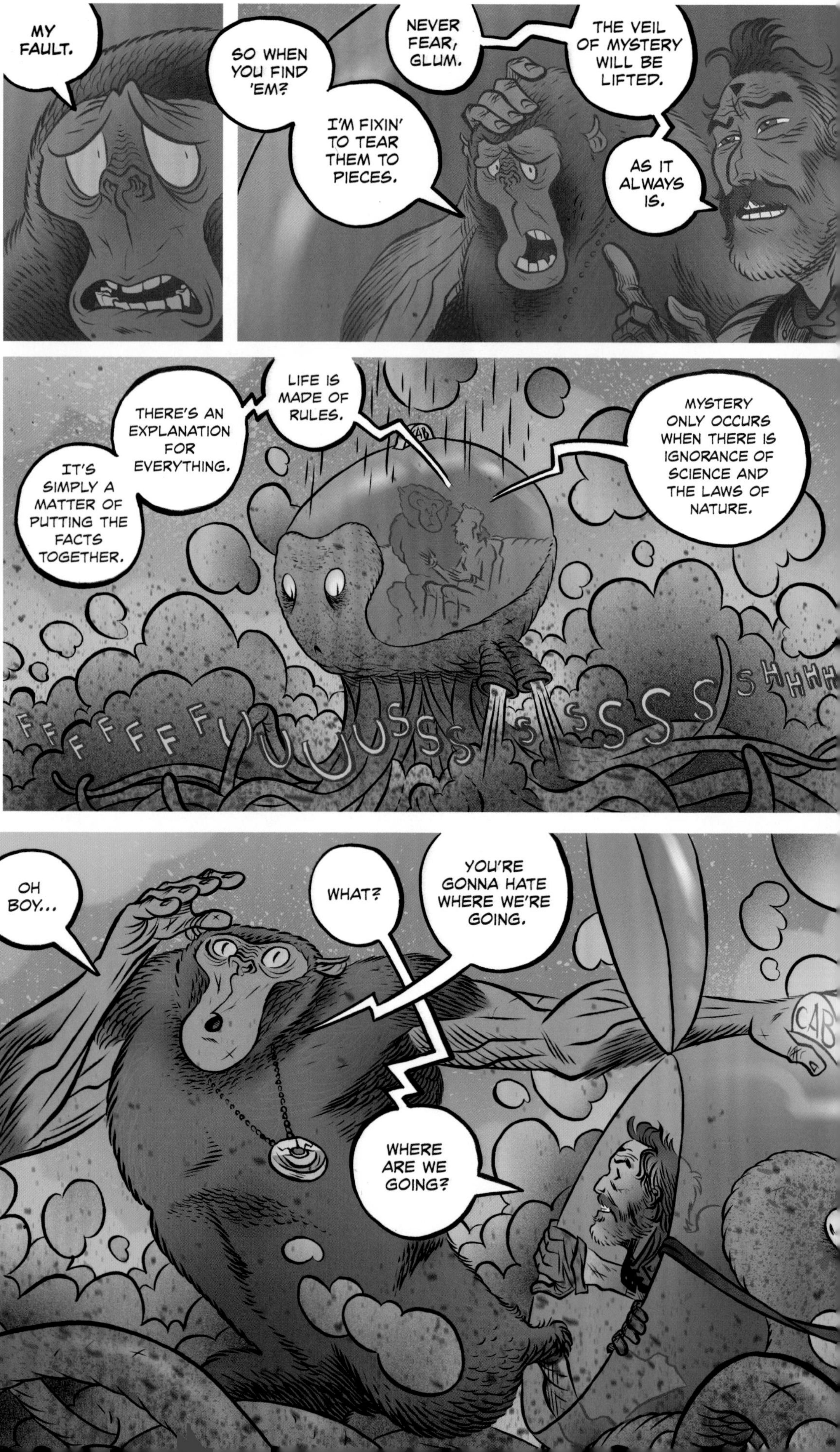
MY FAULT.
SO WHEN YOU FIND 'EM?
I'M FIXIN' TO TEAR THEM TO PIECES.
NEVER FEAR, GLUM.
THE VEIL OF MYSTERY WILL BE LIFTED.
AS IT ALWAYS IS.
LIFE IS MADE OF RULES.
THERE'S AN EXPLANATION FOR EVERYTHING.
IT'S SIMPLY A MATTER OF PUTTING THE FACTS TOGETHER.
MYSTERY ONLY OCCURS WHEN THERE IS IGNORANCE OF SCIENCE AND THE LAWS OF NATURE.
FFFFFFFUUUUUSSSSSSSSSSSSHHHHH
OH BOY...
WHAT?
WHERE ARE WE GOING?
YOU'RE GONNA HATE WHERE WE'RE GOING.

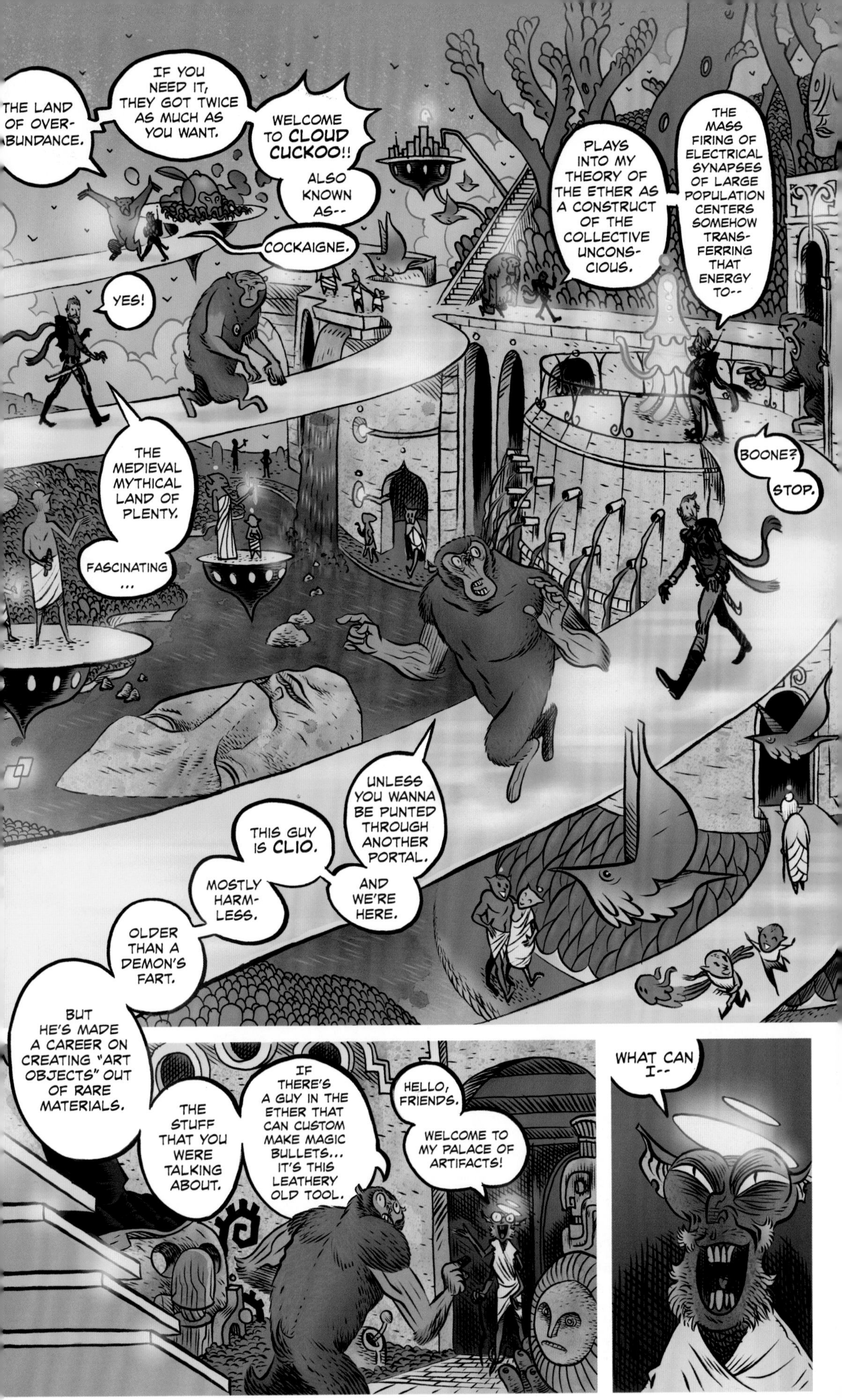

THE LAND OF OVER-BUNDANCE.
IF YOU NEED IT, THEY GOT TWICE AS MUCH AS YOU WANT.
WELCOME TO CLOUD CUCKOO!!
ALSO KNOWN AS--
COCKAIGNE.
YES!
THE MEDIEVAL MYTHICAL LAND OF PLENTY.
FASCINATING...
PLAYS INTO MY THEORY OF THE ETHER AS A CONSTRUCT OF THE COLLECTIVE UNCONSCIOUS.
THE MASS FIRING OF ELECTRICAL SYNAPSES OF LARGE POPULATION CENTERS SOMEHOW TRANSFERRING THAT ENERGY TO--
BOONE?
STOP.
UNLESS YOU WANNA BE PUNTED THROUGH ANOTHER PORTAL.
AND WE'RE HERE.
THIS GUY IS CLIO.
MOSTLY HARMLESS.
OLDER THAN A DEMON'S FART.
BUT HE'S MADE A CAREER ON CREATING "ART OBJECTS" OUT OF RARE MATERIALS.
THE STUFF THAT YOU WERE TALKING ABOUT.
IF THERE'S A GUY IN THE ETHER THAT CAN CUSTOM MAKE MAGIC BULLETS... IT'S THIS LEATHERY OLD TOOL.
HELLO, FRIENDS.
WELCOME TO MY PALACE OF ARTIFACTS!
WHAT CAN I--

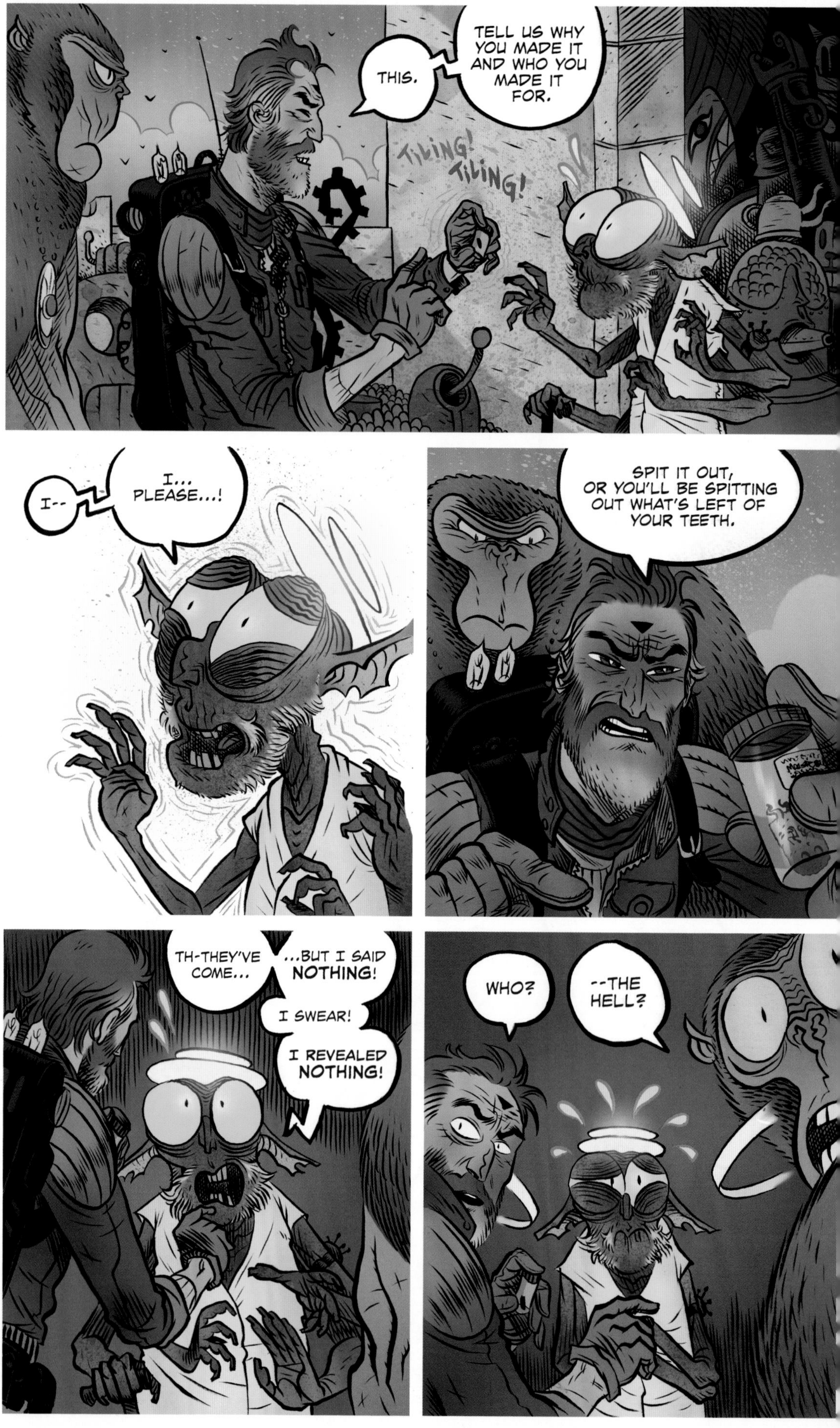
THIS.
TELL US WHY YOU MADE IT AND WHO YOU MADE IT FOR.
TILING! TILING!
I--
I... PLEASE...!
SPIT IT OUT, OR YOU'LL BE SPITTING OUT WHAT'S LEFT OF YOUR TEETH.
TH-THEY'VE COME...
...BUT I SAID NOTHING!
I SWEAR!
I REVEALED NOTHING!
WHO?
--THE HELL?

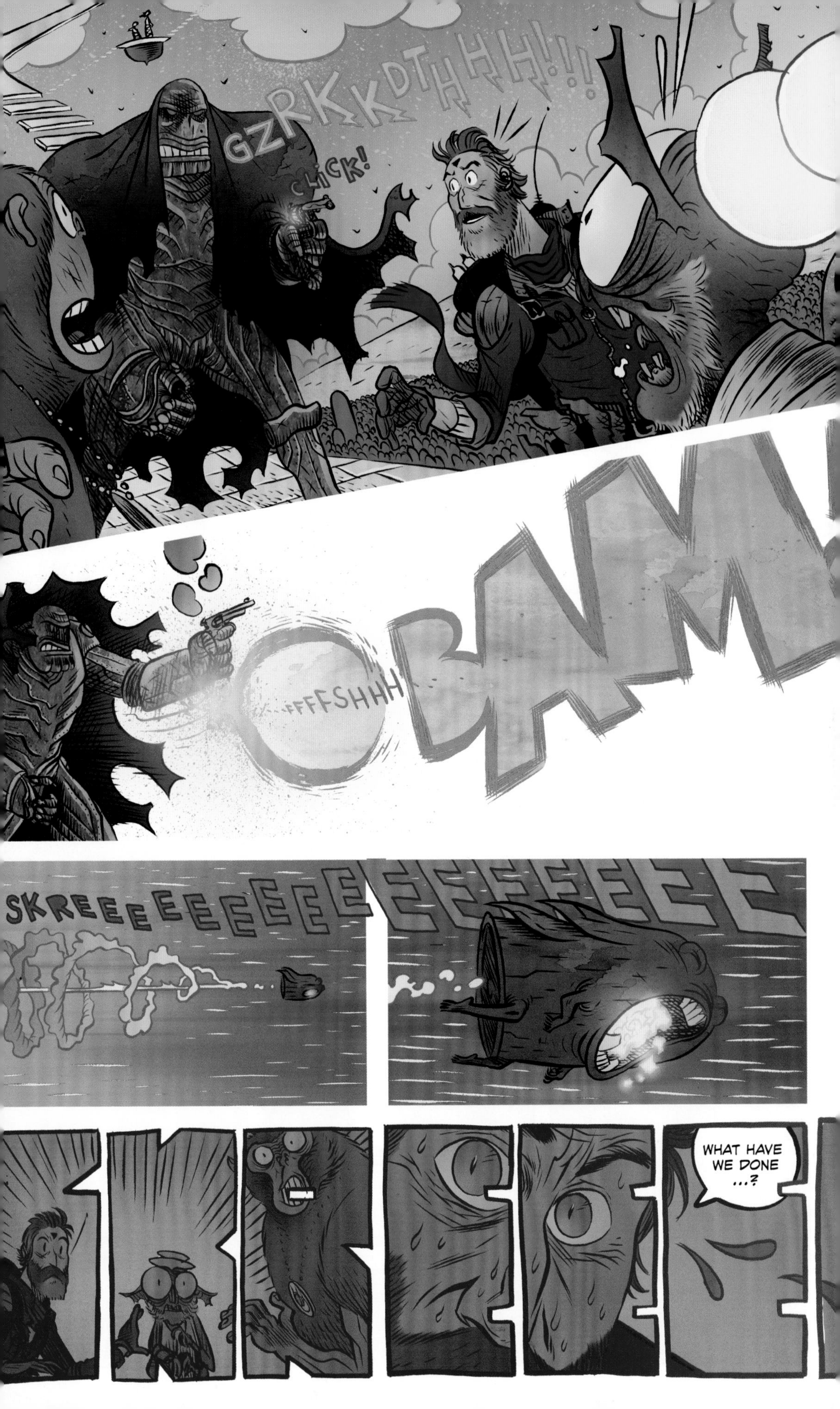
GZRKKDTHHHH!!!
CLICK!
FFFSHHH
BAM!
SKREEEEEEEEEEEEEEEEEEEE
WHAT HAVE WE DONE ...?

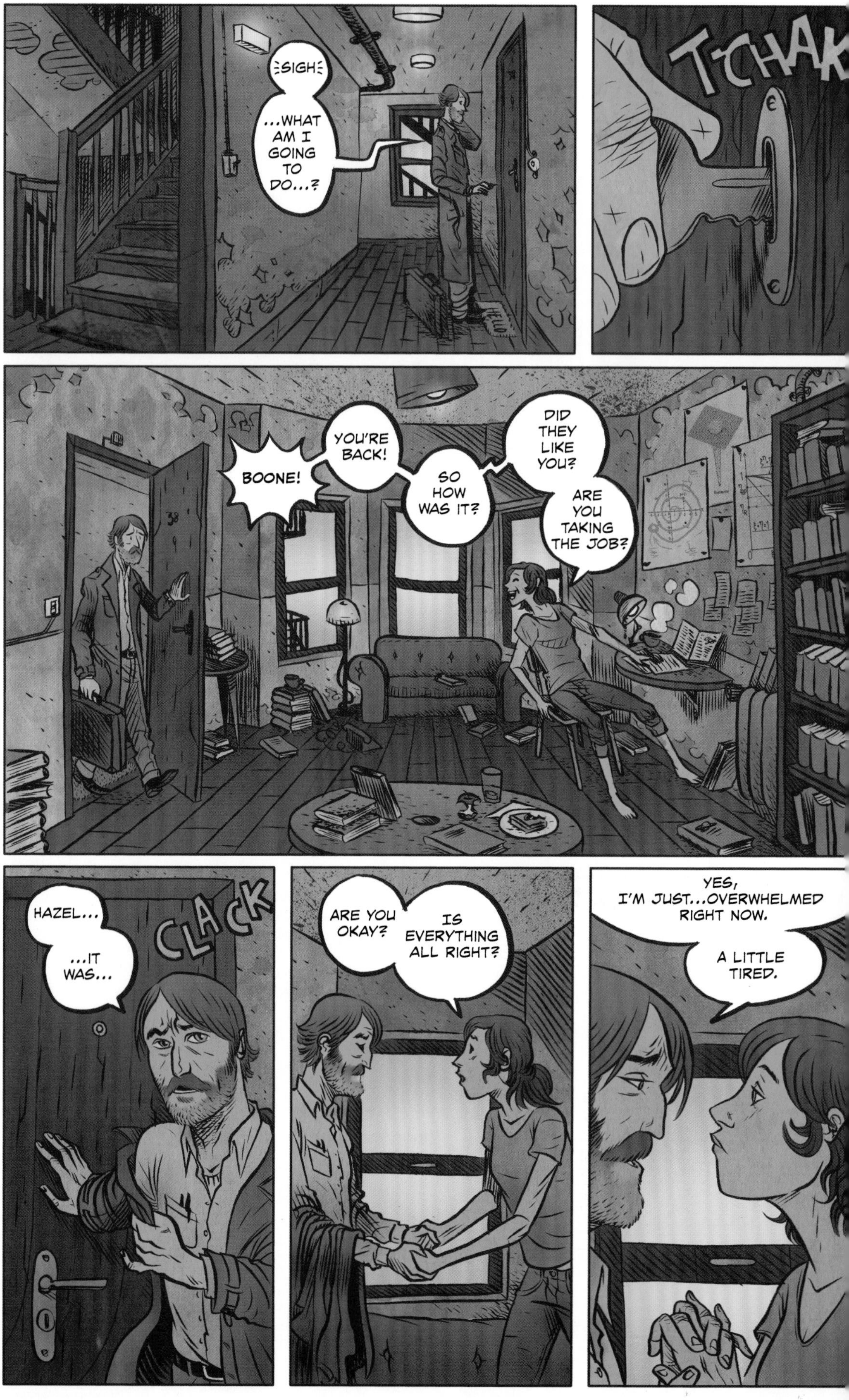

SIGH
...WHAT AM I GOING TO DO...?
T'CHAK
DID THEY LIKE YOU?
ARE YOU TAKING THE JOB?
BOONE!
YOU'RE BACK!
SO HOW WAS IT?
HAZEL...
...IT WAS...
CLACK
ARE YOU OKAY?
IS EVERYTHING ALL RIGHT?
YES, I'M JUST...OVERWHELMED RIGHT NOW.
A LITTLE TIRED.

WHAT WAS THE JOB?

WHAT DID THEY SHOW YOU?

WELL...

...I MET THE GOVERNMENT AGENTS AT THE AIRPORT AS THEY INSTRUCTED ME.

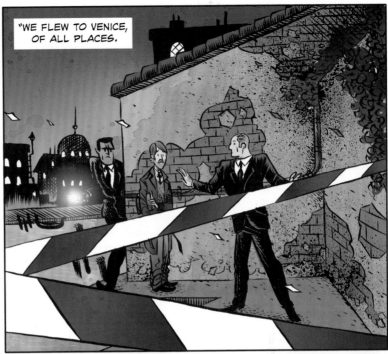

"WE FLEW TO VENICE, OF ALL PLACES.

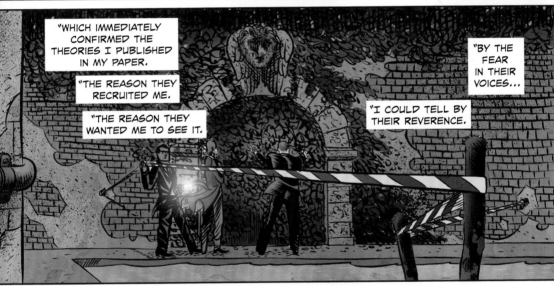

"WHICH IMMEDIATELY CONFIRMED THE THEORIES I PUBLISHED IN MY PAPER.

"THE REASON THEY RECRUITED ME.

"THE REASON THEY WANTED ME TO SEE IT.

"BY THE FEAR IN THEIR VOICES...

"I COULD TELL BY THEIR REVERENCE.

"THEY THOUGHT IT WAS MAGIC."

RUSTLE

RUSTLE

RUST

"THEY WERE CAVEMEN ATTEMPTING TO UNDERSTAND THE THEORY OF RELATIVITY, HAZEL.

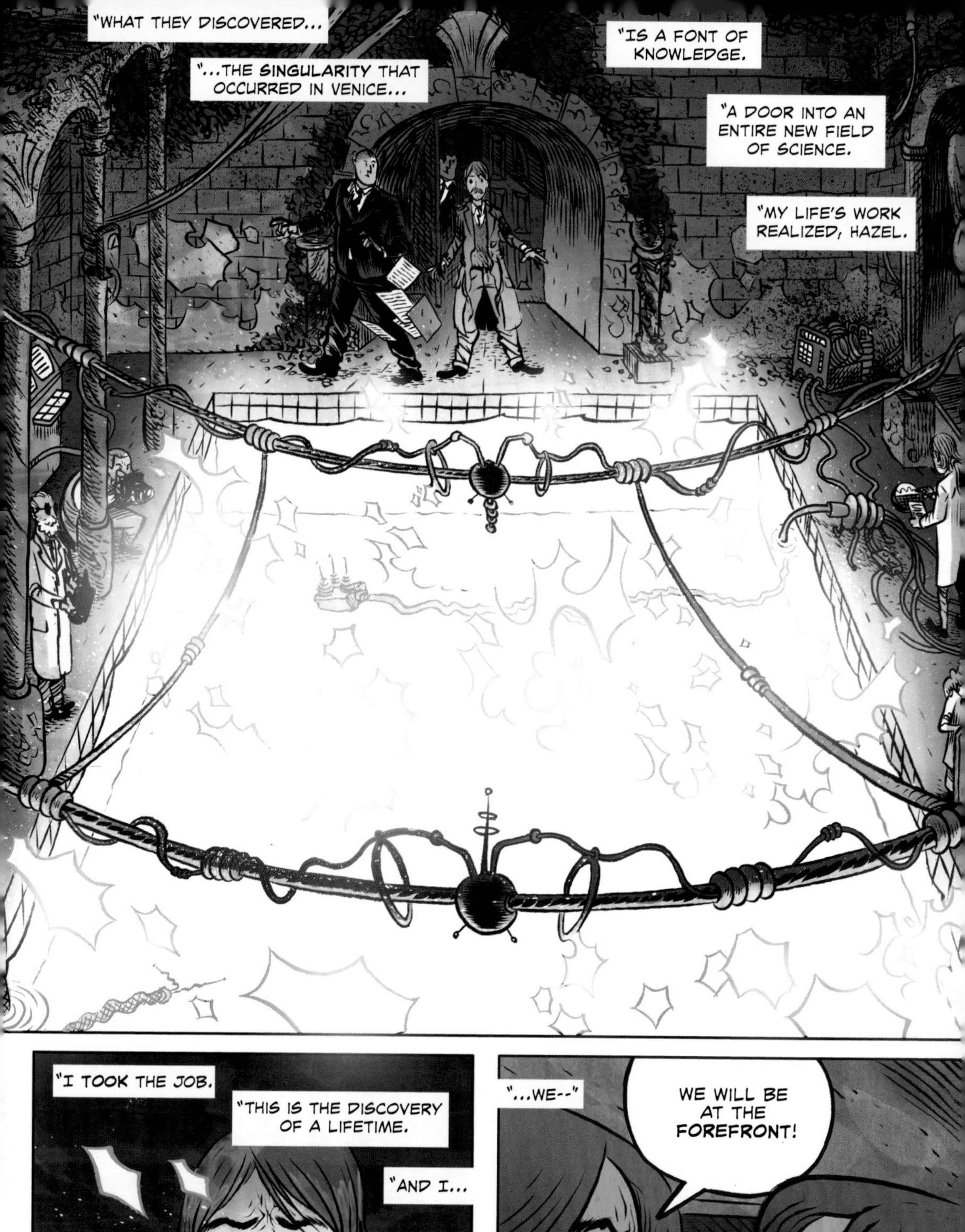
"WHAT THEY DISCOVERED...
"...THE SINGULARITY THAT OCCURRED IN VENICE...
"IS A FONT OF KNOWLEDGE.
"A DOOR INTO AN ENTIRE NEW FIELD OF SCIENCE.
"MY LIFE'S WORK REALIZED, HAZEL.

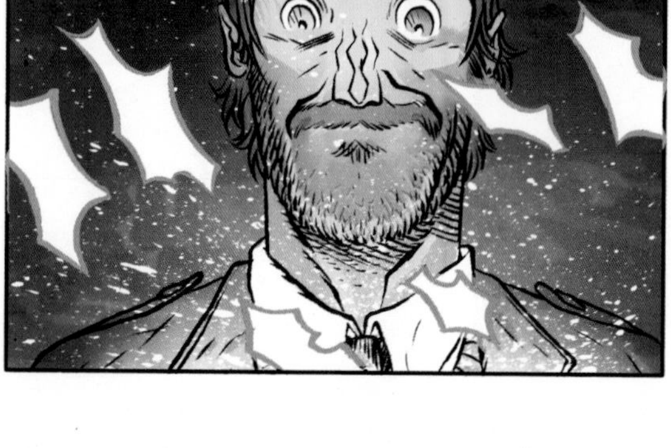
"I TOOK THE JOB.
"THIS IS THE DISCOVERY OF A LIFETIME.
"AND I...

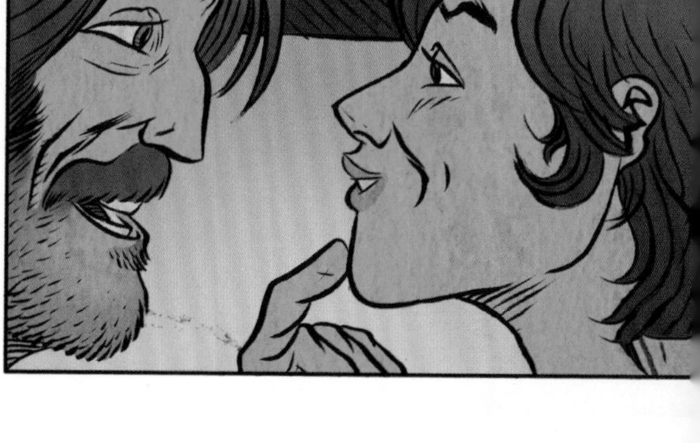
"...WE--"
WE WILL BE AT THE FOREFRONT!

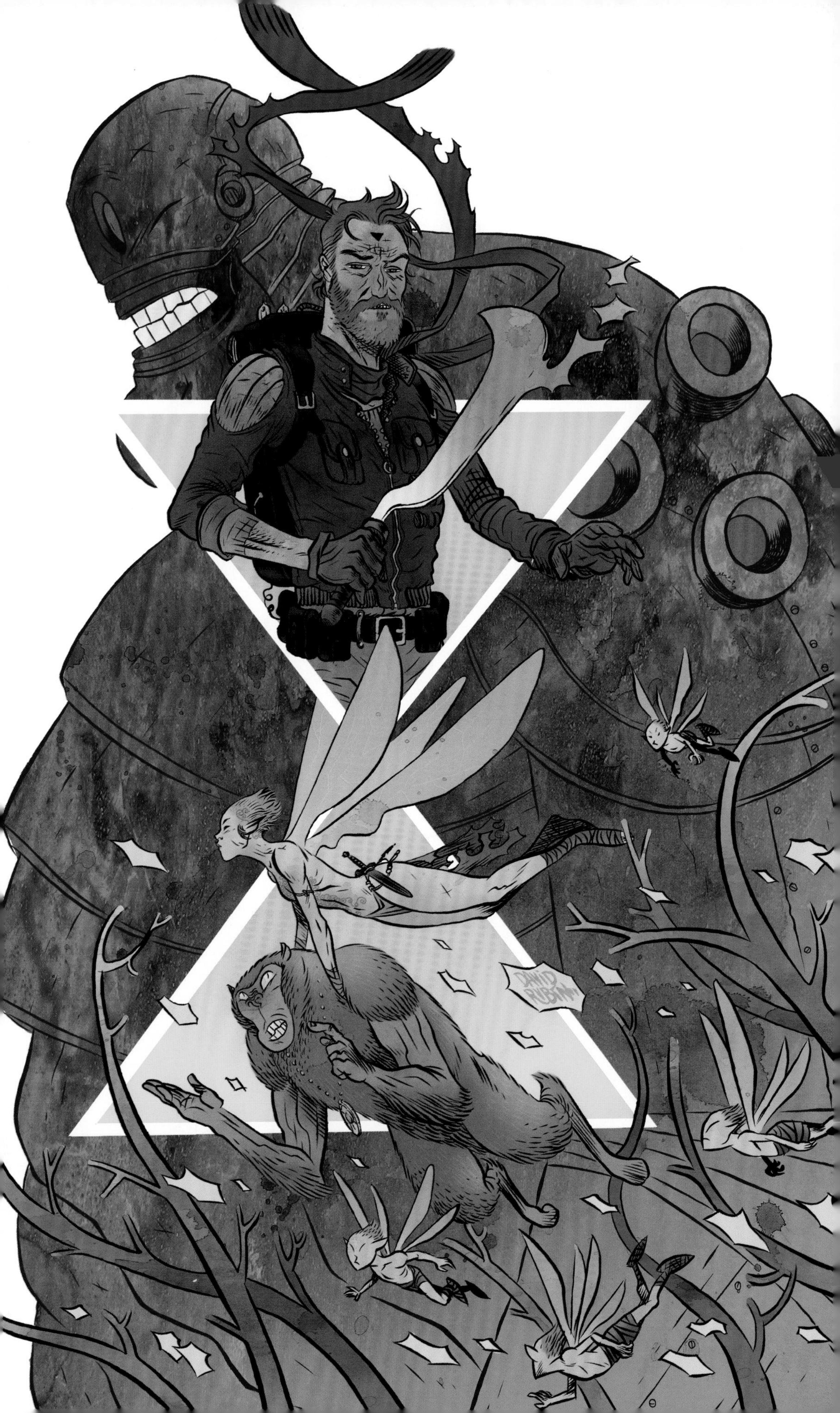
DAVID
RUBÍN

3

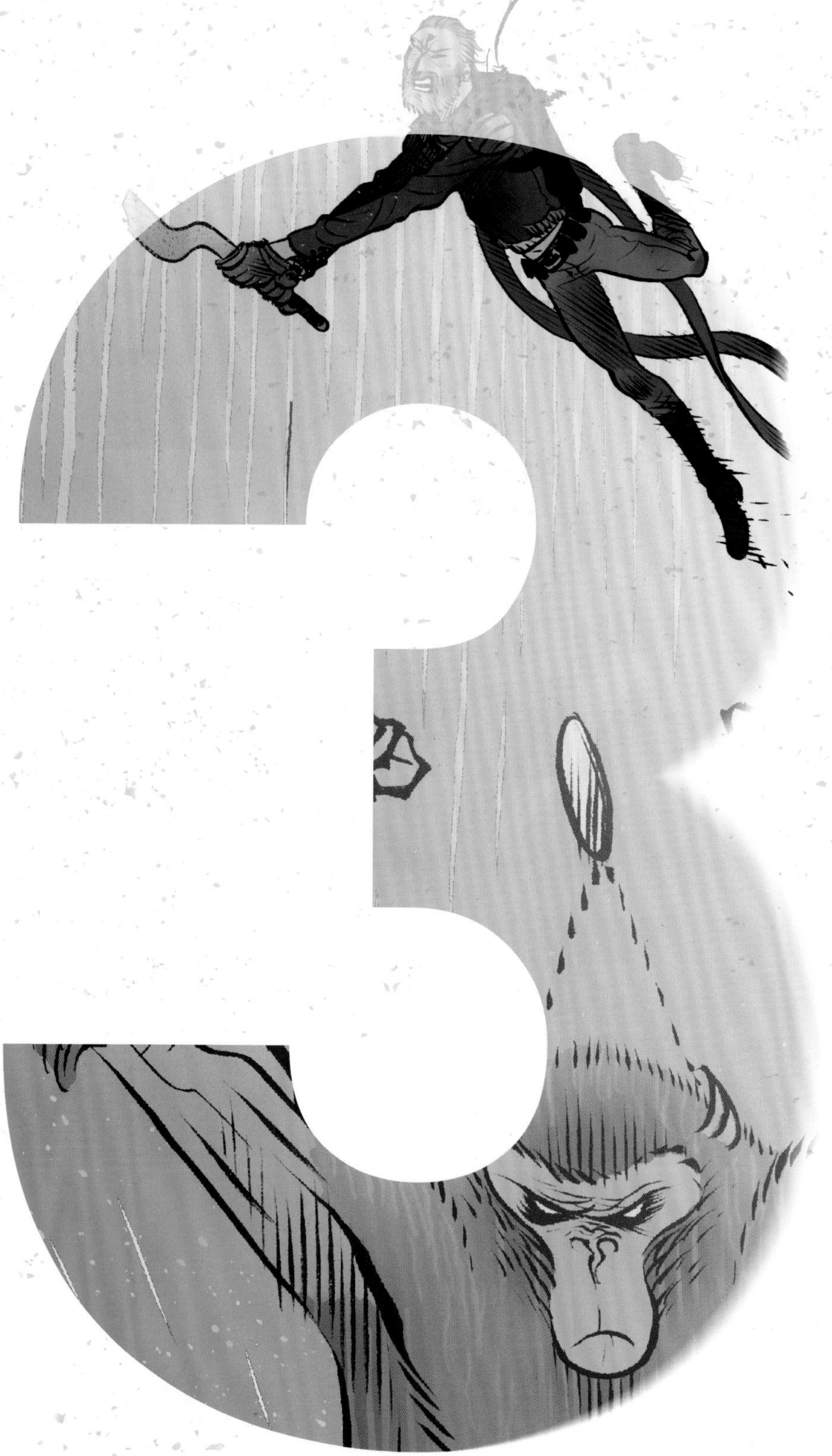

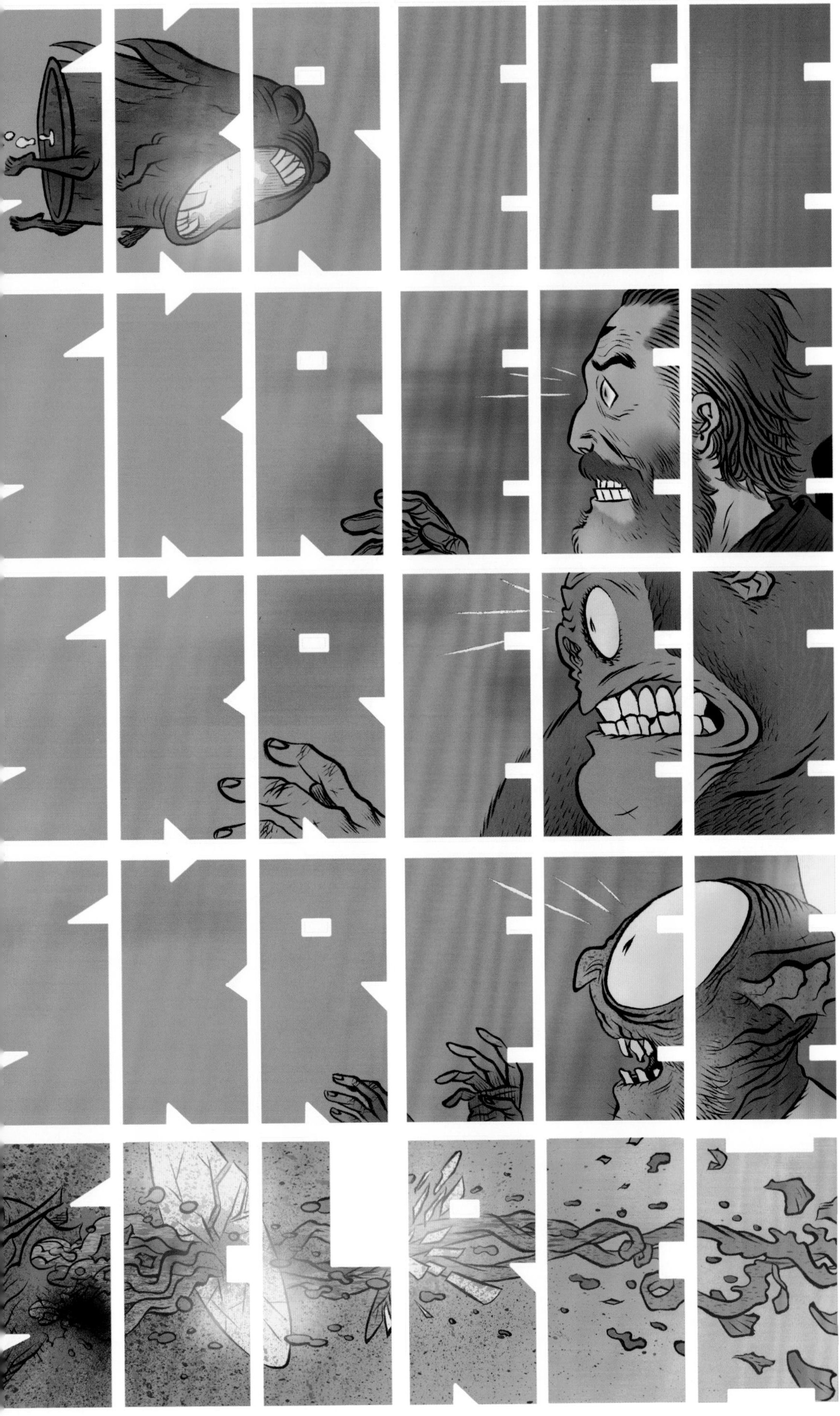
SKREEE
SKREEE
SKREEE
SKREEE

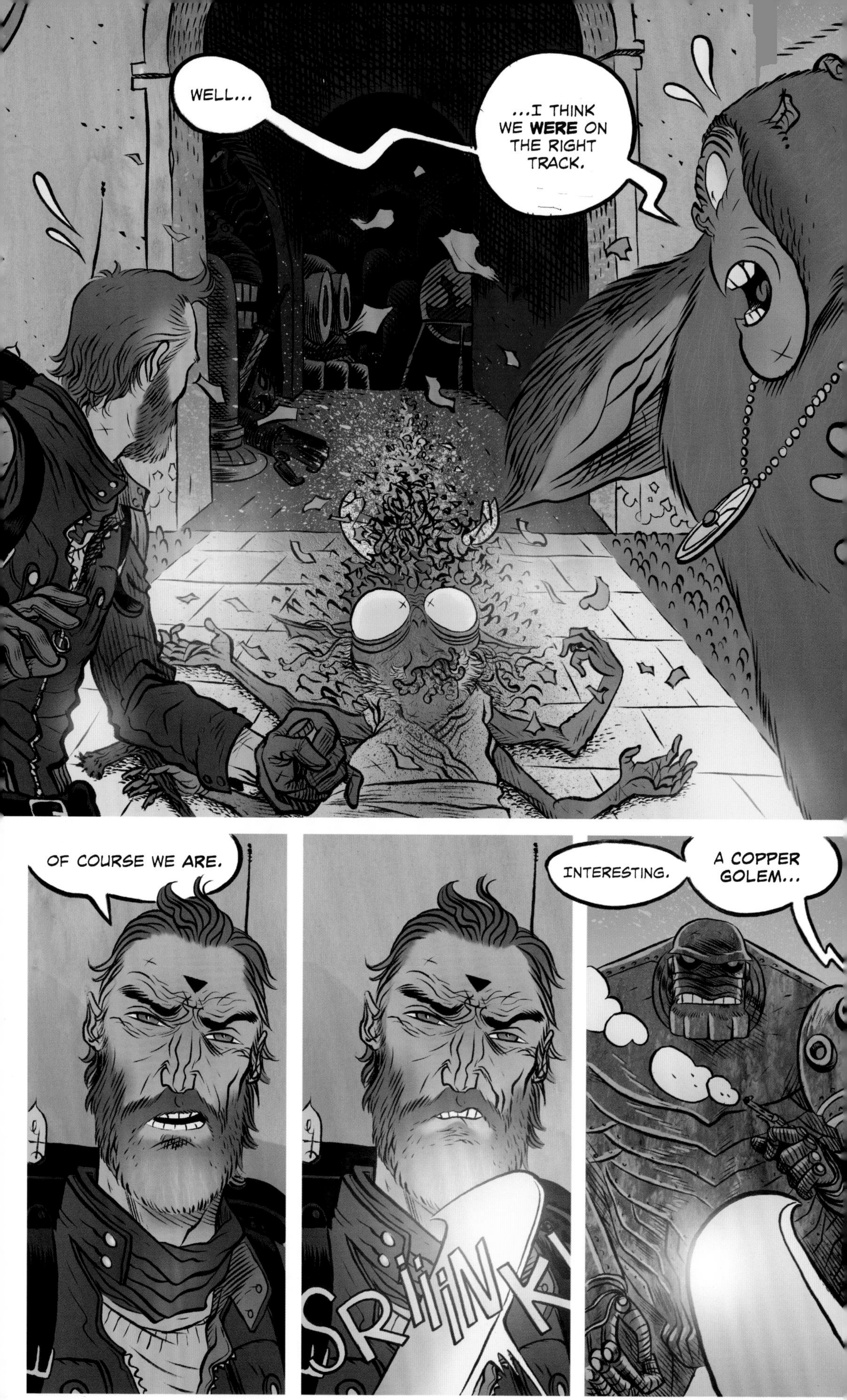
WELL...
...I THINK WE **WERE** ON THE RIGHT TRACK.
OF COURSE WE ARE.
SRIIINK
INTERESTING.
A COPPER GOLEM...

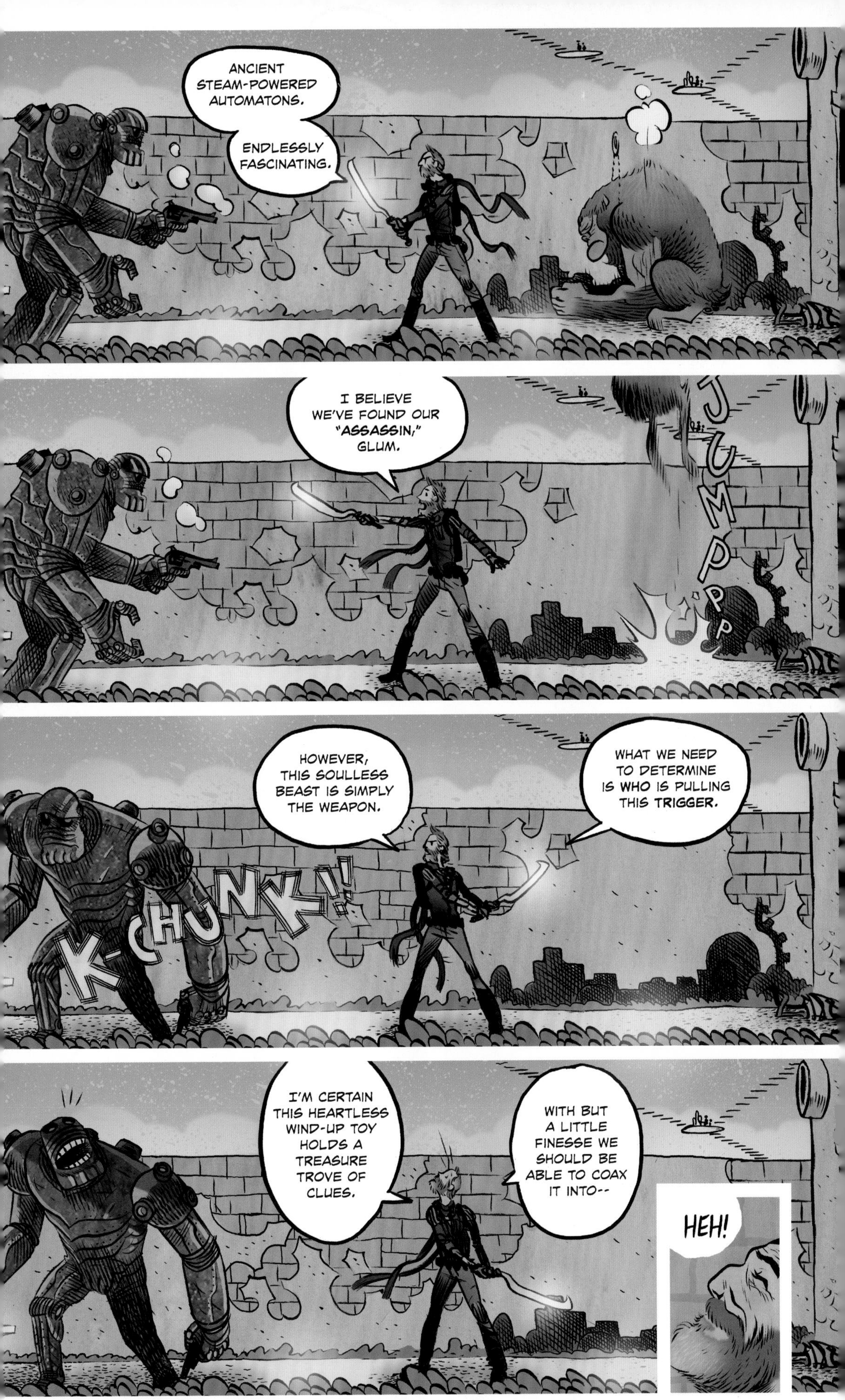

ANCIENT STEAM-POWERED AUTOMATONS.
ENDLESSLY FASCINATING.
I BELIEVE WE'VE FOUND OUR "ASSASSIN," GLUM.
JUMPP
HOWEVER, THIS SOULLESS BEAST IS SIMPLY THE WEAPON.
WHAT WE NEED TO DETERMINE IS WHO IS PULLING THIS TRIGGER.
K-CHUNK!!
I'M CERTAIN THIS HEARTLESS WIND-UP TOY HOLDS A TREASURE TROVE OF CLUES.
WITH BUT A LITTLE FINESSE WE SHOULD BE ABLE TO COAX IT INTO--
HEH!

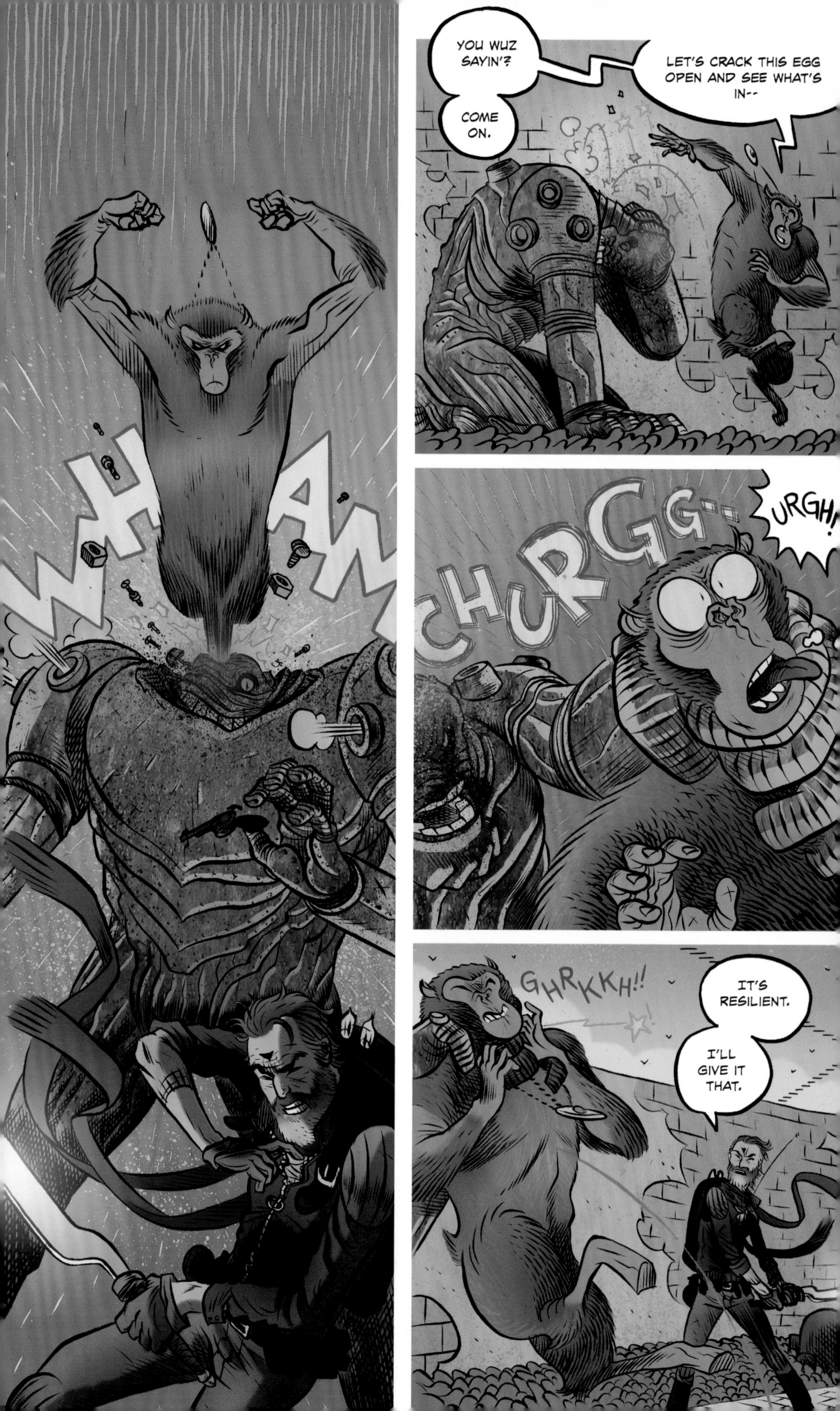
WHAM
YOU WUZ SAYIN'?
COME ON.
LET'S CRACK THIS EGG OPEN AND SEE WHAT'S IN--
CHURGG--
URGH!
GHRKKH!!
IT'S RESILIENT.
I'LL GIVE IT THAT.

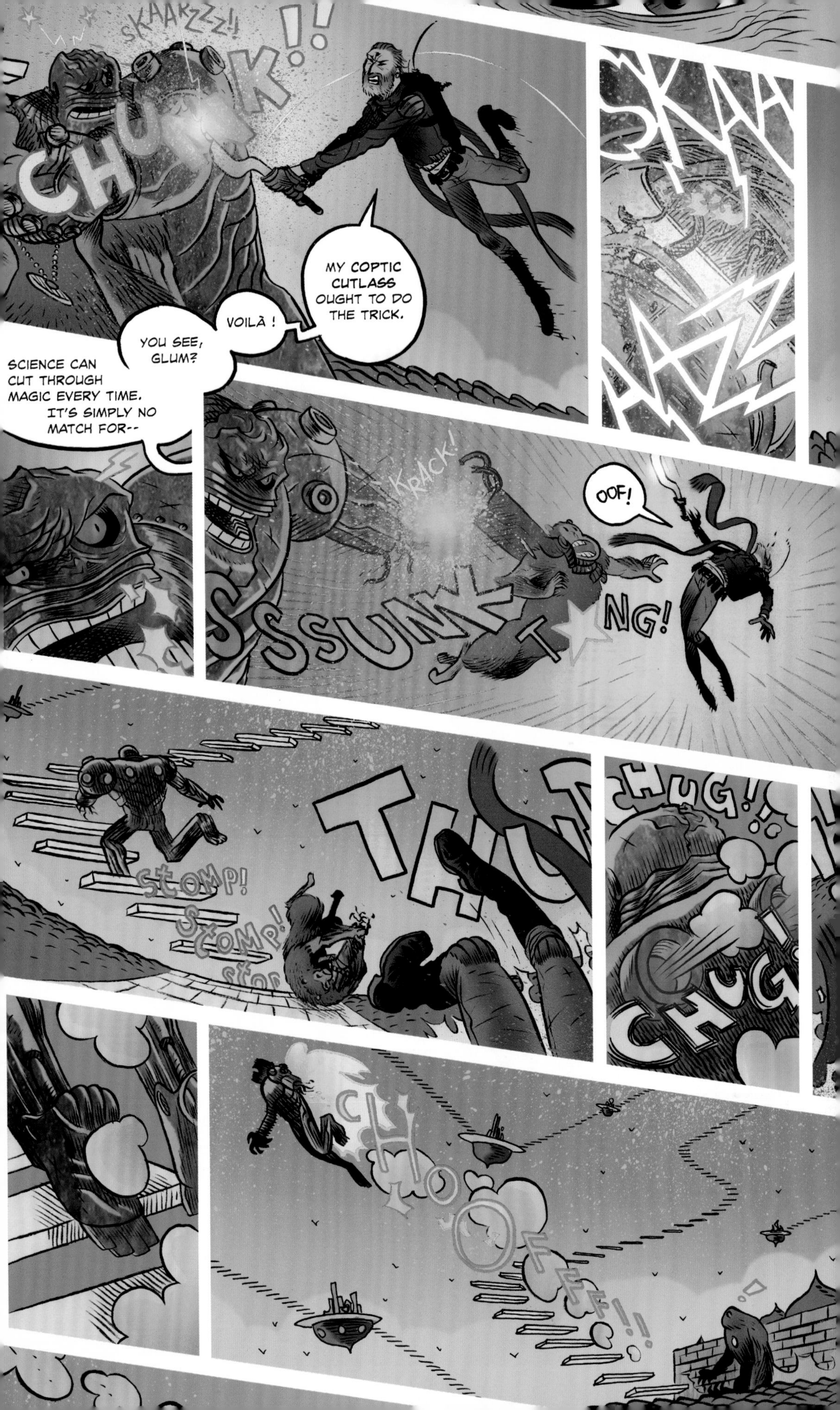

SKAARZZZ!!
CHUNK!!
MY COPTIC CUTLASS OUGHT TO DO THE TRICK.
VOILÀ !
YOU SEE, GLUM?
SCIENCE CAN CUT THROUGH MAGIC EVERY TIME. IT'S SIMPLY NO MATCH FOR--
KRACK!
OOF!
SSSUNK
TING!
STOMP!
STOMP!
THUD
CHUG!!
CHUG!
CHOOFFF!!

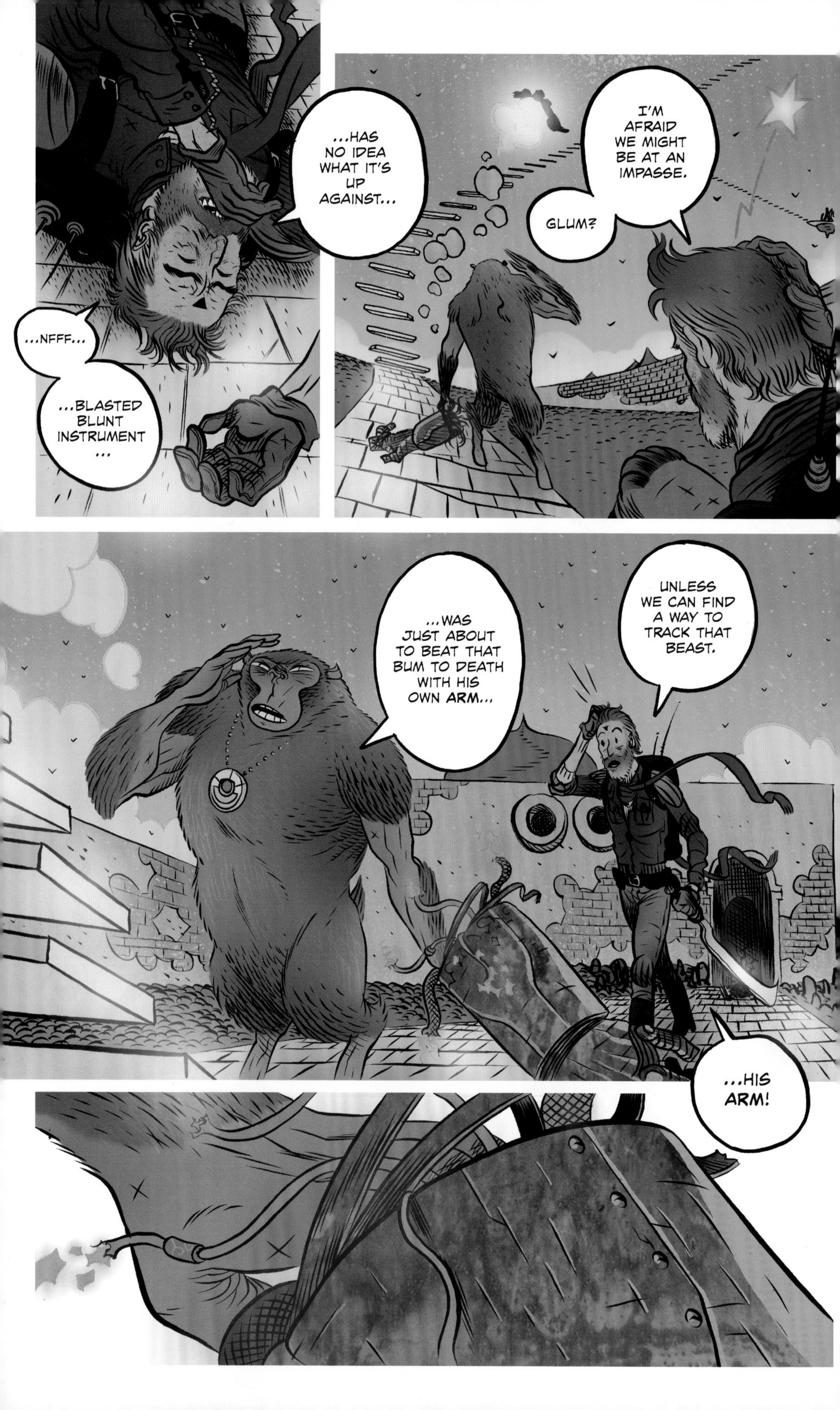
...NFFF...
...BLASTED BLUNT INSTRUMENT ...
...HAS NO IDEA WHAT IT'S UP AGAINST...
I'M AFRAID WE MIGHT BE AT AN IMPASSE.
GLUM?
UNLESS WE CAN FIND A WAY TO TRACK THAT BEAST.
...WAS JUST ABOUT TO BEAT THAT BUM TO DEATH WITH HIS OWN ARM...
...HIS ARM!

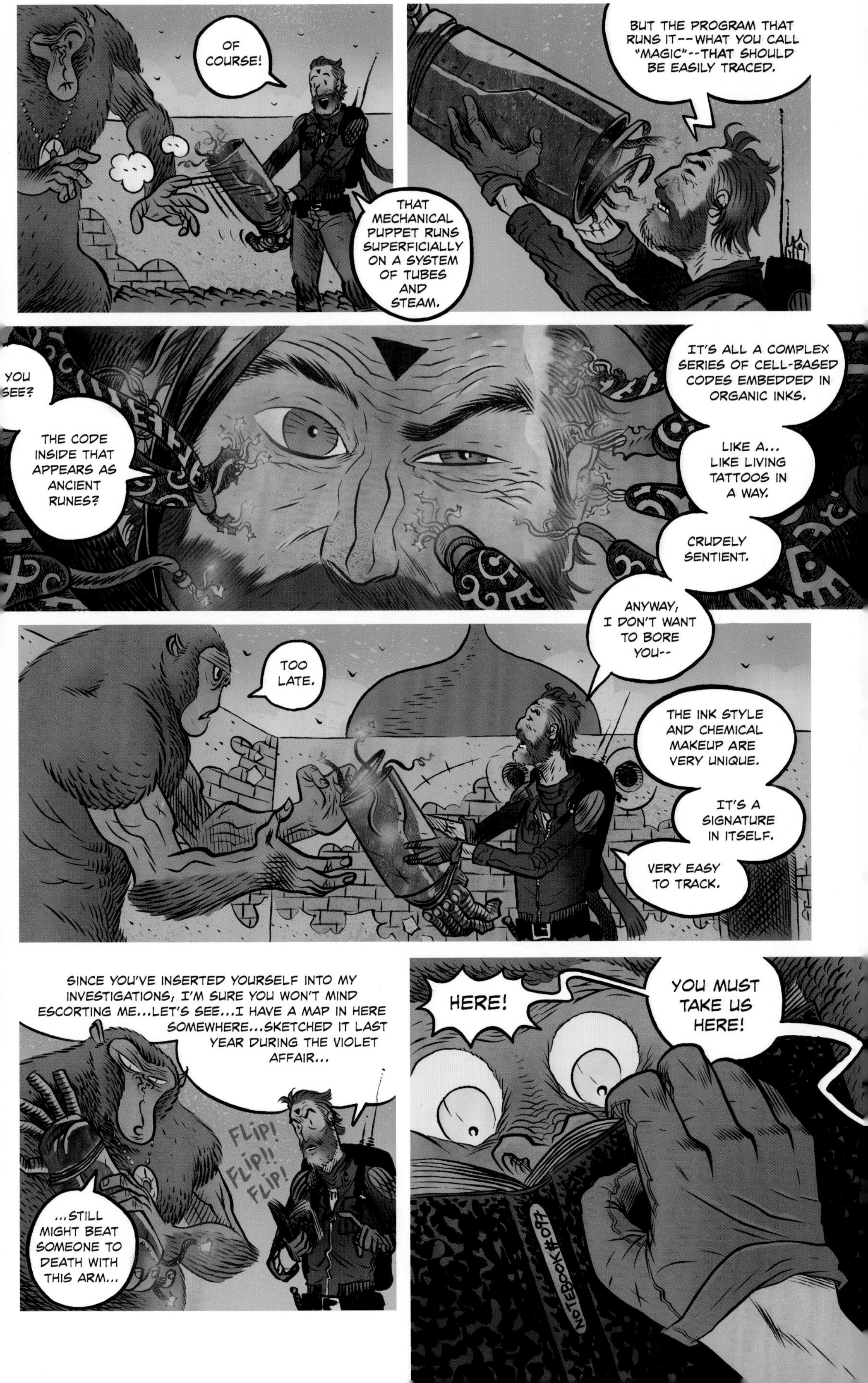
OF COURSE!
THAT MECHANICAL PUPPET RUNS SUPERFICIALLY ON A SYSTEM OF TUBES AND STEAM.
BUT THE PROGRAM THAT RUNS IT--WHAT YOU CALL "MAGIC"--THAT SHOULD BE EASILY TRACED.
YOU SEE?
THE CODE INSIDE THAT APPEARS AS ANCIENT RUNES?
IT'S ALL A COMPLEX SERIES OF CELL-BASED CODES EMBEDDED IN ORGANIC INKS.
LIKE A... LIKE LIVING TATTOOS IN A WAY.
CRUDELY SENTIENT.
TOO LATE.
ANYWAY, I DON'T WANT TO BORE YOU--
THE INK STYLE AND CHEMICAL MAKEUP ARE VERY UNIQUE.
IT'S A SIGNATURE IN ITSELF.
VERY EASY TO TRACK.
SINCE YOU'VE INSERTED YOURSELF INTO MY INVESTIGATIONS, I'M SURE YOU WON'T MIND ESCORTING ME...LET'S SEE...I HAVE A MAP IN HERE SOMEWHERE...SKETCHED IT LAST YEAR DURING THE VIOLET AFFAIR...
FLIP! FLIP!! FLIP!
...STILL MIGHT BEAT SOMEONE TO DEATH WITH THIS ARM...
HERE!
YOU MUST TAKE US HERE!
NOTEBOOK #097

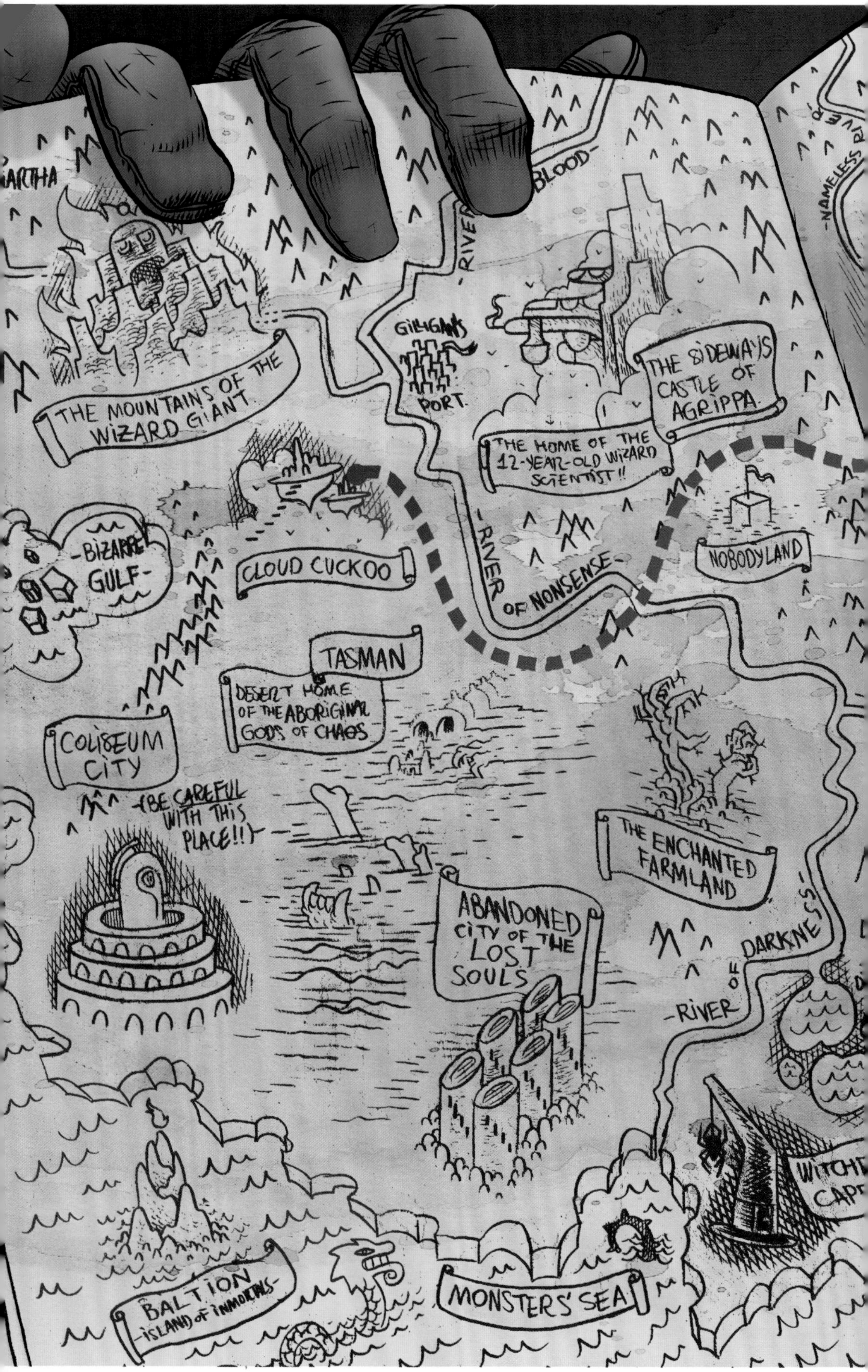
-RIVER OF BLOOD-
THE MOUNTAINS OF THE WIZARD GIANT
GILLIGAN'S PORT
THE SIDEWAYS CASTLE OF AGRIPPA
THE HOME OF THE 12-YEAR-OLD WIZARD SCIENTIST!!
-BIZARRE GULF-
CLOUD CUCKOO
-RIVER OF NONSENSE-
NOBODYLAND
TASMAN
DESERT HOME OF THE ABORIGINAL GODS OF CHAOS
COLISEUM CITY
(BE CAREFUL WITH THIS PLACE!!)
THE ENCHANTED FARMLAND
ABANDONED CITY OF THE LOST SOULS
-RIVER OF DARKNESS-
BALTION -ISLAND OF IMMORTALS-
MONSTERS' SEA

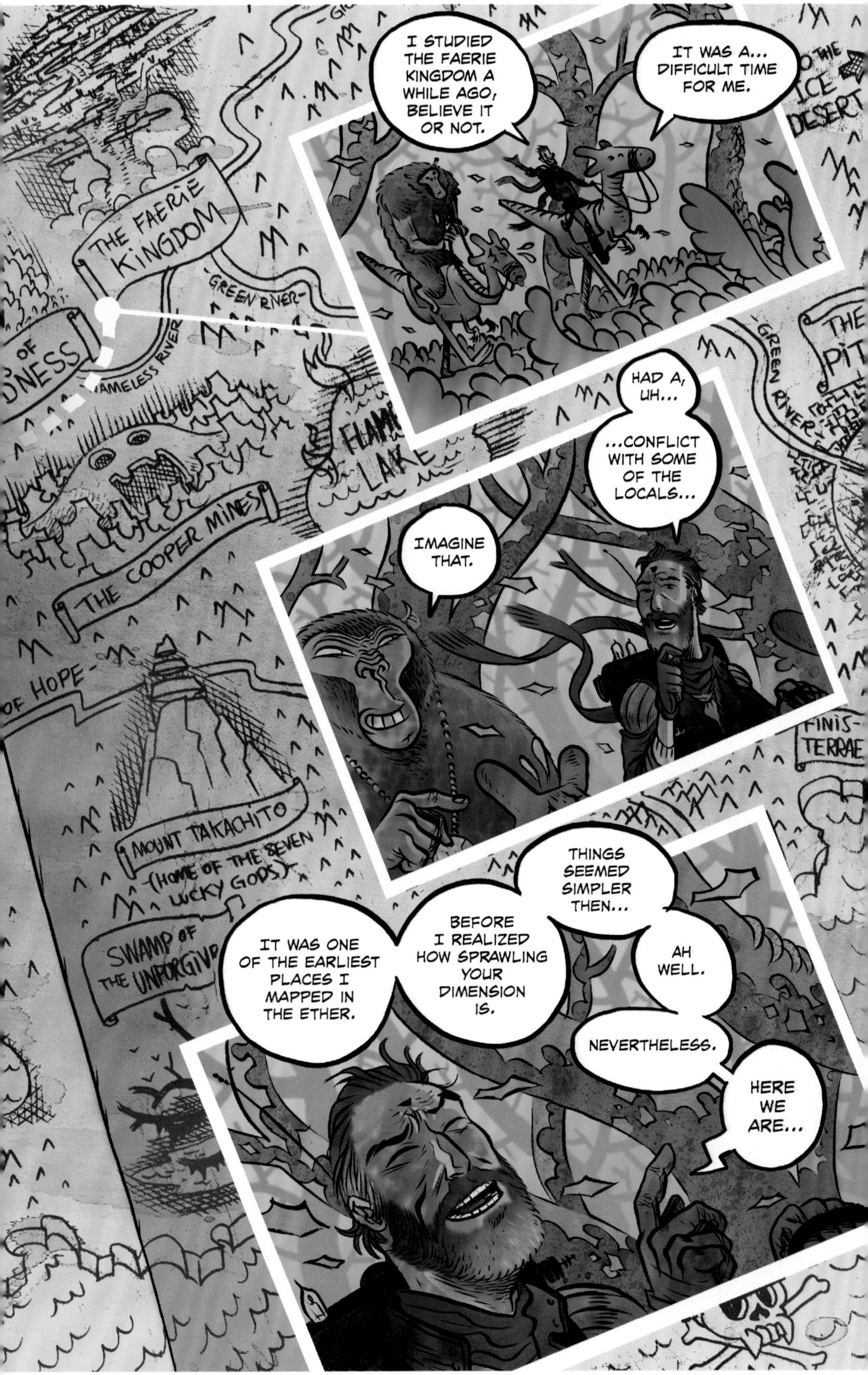
I STUDIED THE FAERIE KINGDOM A WHILE AGO, BELIEVE IT OR NOT.
IT WAS A... DIFFICULT TIME FOR ME.
HAD A, UH...
...CONFLICT WITH SOME OF THE LOCALS...
IMAGINE THAT.
IT WAS ONE OF THE EARLIEST PLACES I MAPPED IN THE ETHER.
BEFORE I REALIZED HOW SPRAWLING YOUR DIMENSION IS.
THINGS SEEMED SIMPLER THEN...
AH WELL.
NEVERTHELESS.
HERE WE ARE...
THE FAERIE KINGDOM
GREEN RIVER
NAMELESS RIVER
THE COOPER MINES
MOUNT TAKACHITO (HOME OF THE SEVEN LUCKY GODS)
FINIS-TERRAE

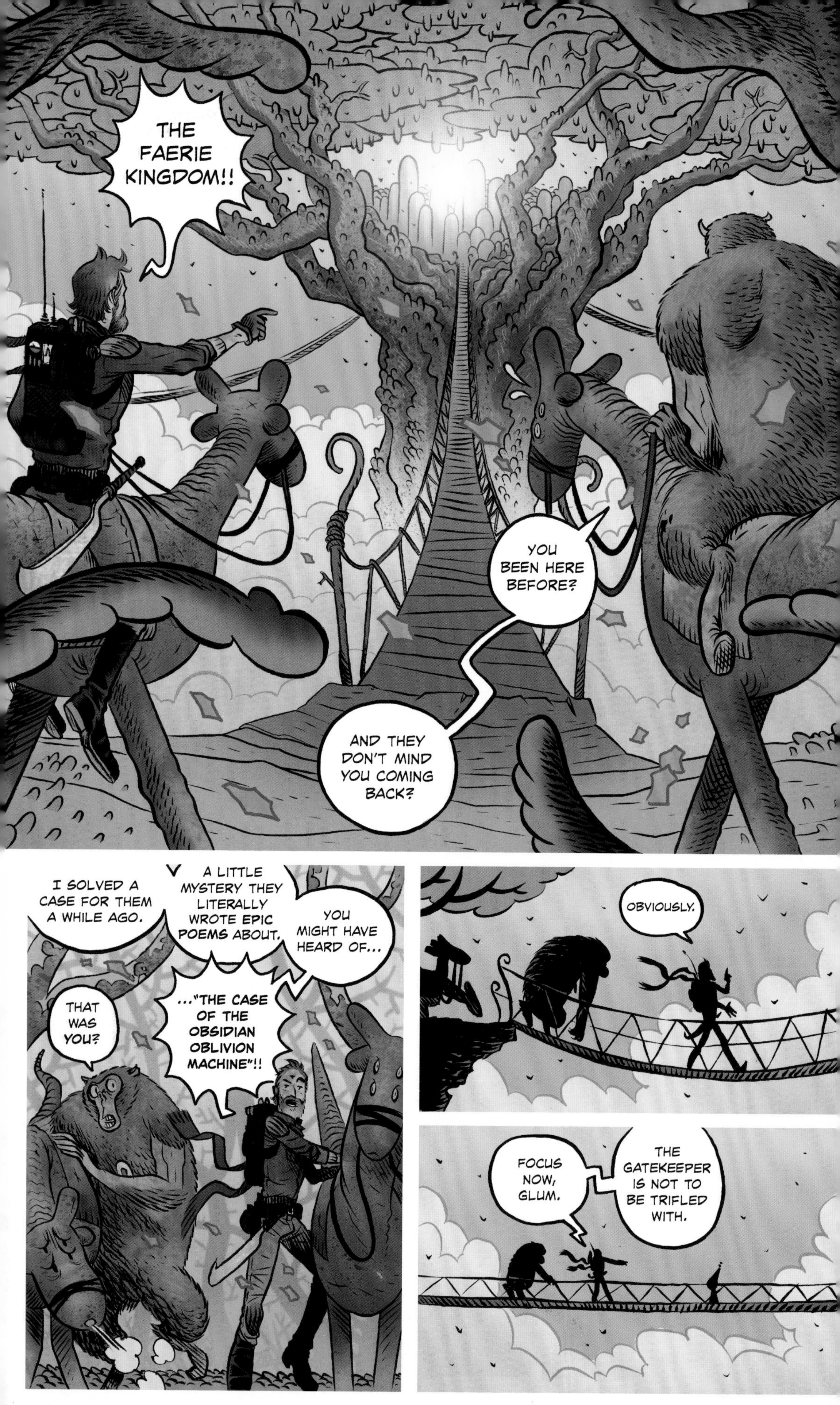
THE FAERIE KINGDOM!!
YOU BEEN HERE BEFORE?
AND THEY DON'T MIND YOU COMING BACK?
I SOLVED A CASE FOR THEM A WHILE AGO.
A LITTLE MYSTERY THEY LITERALLY WROTE EPIC POEMS ABOUT.
YOU MIGHT HAVE HEARD OF...
..."THE CASE OF THE OBSIDIAN OBLIVION MACHINE"!!
THAT WAS YOU?
OBVIOUSLY.
FOCUS NOW, GLUM.
THE GATEKEEPER IS NOT TO BE TRIFLED WITH.

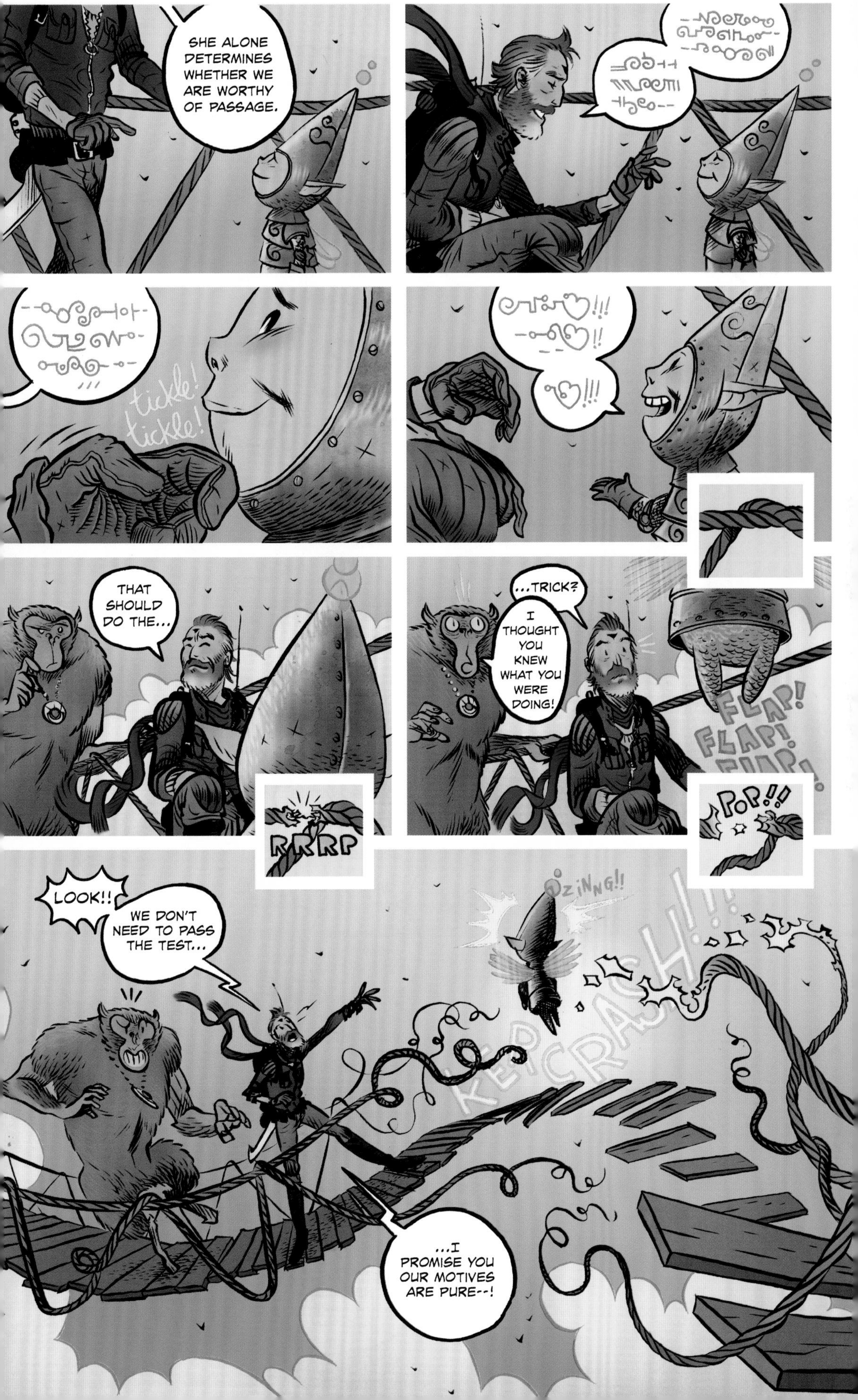
SHE ALONE DETERMINES WHETHER WE ARE WORTHY OF PASSAGE.
tickle! tickle!
THAT SHOULD DO THE...
RRRP
...TRICK?
I THOUGHT YOU KNEW WHAT YOU WERE DOING!
FLAP! FLAP!
POP!!!
LOOK!!
WE DON'T NEED TO PASS THE TEST...
ZINNG!!
KERCRASH!!!
...I PROMISE YOU OUR MOTIVES ARE PURE--!

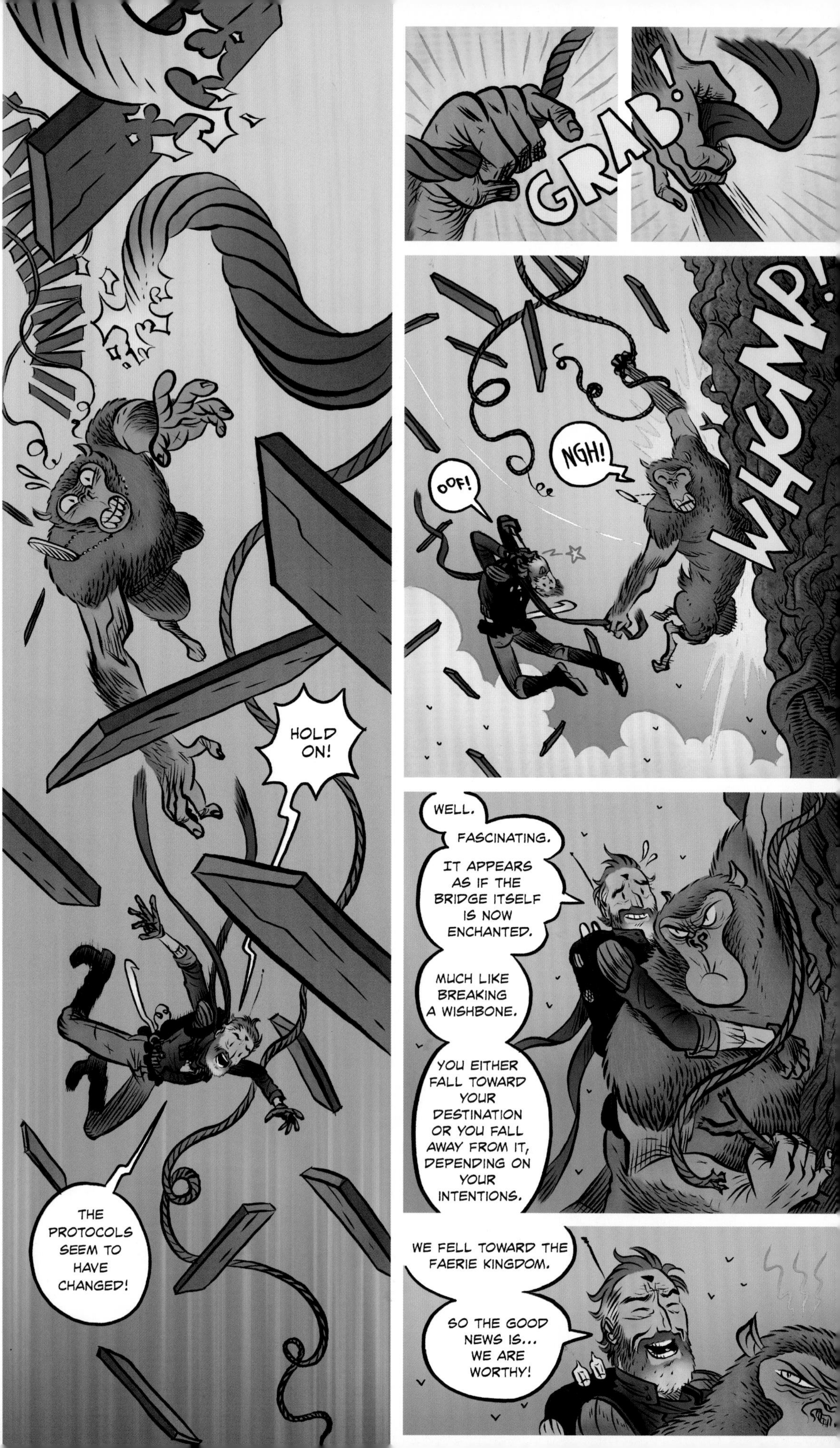
HOLD ON!
THE PROTOCOLS SEEM TO HAVE CHANGED!
GRAB!
NGH!
OOF!
WHUMP!
WELL.
FASCINATING.
IT APPEARS AS IF THE BRIDGE ITSELF IS NOW ENCHANTED.
MUCH LIKE BREAKING A WISHBONE.
YOU EITHER FALL TOWARD YOUR DESTINATION OR YOU FALL AWAY FROM IT, DEPENDING ON YOUR INTENTIONS.
WE FELL TOWARD THE FAERIE KINGDOM.
SO THE GOOD NEWS IS... WE ARE WORTHY!

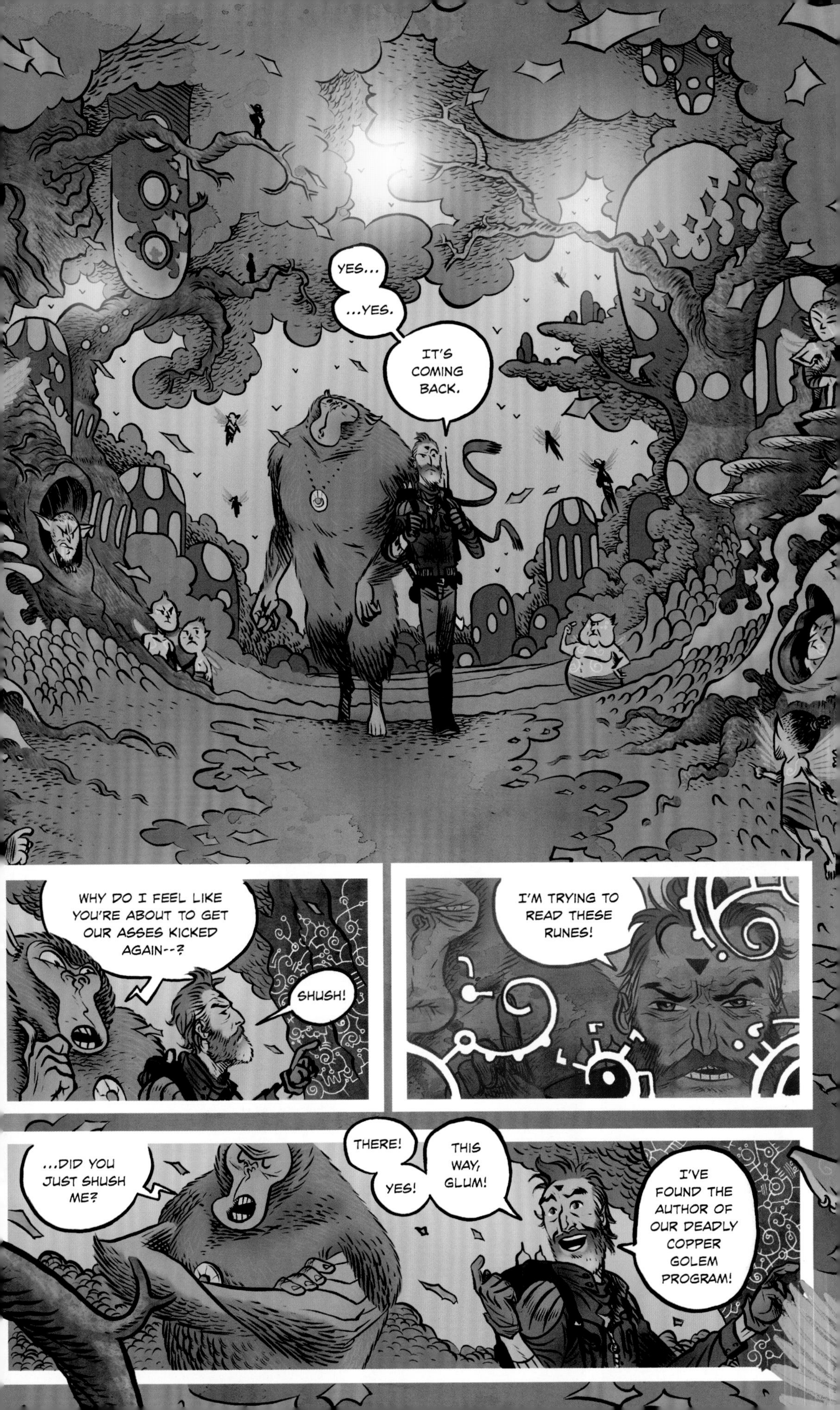
YES...
...YES.
IT'S COMING BACK.
WHY DO I FEEL LIKE YOU'RE ABOUT TO GET OUR ASSES KICKED AGAIN--?
SHUSH!
I'M TRYING TO READ THESE RUNES!
...DID YOU JUST SHUSH ME?
THERE!
YES!
THIS WAY, GLUM!
I'VE FOUND THE AUTHOR OF OUR DEADLY COPPER GOLEM PROGRAM!

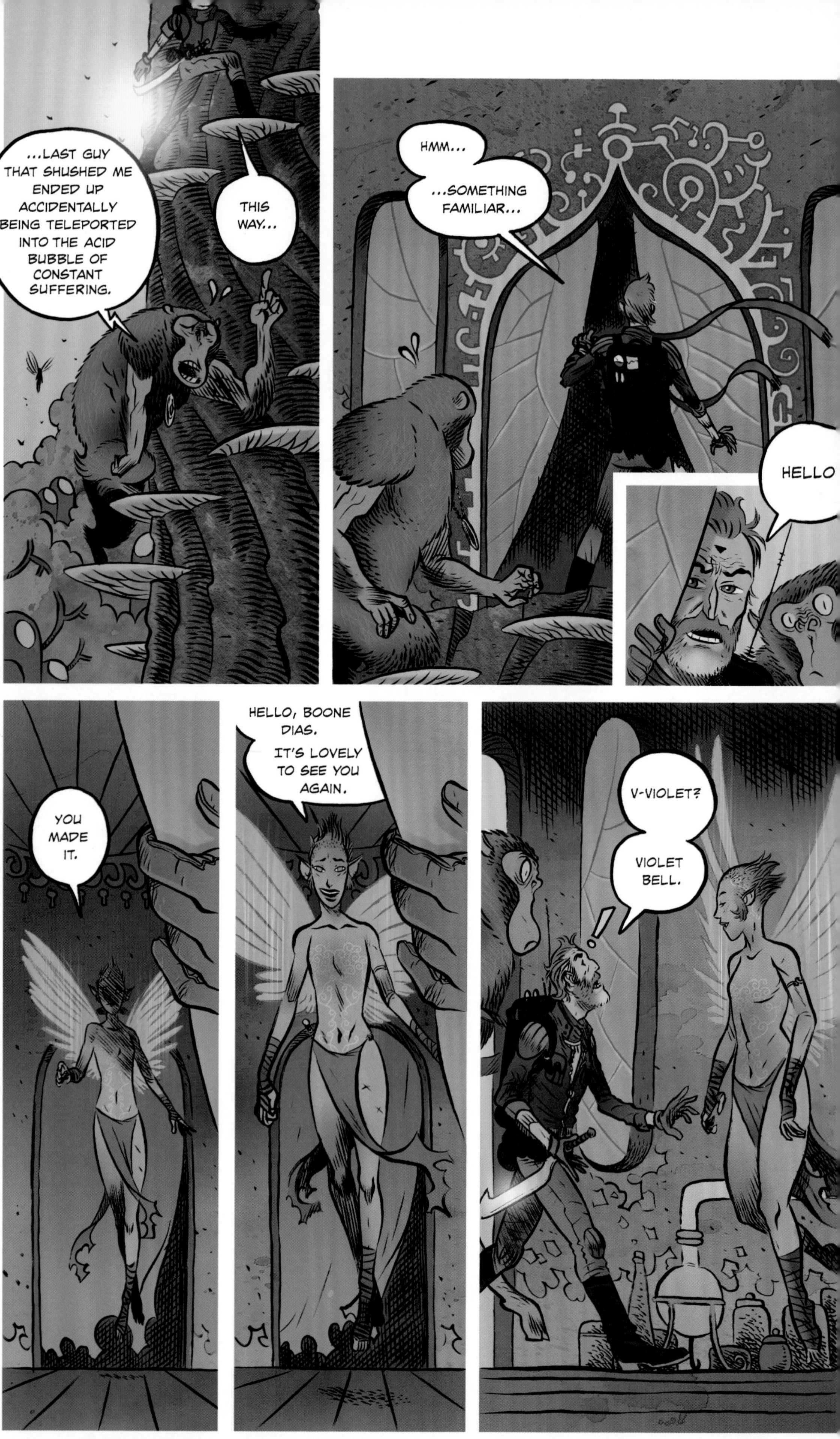
...LAST GUY THAT SHUSHED ME ENDED UP ACCIDENTALLY BEING TELEPORTED INTO THE ACID BUBBLE OF CONSTANT SUFFERING.
THIS WAY...
HMM...
...SOMETHING FAMILIAR...
HELLO
YOU MADE IT.
HELLO, BOONE DIAS.
IT'S LOVELY TO SEE YOU AGAIN.
V-VIOLET?
VIOLET BELL.

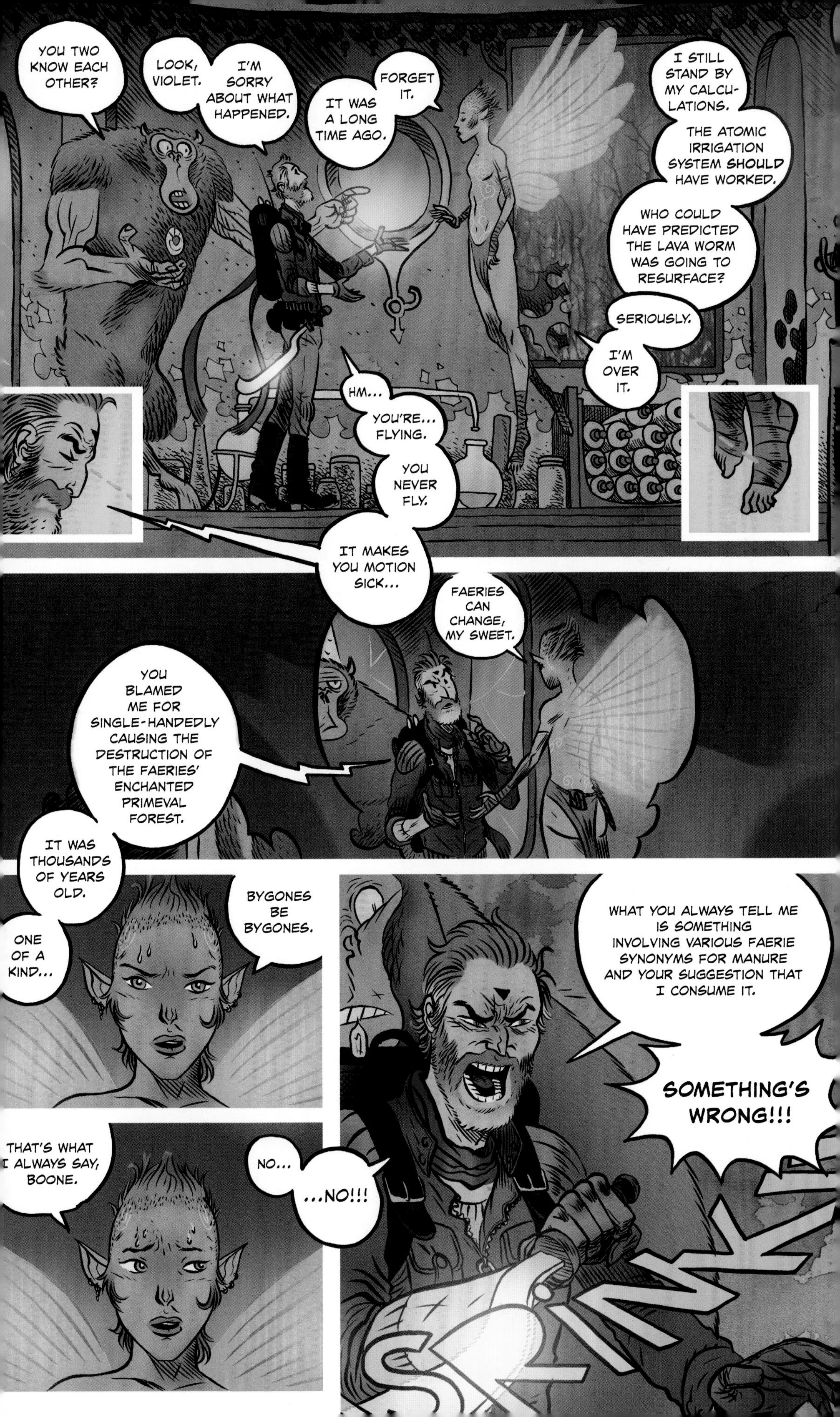
YOU TWO KNOW EACH OTHER?
LOOK, VIOLET.
I'M SORRY ABOUT WHAT HAPPENED.
FORGET IT.
IT WAS A LONG TIME AGO.
I STILL STAND BY MY CALCU-LATIONS.
THE ATOMIC IRRIGATION SYSTEM SHOULD HAVE WORKED.
WHO COULD HAVE PREDICTED THE LAVA WORM WAS GOING TO RESURFACE?
SERIOUSLY.
I'M OVER IT.
HM...
YOU'RE... FLYING.
YOU NEVER FLY.
IT MAKES YOU MOTION SICK...
FAERIES CAN CHANGE, MY SWEET.
YOU BLAMED ME FOR SINGLE-HANDEDLY CAUSING THE DESTRUCTION OF THE FAERIES' ENCHANTED PRIMEVAL FOREST.
IT WAS THOUSANDS OF YEARS OLD.
ONE OF A KIND...
BYGONES BE BYGONES.
THAT'S WHAT I ALWAYS SAY, BOONE.
NO...
...NO!!!
WHAT YOU ALWAYS TELL ME IS SOMETHING INVOLVING VARIOUS FAERIE SYNONYMS FOR MANURE AND YOUR SUGGESTION THAT I CONSUME IT.
SOMETHING'S WRONG!!!

GAHH!!

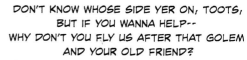

DON'T KNOW WHOSE SIDE YER ON, TOOTS,
BUT IF YOU WANNA HELP--
WHY DON'T YOU FLY US AFTER THAT GOLEM
AND YOUR OLD FRIEND?

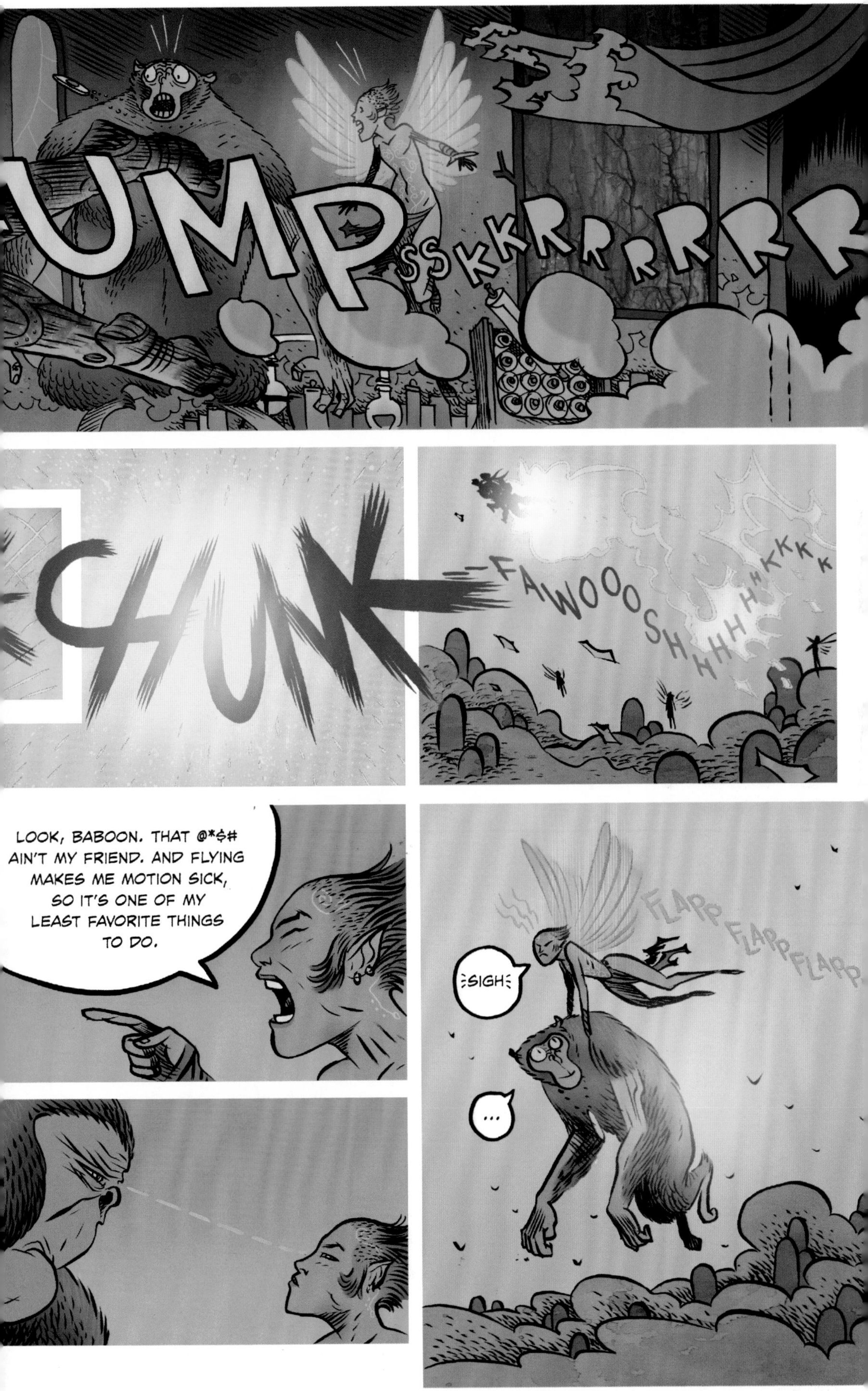

UMP
SSKKRRRRRRRR
CHUNK
FAWOOOSHHHHHKKKK
LOOK, BABOON. THAT @*$# AIN'T MY FRIEND. AND FLYING MAKES ME MOTION SICK, SO IT'S ONE OF MY LEAST FAVORITE THINGS TO DO.
SIGH
FLAPP FLAPP FLAPP
...

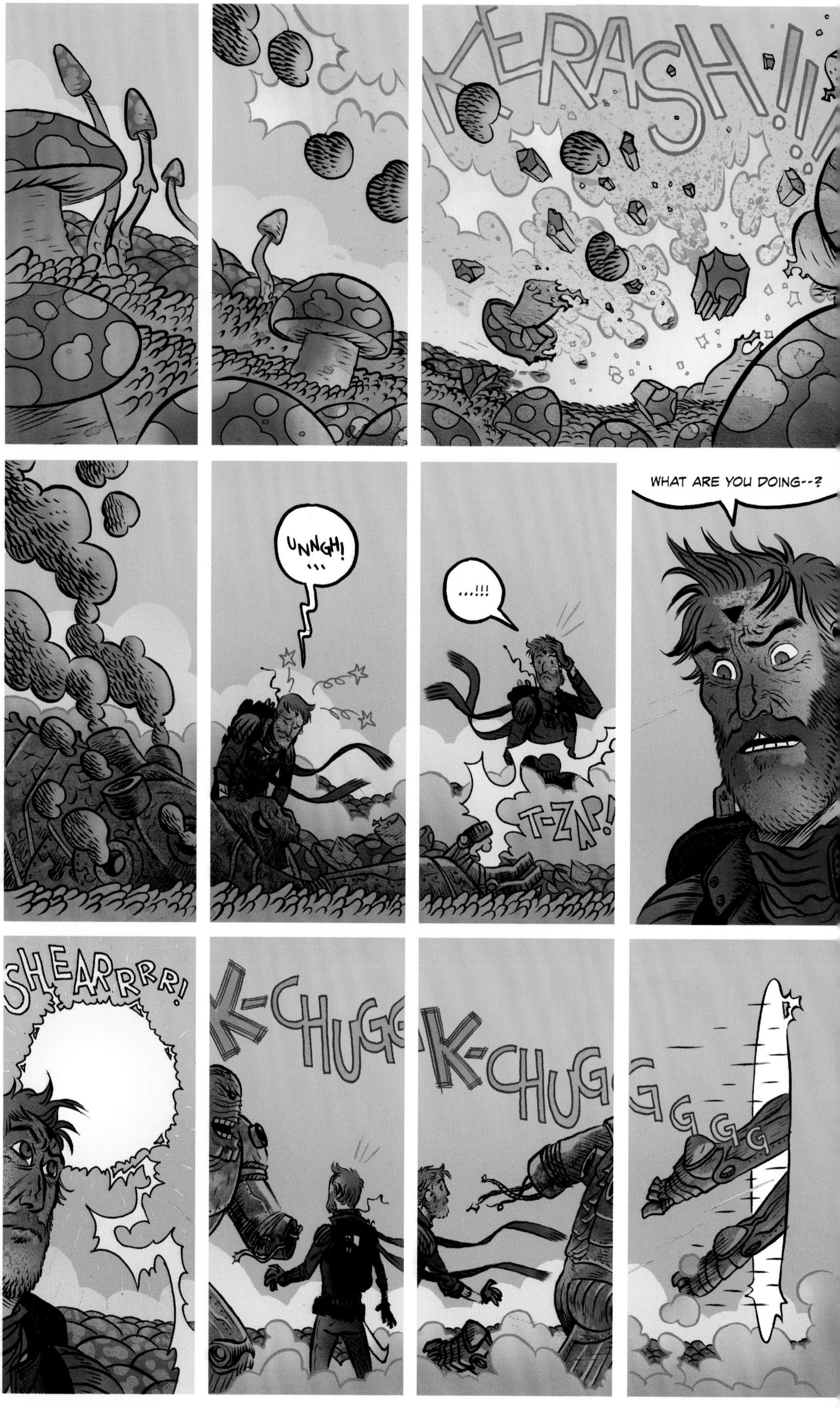
KERASH!!!
UNNGH! ...
...!!!
T-ZAP!
WHAT ARE YOU DOING--?
SHEARRRRR!
K-CHUGG
K-CHUGG
GGGG

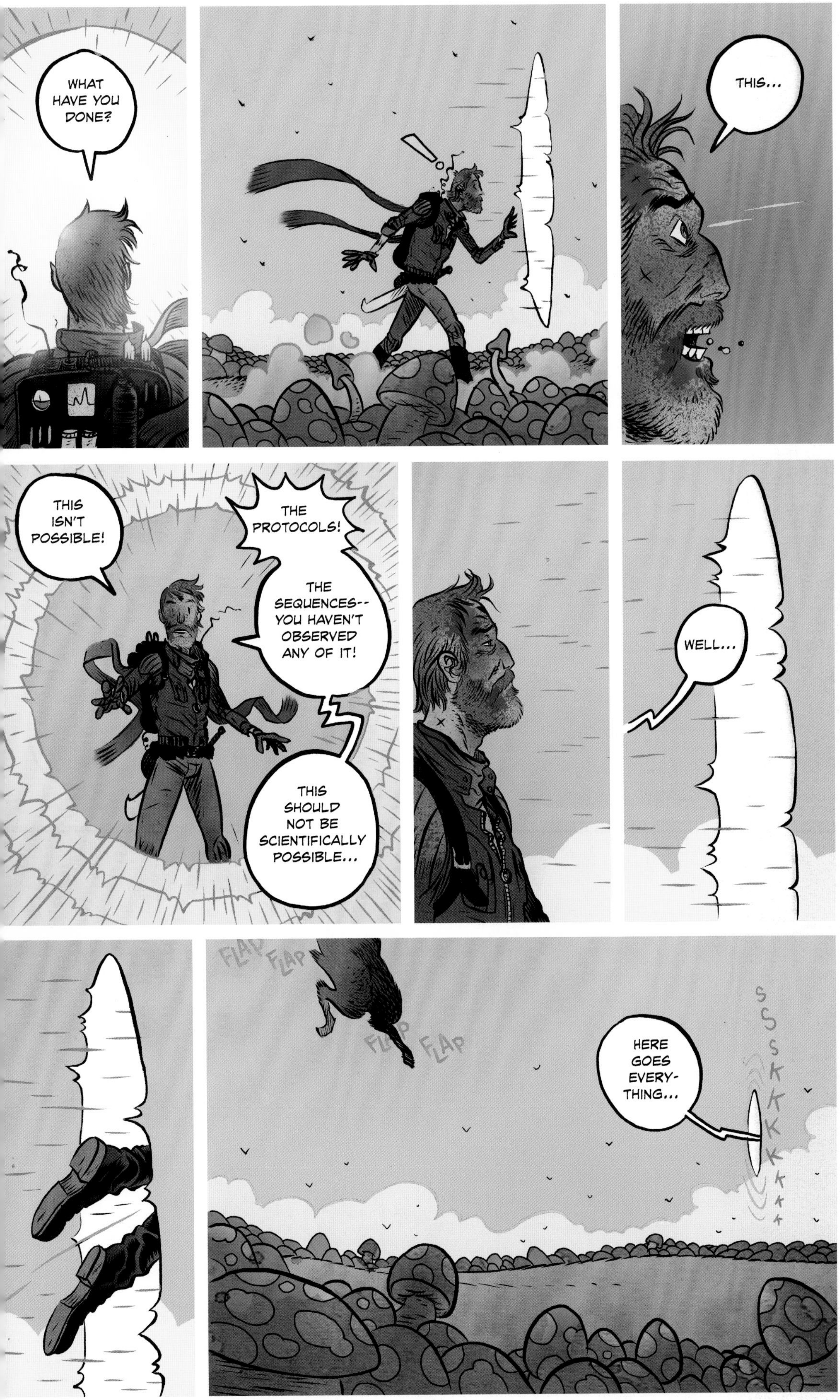
WHAT HAVE YOU DONE?
!
THIS...
THIS ISN'T POSSIBLE!
THE PROTOCOLS!
THE SEQUENCES--YOU HAVEN'T OBSERVED ANY OF IT!
THIS SHOULD NOT BE SCIENTIFICALLY POSSIBLE...
WELL...
FLAP FLAP
FLAP FLAP
HERE GOES EVERY-THING...
SSSKKKKKKKK

FLAP FLAP FLAP FLAP FLAP FLAP FLAP

FWUUMP!!!

THEY WENT THROUGH HERE.

USED A SPELL.

ONE A YERS, IT LOOKS LIKE.

RRRRRKCHHKK..

SSSSKKKK

SOME KINDA PORTAL.

MORE LIKE A TEAR, THOUGH.

YEAH.

I KNOW.

THE COPPER GOLEM MADE ME MAKE IT.

HELD MY GRANDMA HOSTAGE.

I HAD TO.

YOU MADE A HOLE IN REALITY, BABE.

A TUNNEL WE CAN'T GO THROUGH.

WE CAN'T FOLLOW BOONE...

WE AIN'T ALLOWED THERE.

CROSBY ST

ONKEY ING!

PARKING 24H

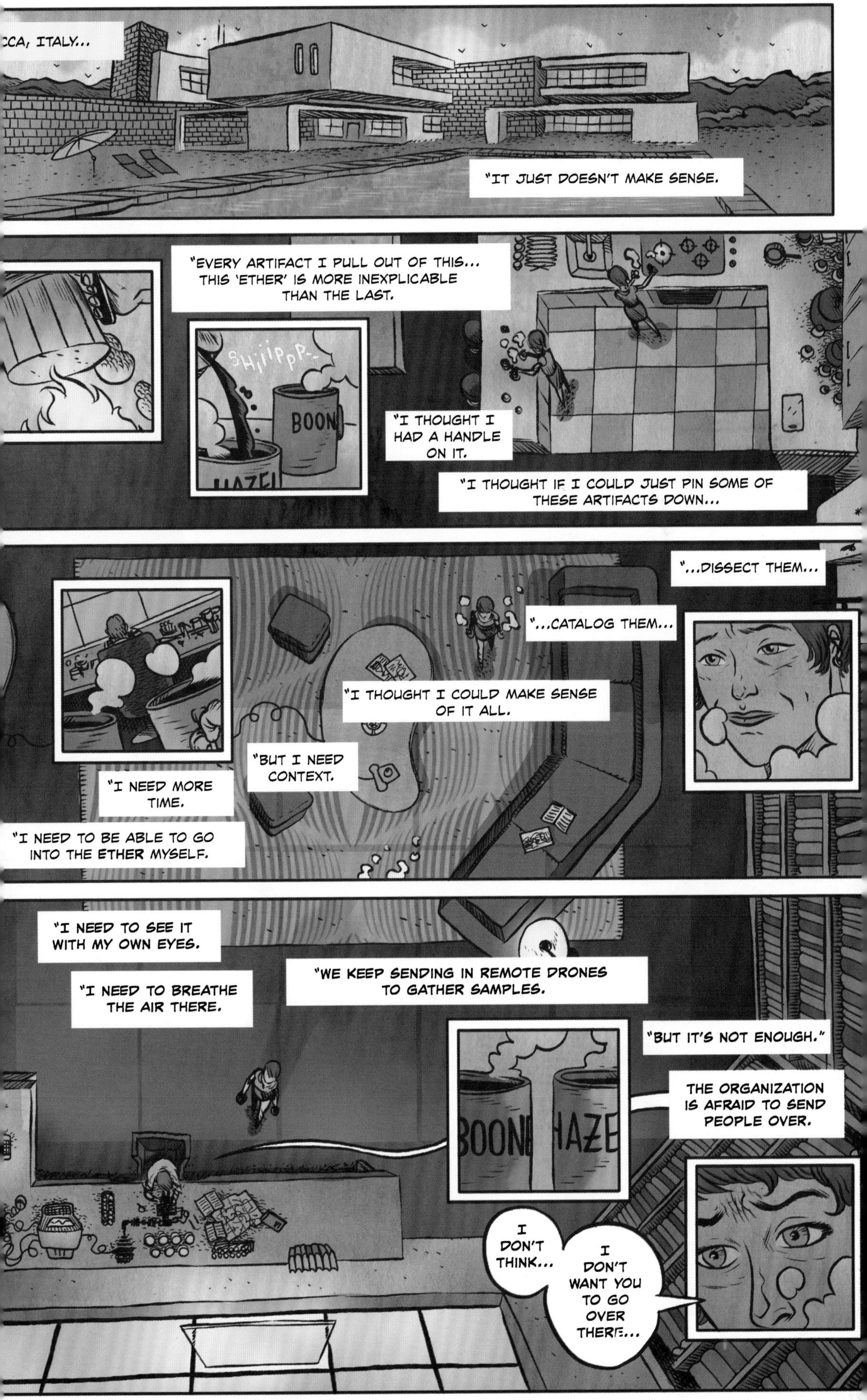
CCA, ITALY...
"IT JUST DOESN'T MAKE SENSE.
"EVERY ARTIFACT I PULL OUT OF THIS... THIS 'ETHER' IS MORE INEXPLICABLE THAN THE LAST.
SHIIIPPP--
BOON
HAZEL
"I THOUGHT I HAD A HANDLE ON IT.
"I THOUGHT IF I COULD JUST PIN SOME OF THESE ARTIFACTS DOWN...
"...DISSECT THEM...
"...CATALOG THEM...
"I THOUGHT I COULD MAKE SENSE OF IT ALL.
"BUT I NEED CONTEXT.
"I NEED MORE TIME.
"I NEED TO BE ABLE TO GO INTO THE ETHER MYSELF.
"I NEED TO SEE IT WITH MY OWN EYES.
"I NEED TO BREATHE THE AIR THERE.
"WE KEEP SENDING IN REMOTE DRONES TO GATHER SAMPLES.
"BUT IT'S NOT ENOUGH."
BOONE
HAZE
THE ORGANIZATION IS AFRAID TO SEND PEOPLE OVER.
I DON'T THINK...
I DON'T WANT YOU TO GO OVER THERE...

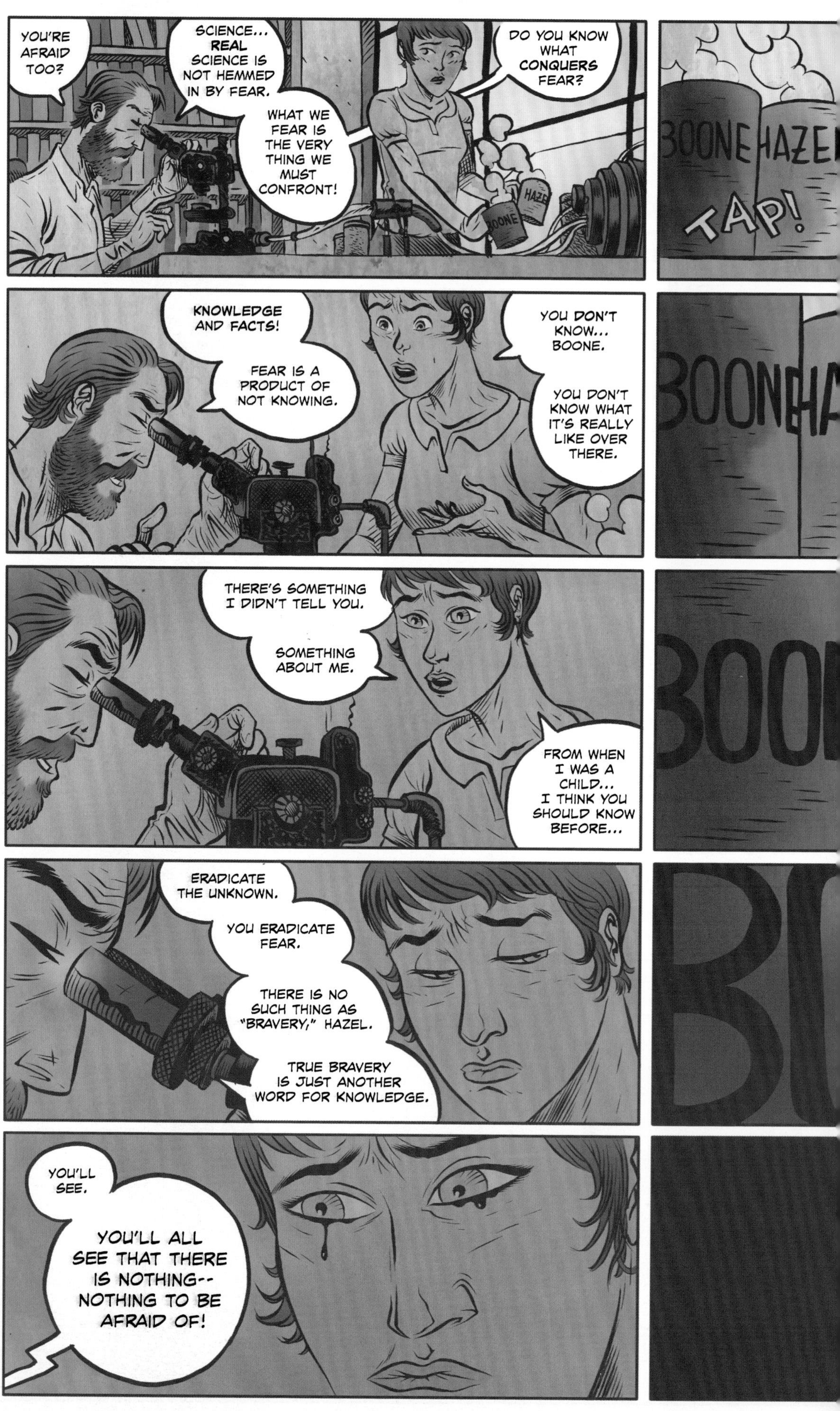

YOU'RE AFRAID TOO?
SCIENCE... REAL SCIENCE IS NOT HEMMED IN BY FEAR.
WHAT WE FEAR IS THE VERY THING WE MUST CONFRONT!
DO YOU KNOW WHAT CONQUERS FEAR?
BOONE
HAZE
BOONE HAZE
TAP!
KNOWLEDGE AND FACTS!
FEAR IS A PRODUCT OF NOT KNOWING.
YOU DON'T KNOW... BOONE.
YOU DON'T KNOW WHAT IT'S REALLY LIKE OVER THERE.
THERE'S SOMETHING I DIDN'T TELL YOU.
SOMETHING ABOUT ME.
FROM WHEN I WAS A CHILD... I THINK YOU SHOULD KNOW BEFORE...
ERADICATE THE UNKNOWN.
YOU ERADICATE FEAR.
THERE IS NO SUCH THING AS "BRAVERY," HAZEL.
TRUE BRAVERY IS JUST ANOTHER WORD FOR KNOWLEDGE.
YOU'LL SEE.
YOU'LL ALL SEE THAT THERE IS NOTHING-- NOTHING TO BE AFRAID OF!

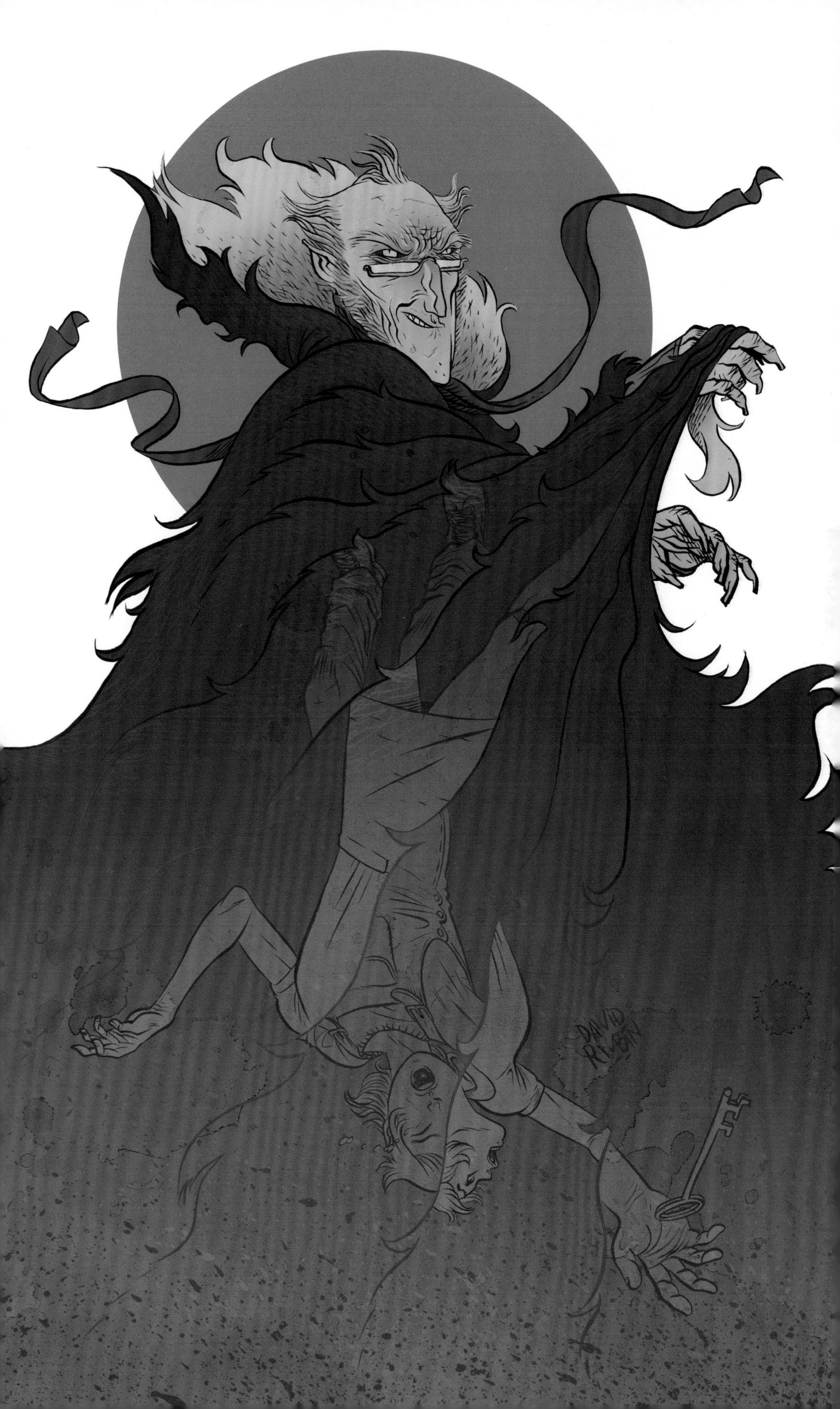
DAVID
RUBIN

4

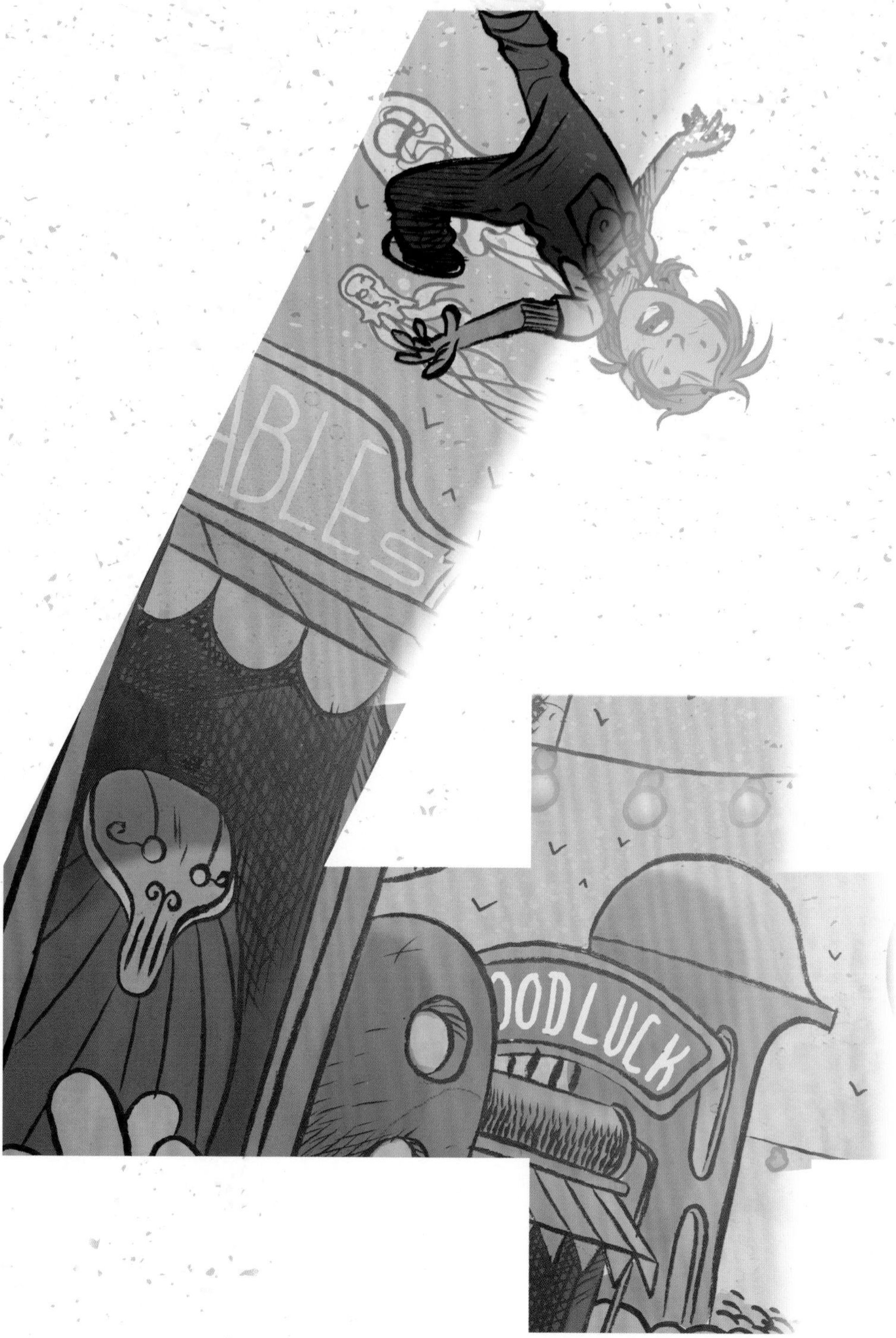
ABLES
OODLUCK

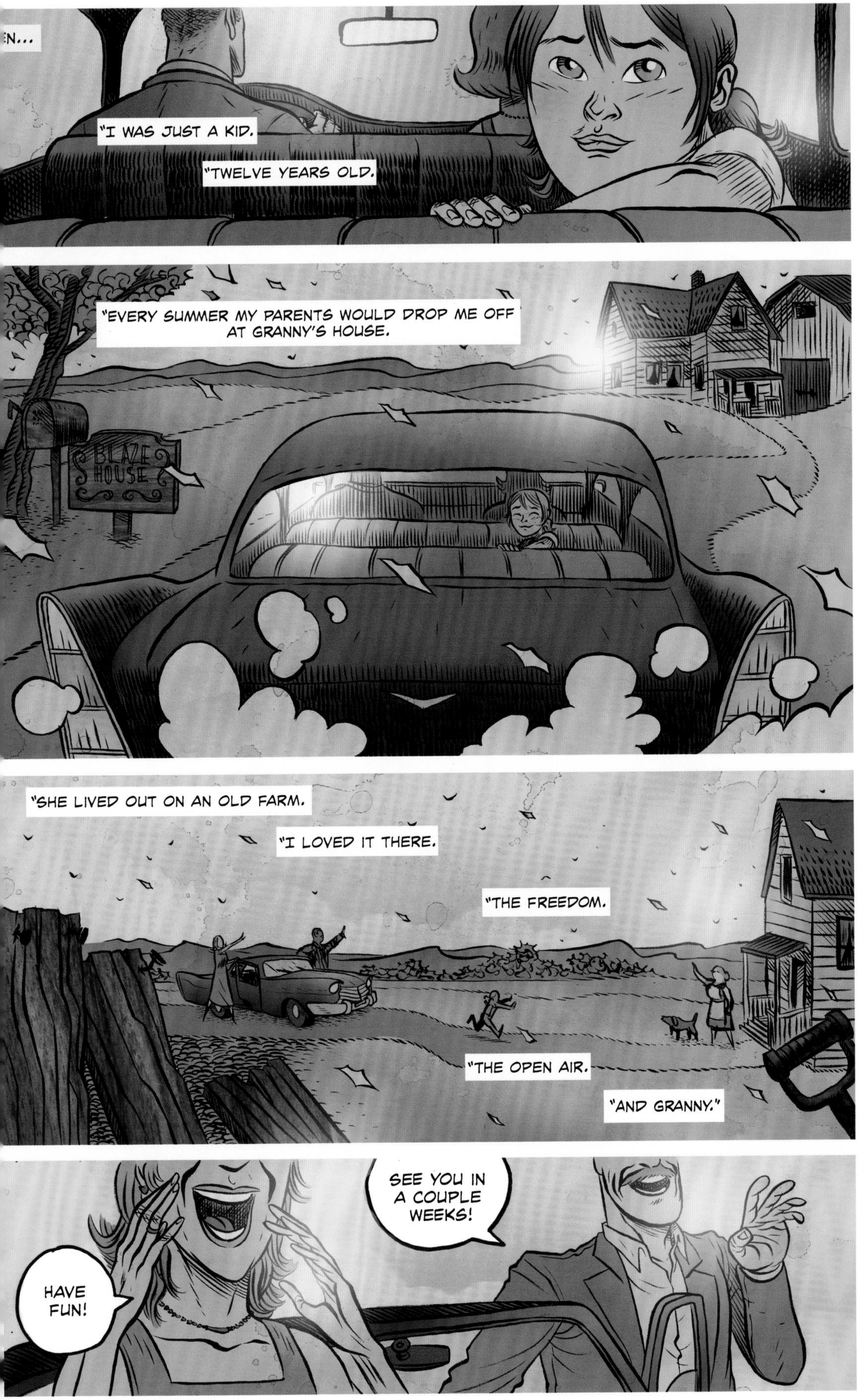

N...
"I WAS JUST A KID.
"TWELVE YEARS OLD.
"EVERY SUMMER MY PARENTS WOULD DROP ME OFF AT GRANNY'S HOUSE.
BLAZE HOUSE
"SHE LIVED OUT ON AN OLD FARM.
"I LOVED IT THERE.
"THE FREEDOM.
"THE OPEN AIR.
"AND GRANNY."
SEE YOU IN A COUPLE WEEKS!
HAVE FUN!

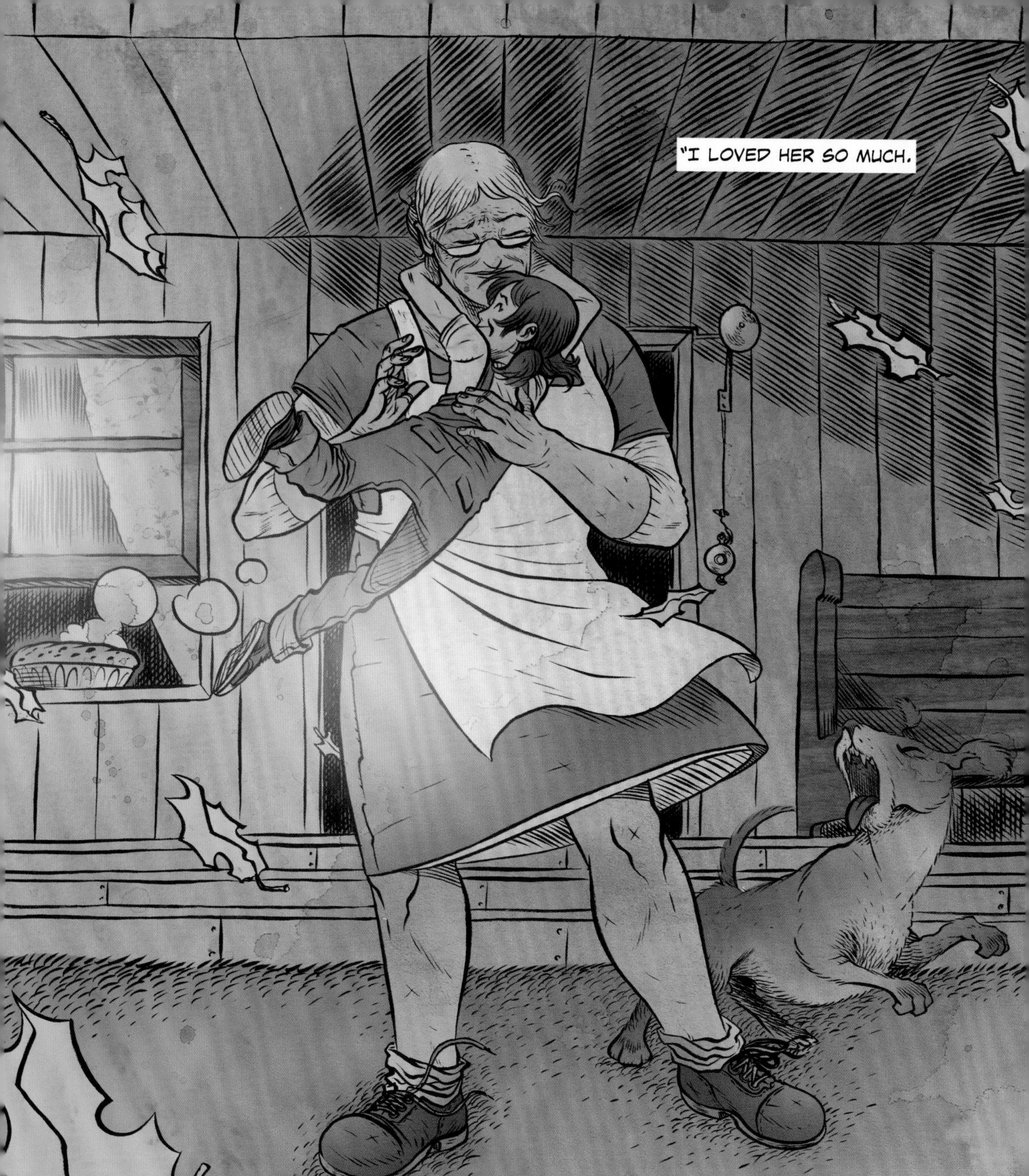
"I LOVED HER SO MUCH.

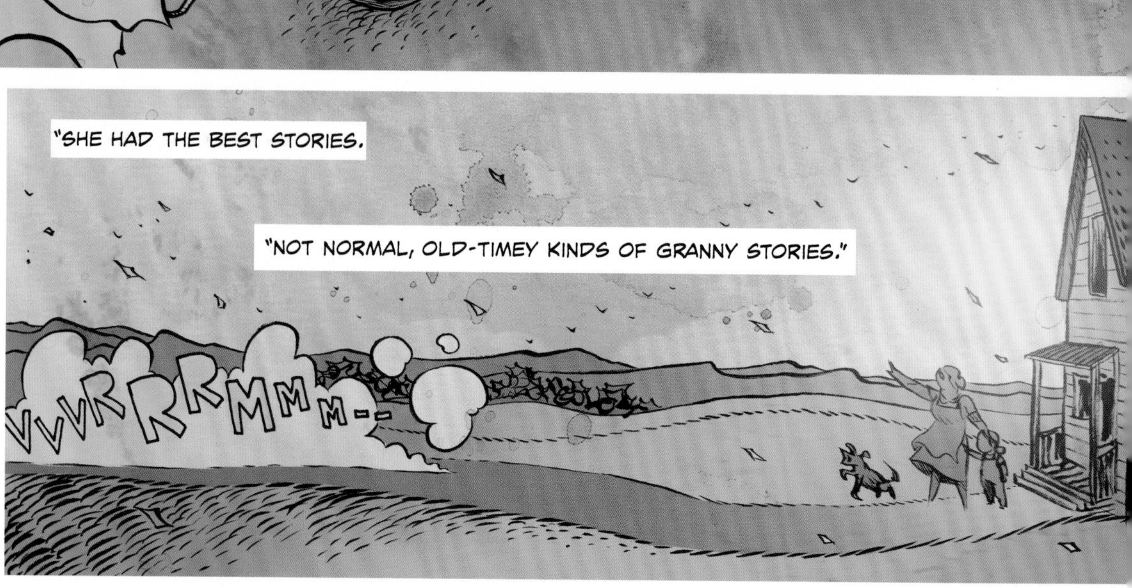
"SHE HAD THE BEST STORIES.
"NOT NORMAL, OLD-TIMEY KINDS OF GRANNY STORIES."
VVVRRRMMMM--

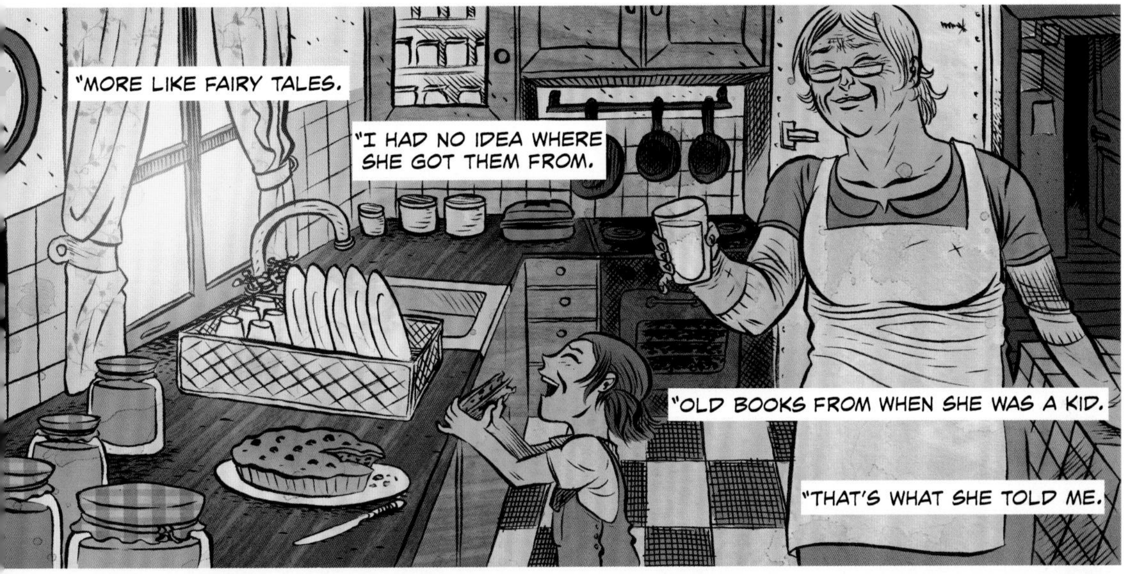
"MORE LIKE FAIRY TALES.
"I HAD NO IDEA WHERE SHE GOT THEM FROM.
"OLD BOOKS FROM WHEN SHE WAS A KID.
"THAT'S WHAT SHE TOLD ME.

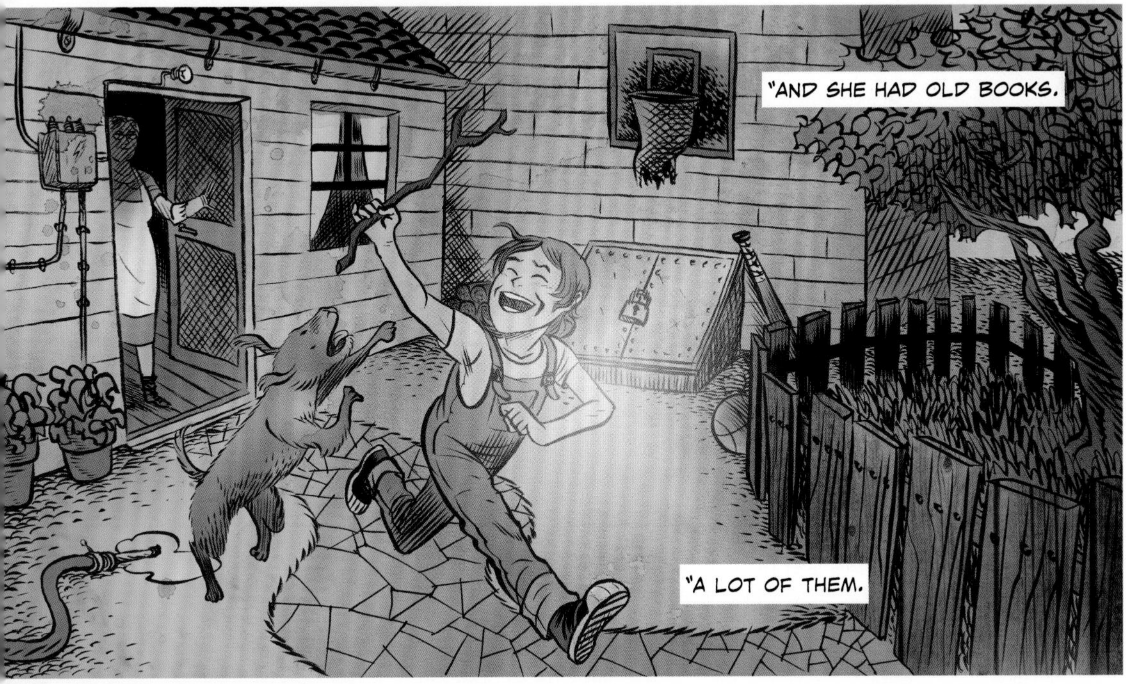
"AND SHE HAD OLD BOOKS.
"A LOT OF THEM.

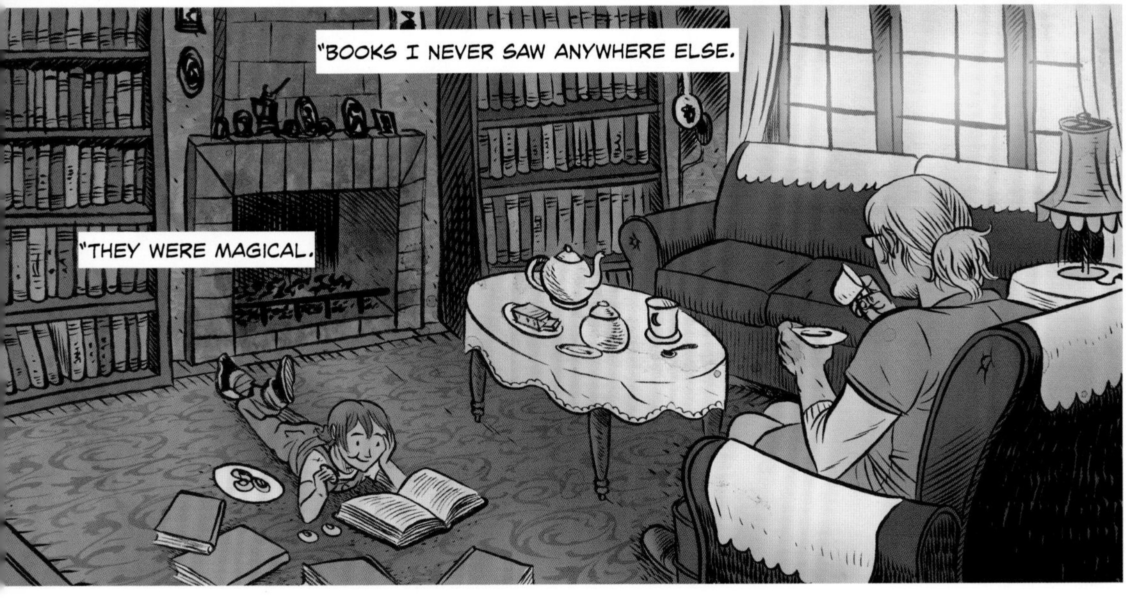
"BOOKS I NEVER SAW ANYWHERE ELSE.
"THEY WERE MAGICAL.

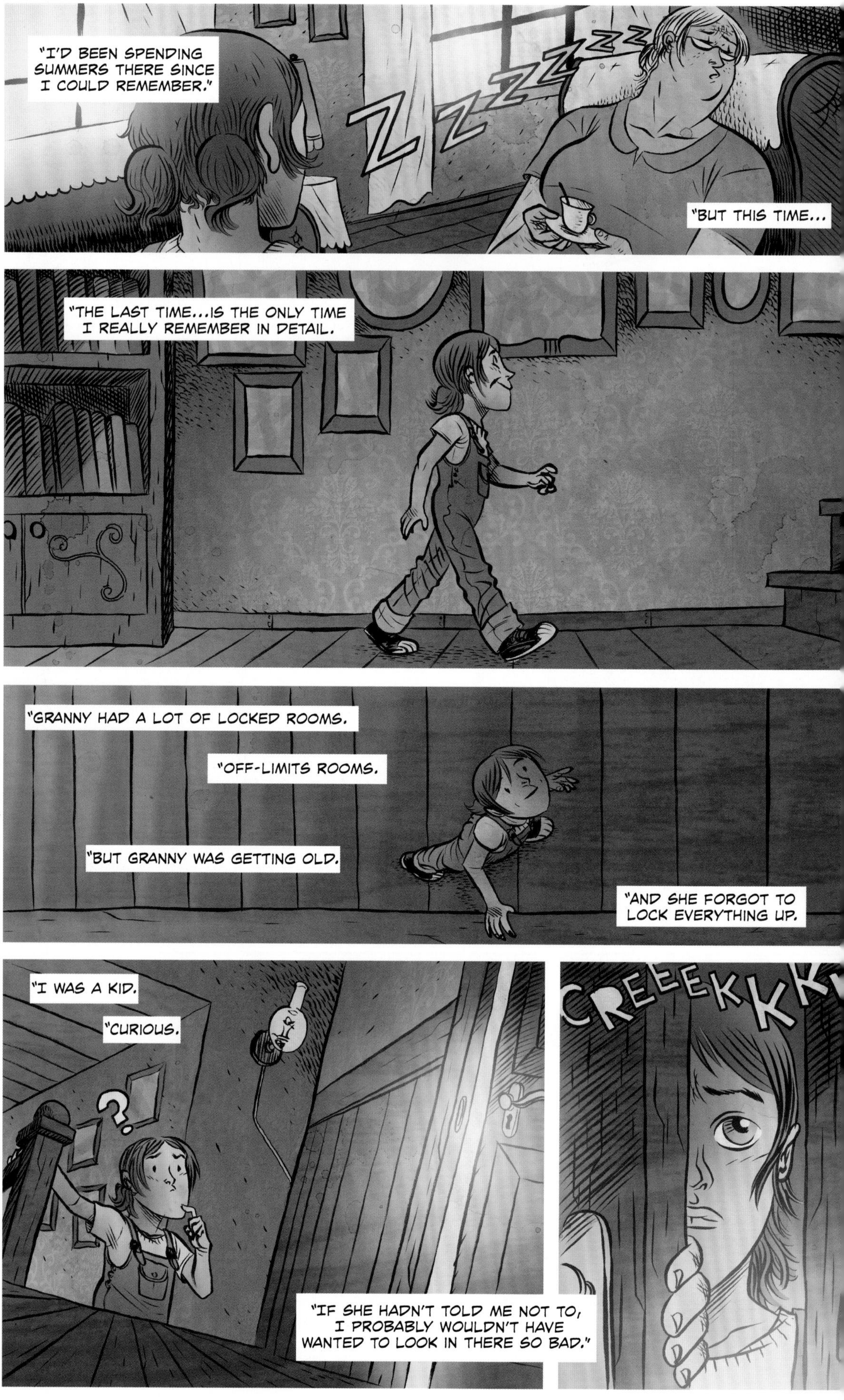
"I'D BEEN SPENDING SUMMERS THERE SINCE I COULD REMEMBER."
ZZZZZZZ
"BUT THIS TIME...
"THE LAST TIME...IS THE ONLY TIME I REALLY REMEMBER IN DETAIL.
"GRANNY HAD A LOT OF LOCKED ROOMS.
"OFF-LIMITS ROOMS.
"BUT GRANNY WAS GETTING OLD.
"AND SHE FORGOT TO LOCK EVERYTHING UP.
"I WAS A KID.
"CURIOUS.
?
"IF SHE HADN'T TOLD ME NOT TO, I PROBABLY WOULDN'T HAVE WANTED TO LOOK IN THERE SO BAD."
CREEEKKK

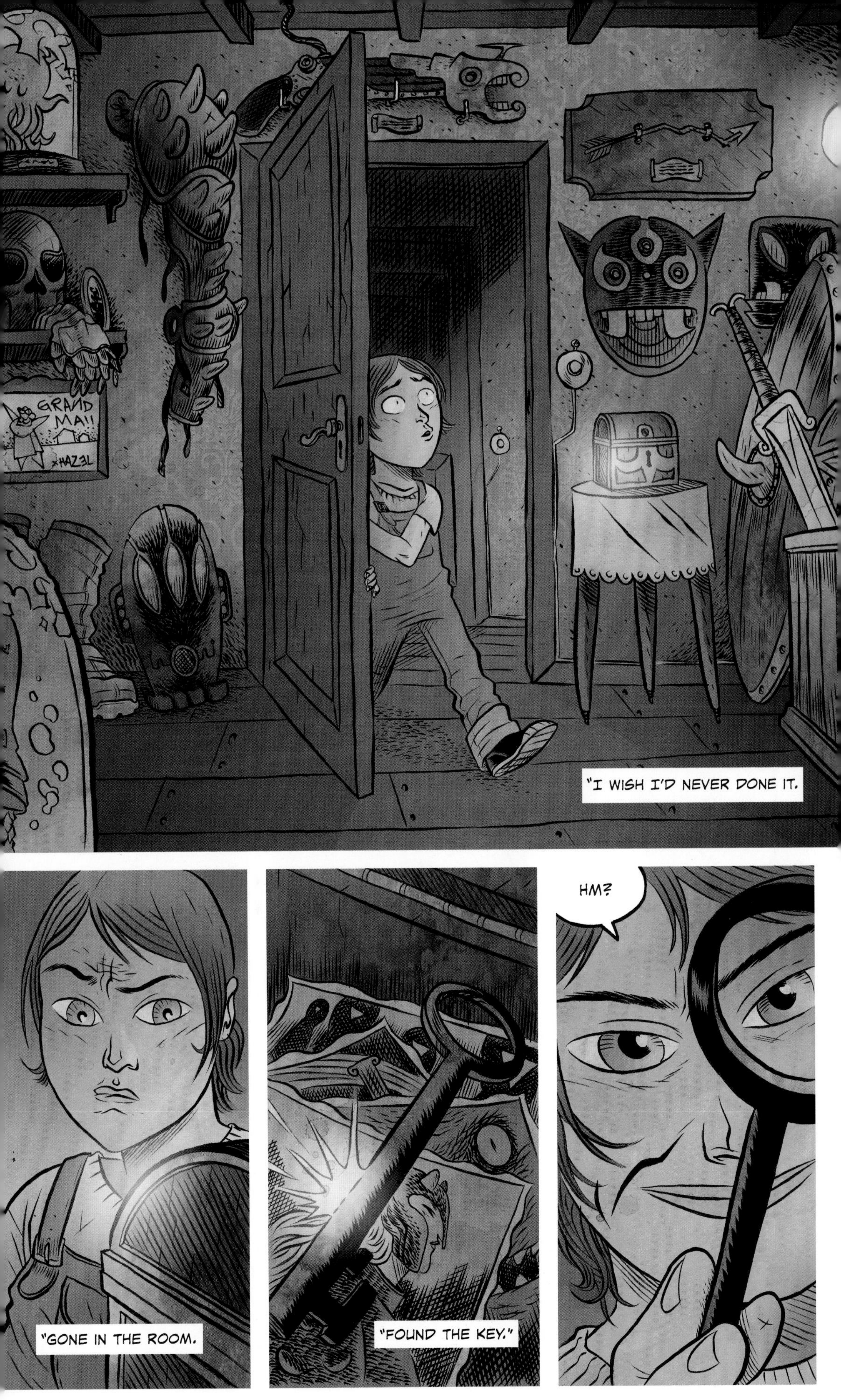
GRAND MA!!
HAZ3L
"I WISH I'D NEVER DONE IT.
"GONE IN THE ROOM.
"FOUND THE KEY."
HM?

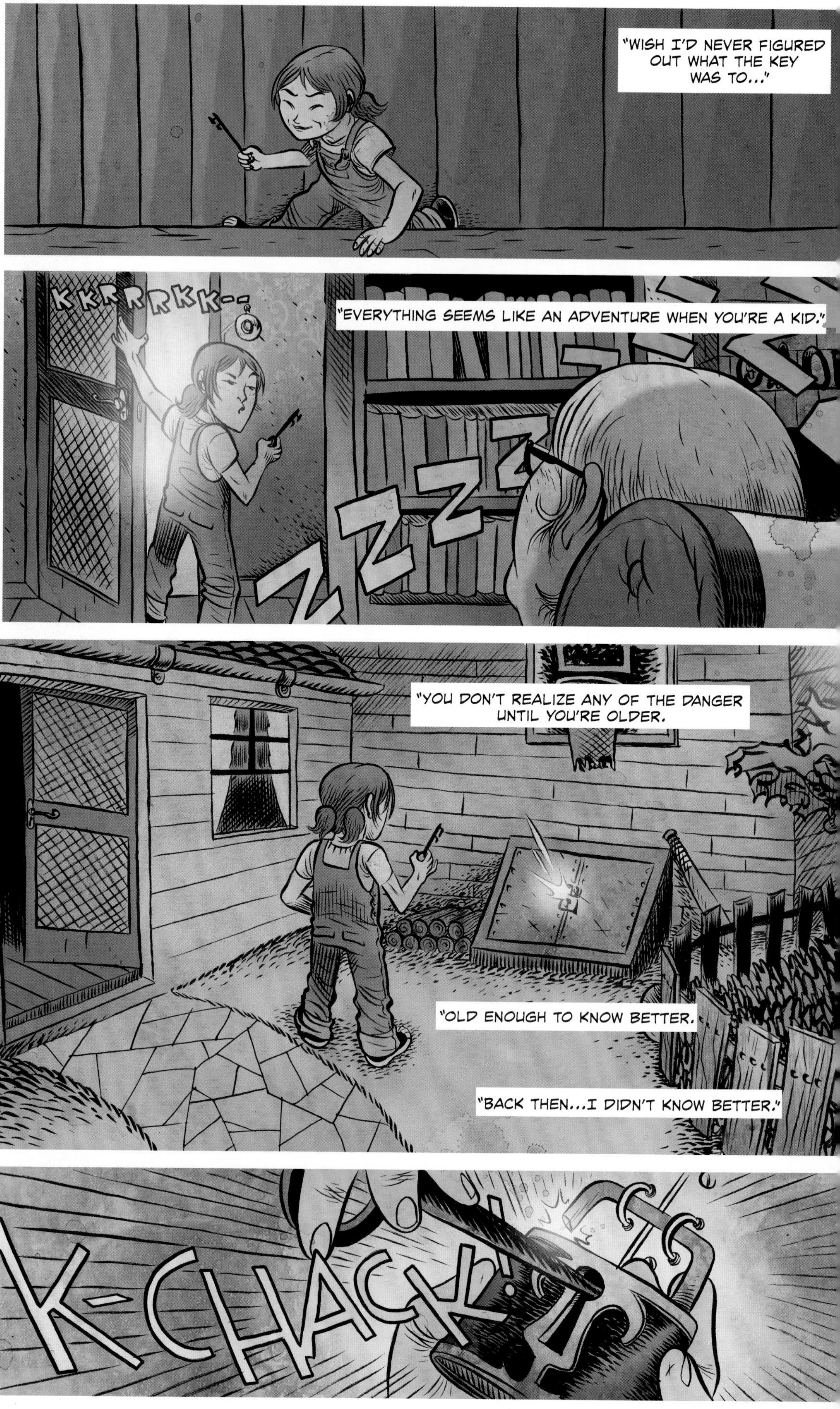
"WISH I'D NEVER FIGURED OUT WHAT THE KEY WAS TO..."
KKRRRKK--
"EVERYTHING SEEMS LIKE AN ADVENTURE WHEN YOU'RE A KID."
ZZZZ
"YOU DON'T REALIZE ANY OF THE DANGER UNTIL YOU'RE OLDER.
"OLD ENOUGH TO KNOW BETTER.
"BACK THEN...I DIDN'T KNOW BETTER."
K-CHACK!

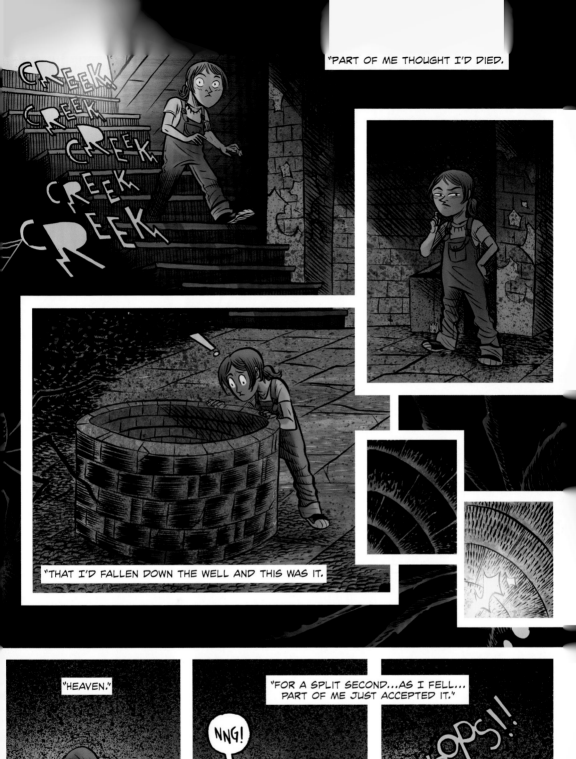

"PART OF ME THOUGHT I'D DIED.

CREEK! CREEK CREEK CREEK CREEK CREEK

"THAT I'D FALLEN DOWN THE WELL AND THIS WAS IT.

"HEAVEN."

"FOR A SPLIT SECOND...AS I FELL...
PART OF ME JUST ACCEPTED IT."

NNG!

WOOPS!!

"THAT I'D MADE A MISTAKE AND I WAS DYING.

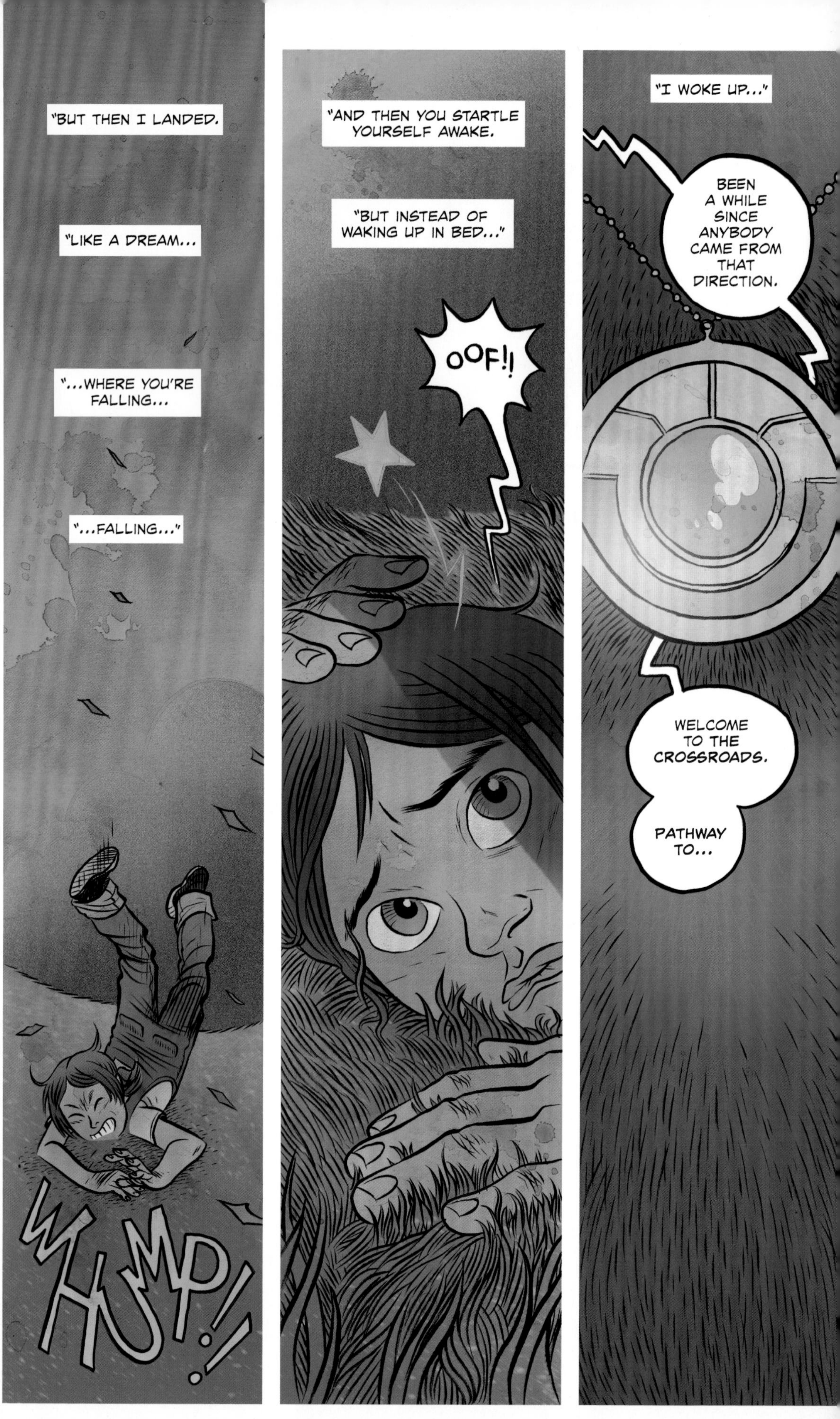
"BUT THEN I LANDED.
"LIKE A DREAM...
"...WHERE YOU'RE FALLING...
"...FALLING..."
WHUMP!!
"AND THEN YOU STARTLE YOURSELF AWAKE.
"BUT INSTEAD OF WAKING UP IN BED..."
OOF!!
"I WOKE UP..."
BEEN A WHILE SINCE ANYBODY CAME FROM THAT DIRECTION.
WELCOME TO THE CROSSROADS.
PATHWAY TO...

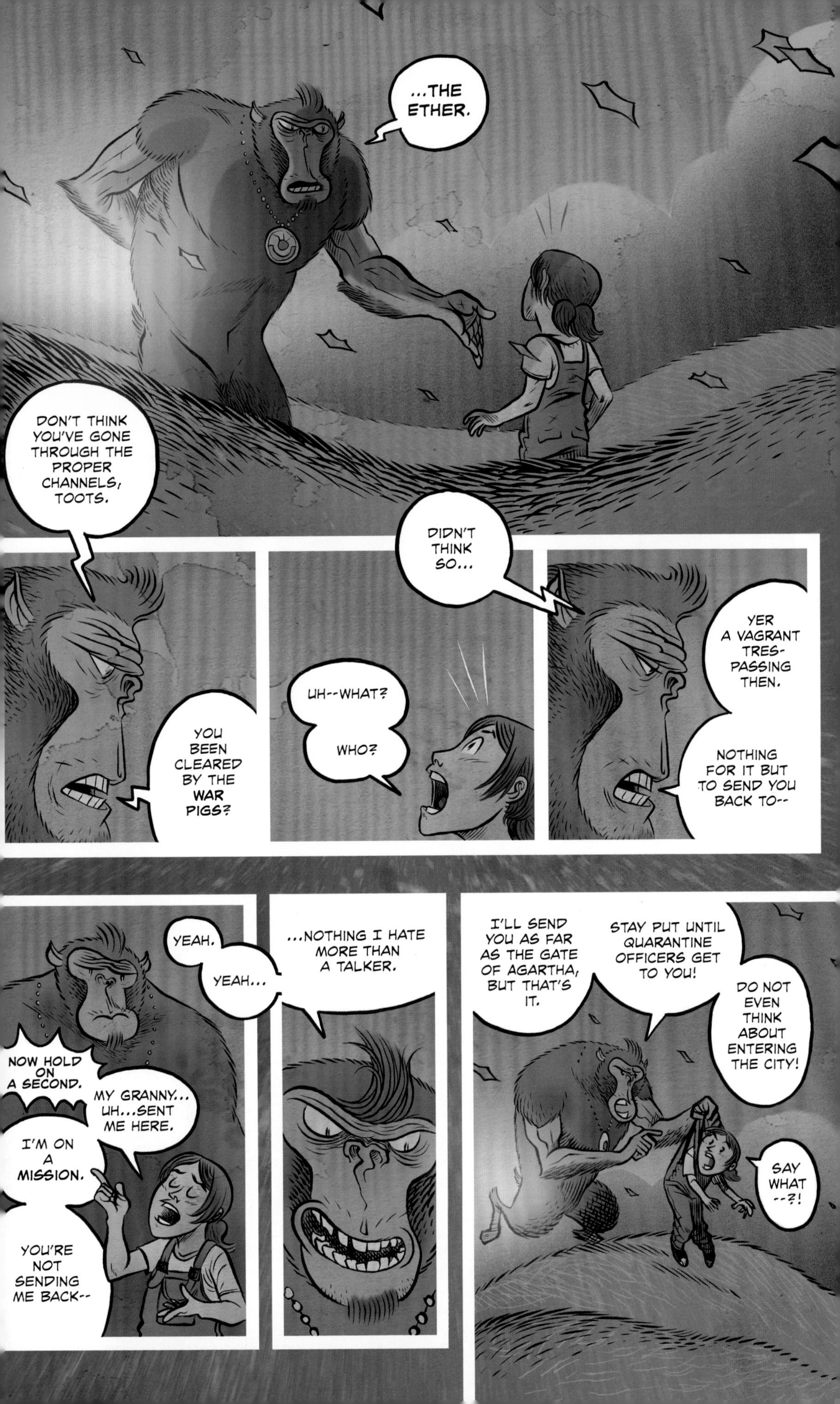
...THE ETHER.
DON'T THINK YOU'VE GONE THROUGH THE PROPER CHANNELS, TOOTS.
YOU BEEN CLEARED BY THE WAR PIGS?
UH--WHAT?
WHO?
DIDN'T THINK SO...
YER A VAGRANT TRES-PASSING THEN.
NOTHING FOR IT BUT TO SEND YOU BACK TO--
NOW HOLD ON A SECOND.
MY GRANNY... UH...SENT ME HERE.
I'M ON A MISSION.
YOU'RE NOT SENDING ME BACK--
YEAH.
YEAH...
...NOTHING I HATE MORE THAN A TALKER.
I'LL SEND YOU AS FAR AS THE GATE OF AGARTHA, BUT THAT'S IT.
STAY PUT UNTIL QUARANTINE OFFICERS GET TO YOU!
DO NOT EVEN THINK ABOUT ENTERING THE CITY!
SAY WHAT --?!

THUMP!!

WHOOA!!!

WHAM

MORE THAN JUST A LITTLE BIT RUDE...

STAY PUT...?

HMM...

"IT ALL HAPPENED SO FAST.

"I'D NEVER BEEN TO NEW YORK CITY BEFORE..."

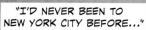

WELL...

...I AIN'T WAITING AROUND FOREVER.

"THIS WAS WHAT I'D IMAGINED IT WAS LIKE...BUT...STRANGE.

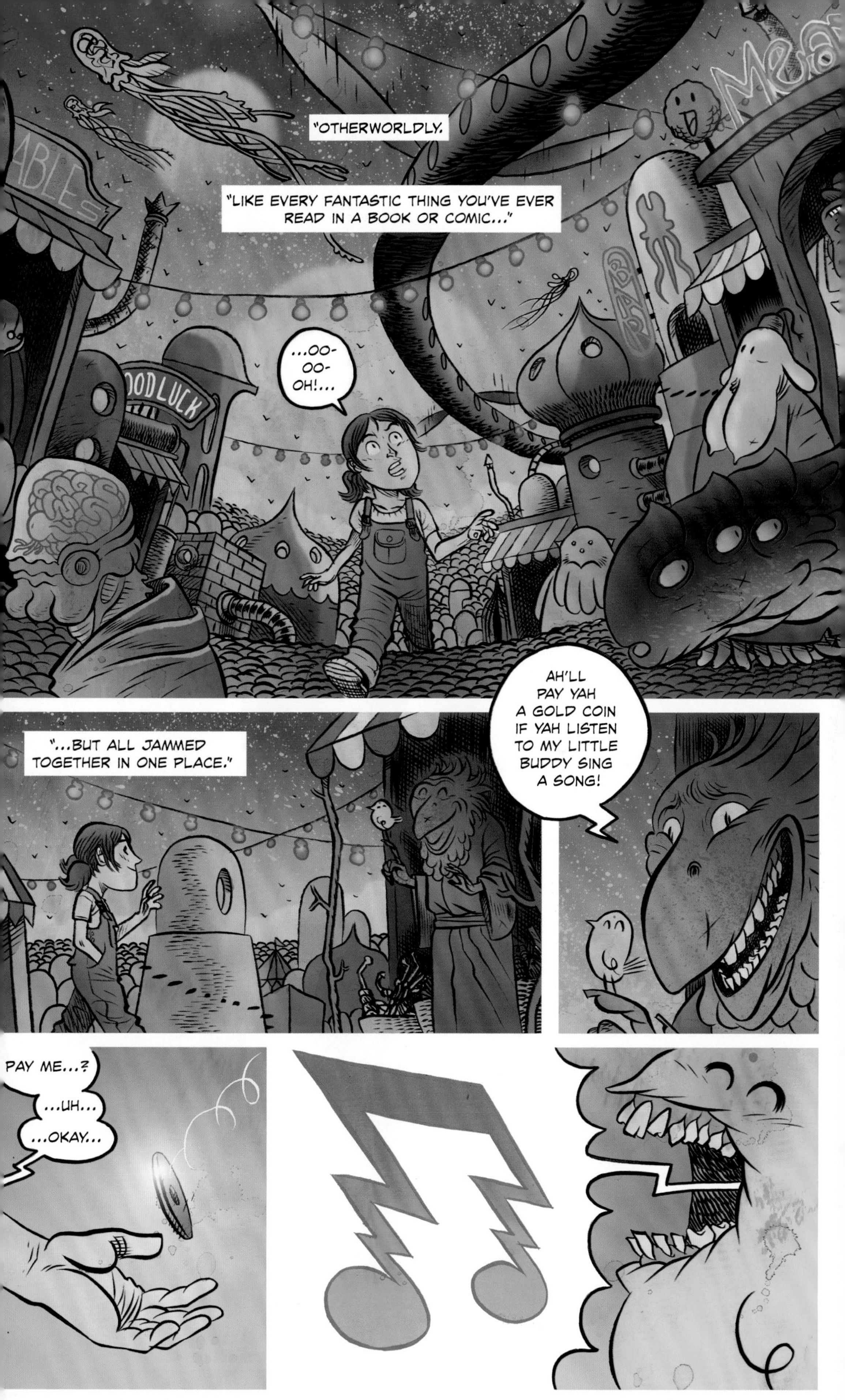
"OTHERWORLDLY.
"LIKE EVERY FANTASTIC THING YOU'VE EVER READ IN A BOOK OR COMIC..."
...OO-OO-OH!...
"...BUT ALL JAMMED TOGETHER IN ONE PLACE."
AH'LL PAY YAH A GOLD COIN IF YAH LISTEN TO MY LITTLE BUDDY SING A SONG!
PAY ME...?
...UH...
...OKAY...

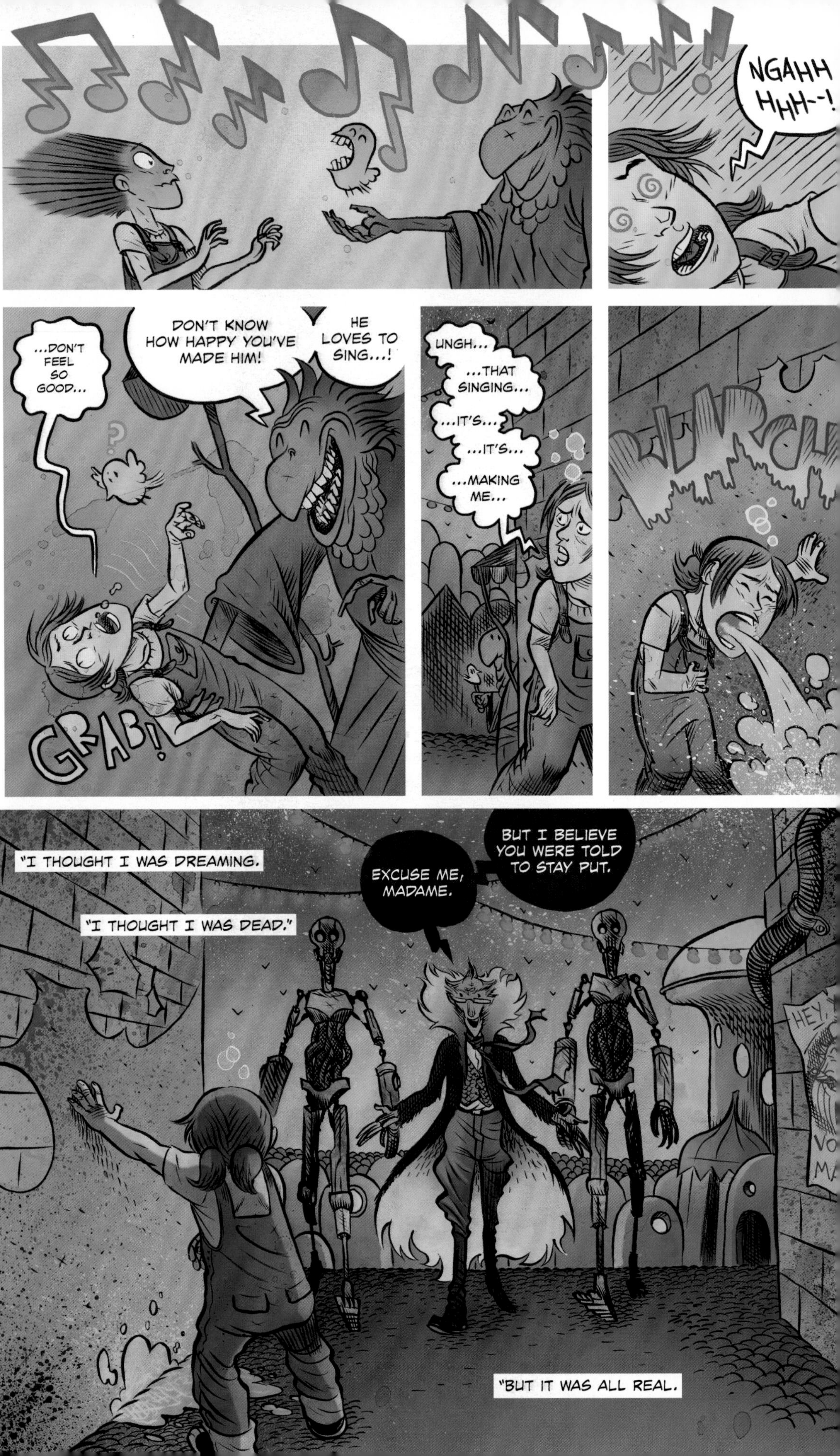
NGAHH HHH--!
...DON'T FEEL SO GOOD...
DON'T KNOW HOW HAPPY YOU'VE MADE HIM!
HE LOVES TO SING...!
GRAB!
UNGH...
...THAT SINGING...
...IT'S...
...IT'S...
...MAKING ME...
"I THOUGHT I WAS DREAMING.
"I THOUGHT I WAS DEAD."
EXCUSE ME, MADAME.
BUT I BELIEVE YOU WERE TOLD TO STAY PUT.
"BUT IT WAS ALL REAL.

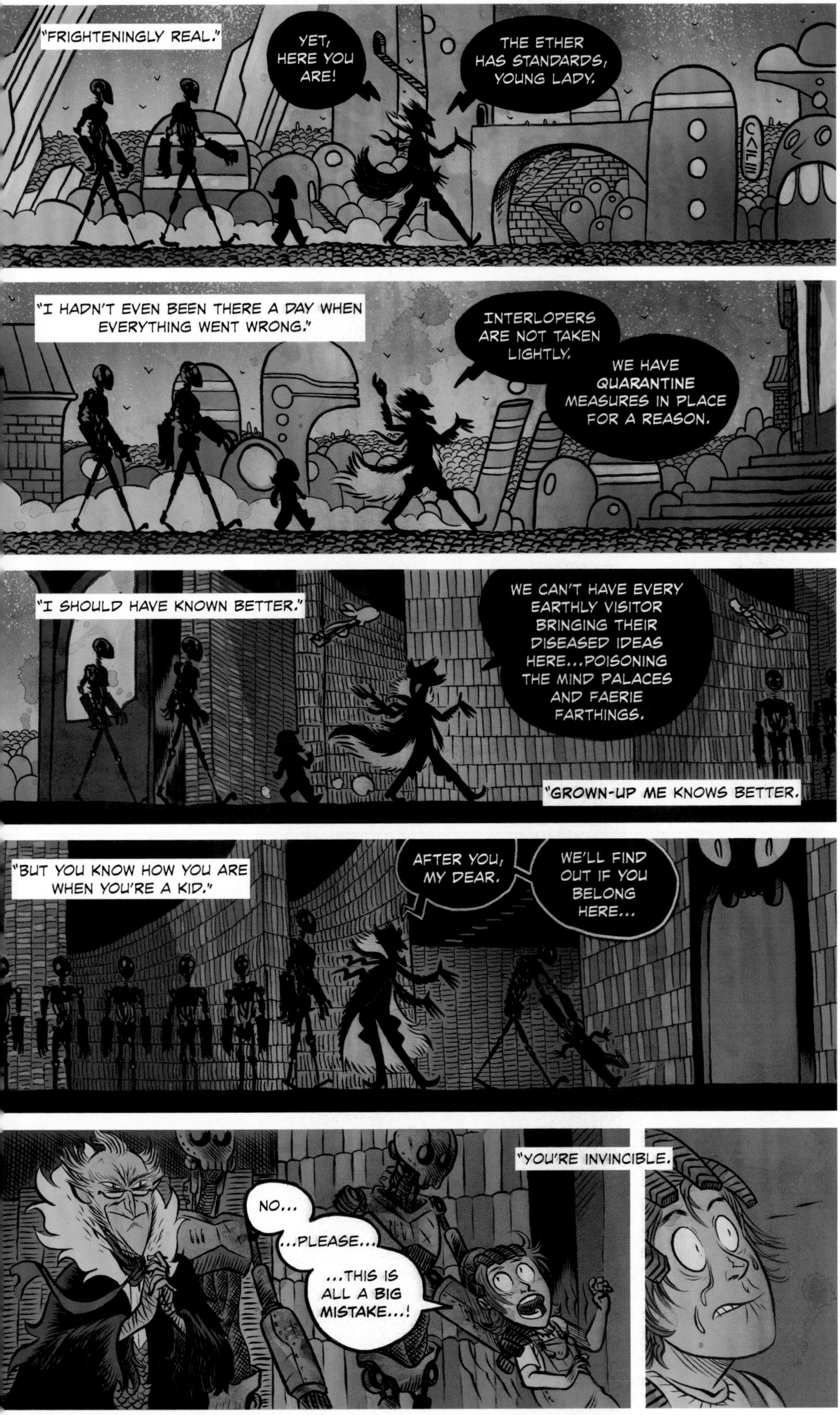
"FRIGHTENINGLY REAL."
YET, HERE YOU ARE!
THE ETHER HAS STANDARDS, YOUNG LADY.
CAFE
"I HADN'T EVEN BEEN THERE A DAY WHEN EVERYTHING WENT WRONG."
INTERLOPERS ARE NOT TAKEN LIGHTLY.
WE HAVE QUARANTINE MEASURES IN PLACE FOR A REASON.
"I SHOULD HAVE KNOWN BETTER."
WE CAN'T HAVE EVERY EARTHLY VISITOR BRINGING THEIR DISEASED IDEAS HERE...POISONING THE MIND PALACES AND FAERIE FARTHINGS.
"GROWN-UP ME KNOWS BETTER.
"BUT YOU KNOW HOW YOU ARE WHEN YOU'RE A KID."
AFTER YOU, MY DEAR.
WE'LL FIND OUT IF YOU BELONG HERE...
NO...
...PLEASE...
...THIS IS ALL A BIG MISTAKE...!
"YOU'RE INVINCIBLE.

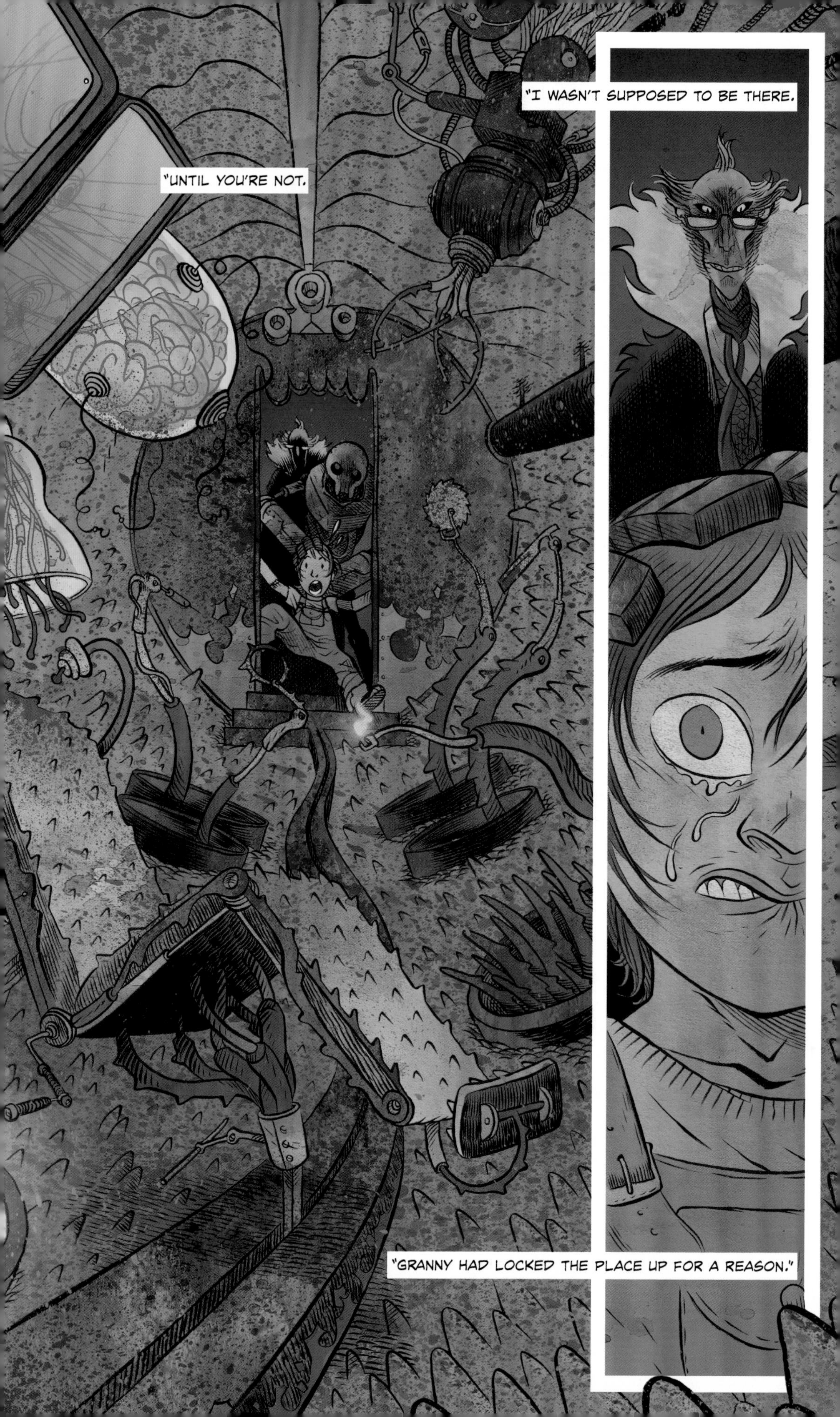
"I WASN'T SUPPOSED TO BE THERE.
"UNTIL YOU'RE NOT.
"GRANNY HAD LOCKED THE PLACE UP FOR A REASON."

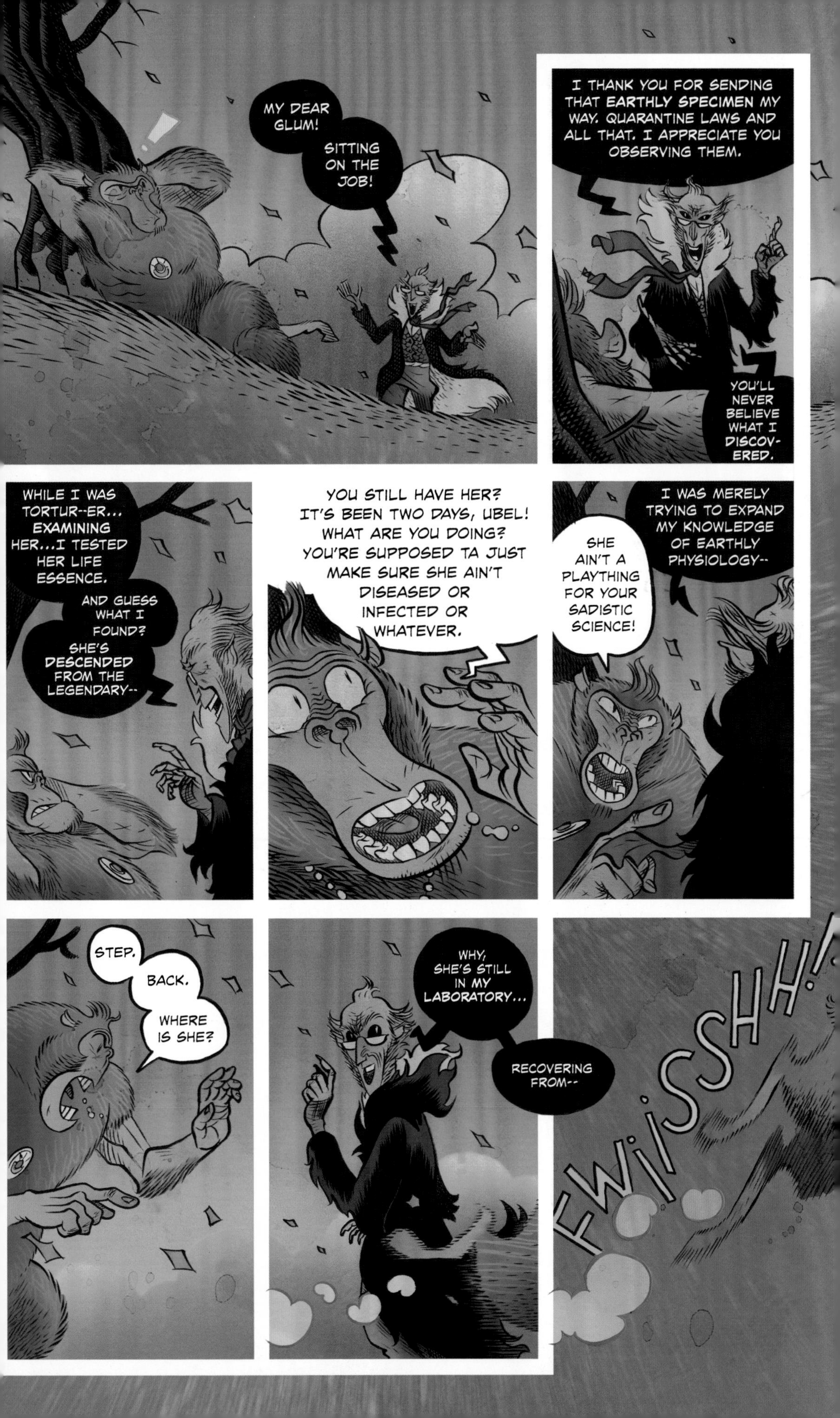
MY DEAR GLUM!
SITTING ON THE JOB!
I THANK YOU FOR SENDING THAT EARTHLY SPECIMEN MY WAY. QUARANTINE LAWS AND ALL THAT. I APPRECIATE YOU OBSERVING THEM.
YOU'LL NEVER BELIEVE WHAT I DISCOV-ERED.
WHILE I WAS TORTUR--ER... EXAMINING HER...I TESTED HER LIFE ESSENCE.
AND GUESS WHAT I FOUND?
SHE'S DESCENDED FROM THE LEGENDARY--
YOU STILL HAVE HER? IT'S BEEN TWO DAYS, UBEL! WHAT ARE YOU DOING? YOU'RE SUPPOSED TA JUST MAKE SURE SHE AIN'T DISEASED OR INFECTED OR WHATEVER.
I WAS MERELY TRYING TO EXPAND MY KNOWLEDGE OF EARTHLY PHYSIOLOGY--
SHE AIN'T A PLAYTHING FOR YOUR SADISTIC SCIENCE!
STEP.
BACK.
WHERE IS SHE?
WHY, SHE'S STILL IN MY LABORATORY...
RECOVERING FROM--
FWISSHH!

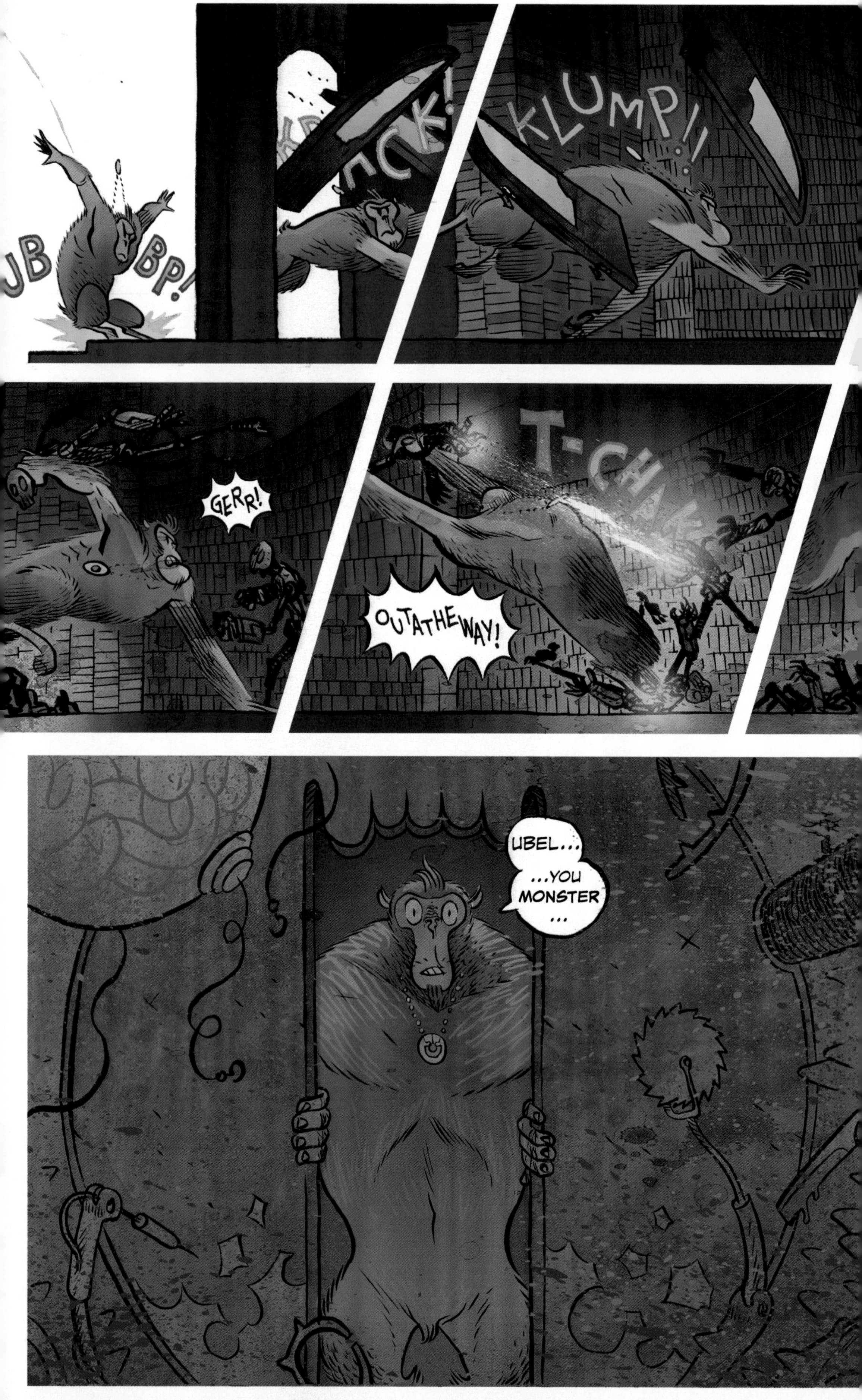
KLUMP!!
GERR!
OUTATHEWAY!
UBEL...
...YOU MONSTER ...

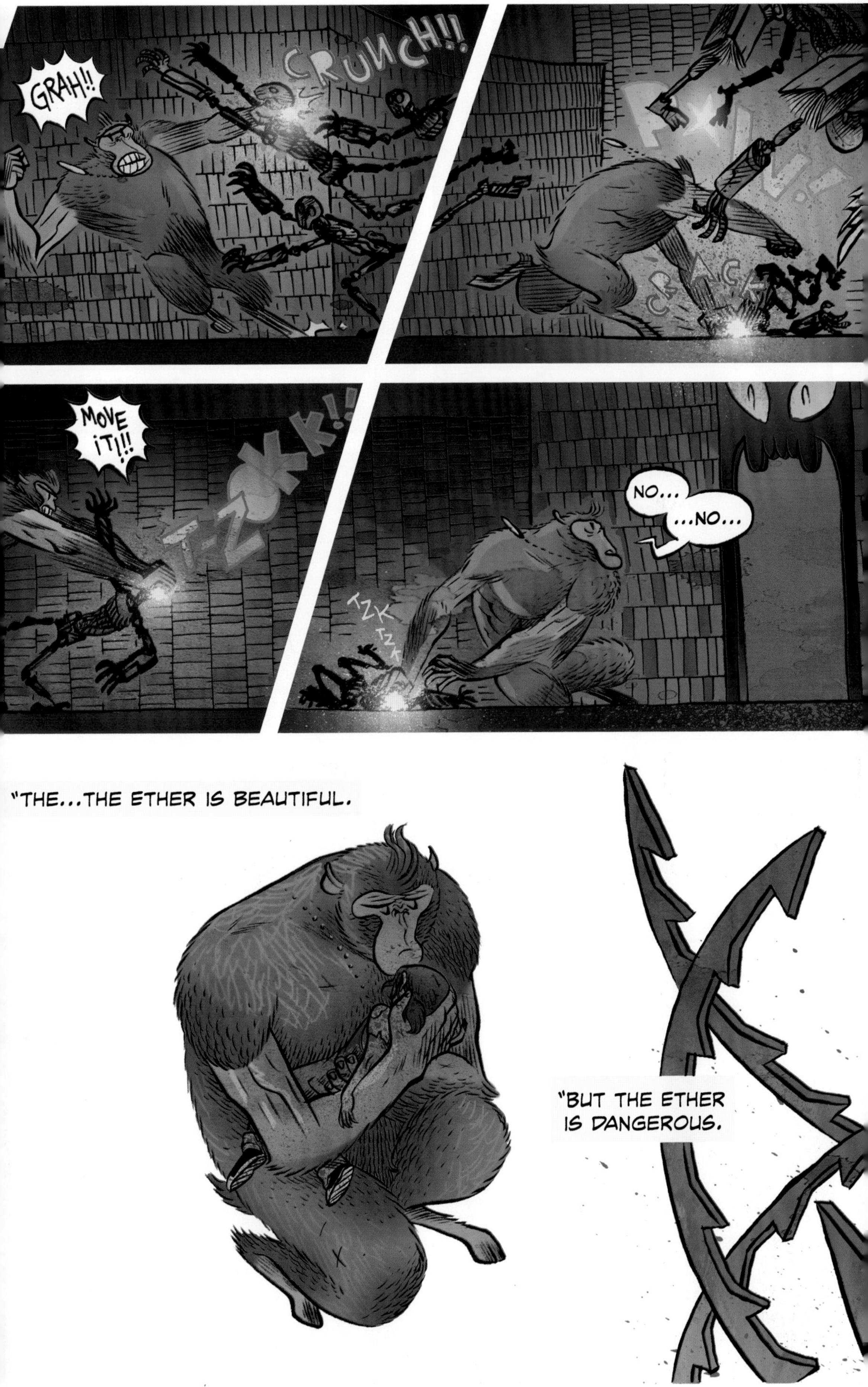
GRAH!!
CRUNCH!!
MOVE IT!!!
NO...
...NO...
TZK
TZK
"THE...THE ETHER IS BEAUTIFUL.
"BUT THE ETHER IS DANGEROUS.

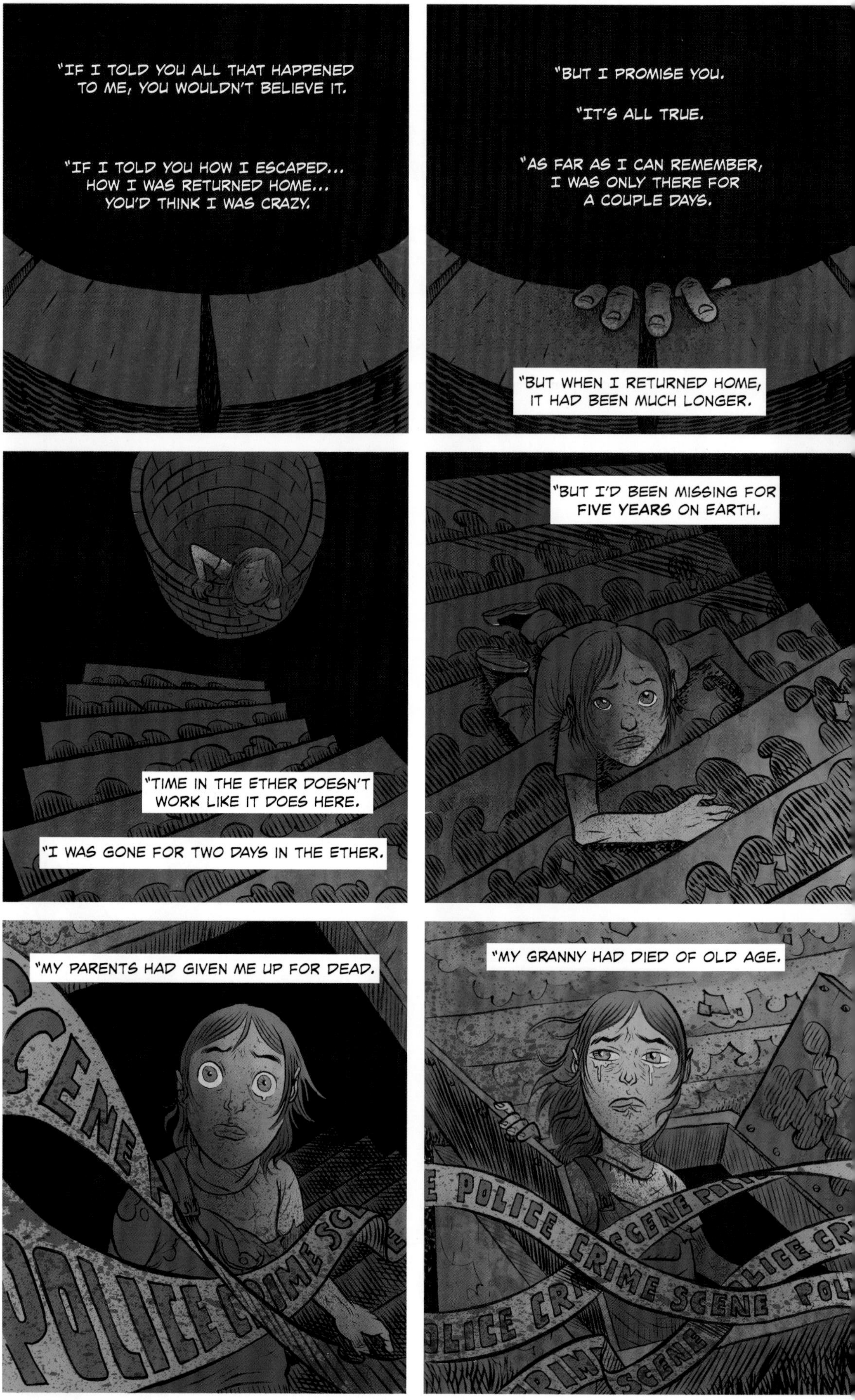
"IF I TOLD YOU ALL THAT HAPPENED TO ME, YOU WOULDN'T BELIEVE IT.
"IF I TOLD YOU HOW I ESCAPED... HOW I WAS RETURNED HOME... YOU'D THINK I WAS CRAZY.
"BUT I PROMISE YOU.
"IT'S ALL TRUE.
"AS FAR AS I CAN REMEMBER, I WAS ONLY THERE FOR A COUPLE DAYS.
"BUT WHEN I RETURNED HOME, IT HAD BEEN MUCH LONGER.
"TIME IN THE ETHER DOESN'T WORK LIKE IT DOES HERE.
"I WAS GONE FOR TWO DAYS IN THE ETHER.
"BUT I'D BEEN MISSING FOR FIVE YEARS ON EARTH.
"MY PARENTS HAD GIVEN ME UP FOR DEAD.
POLICE CRIME SCENE
"MY GRANNY HAD DIED OF OLD AGE.
POLICE CRIME SCENE

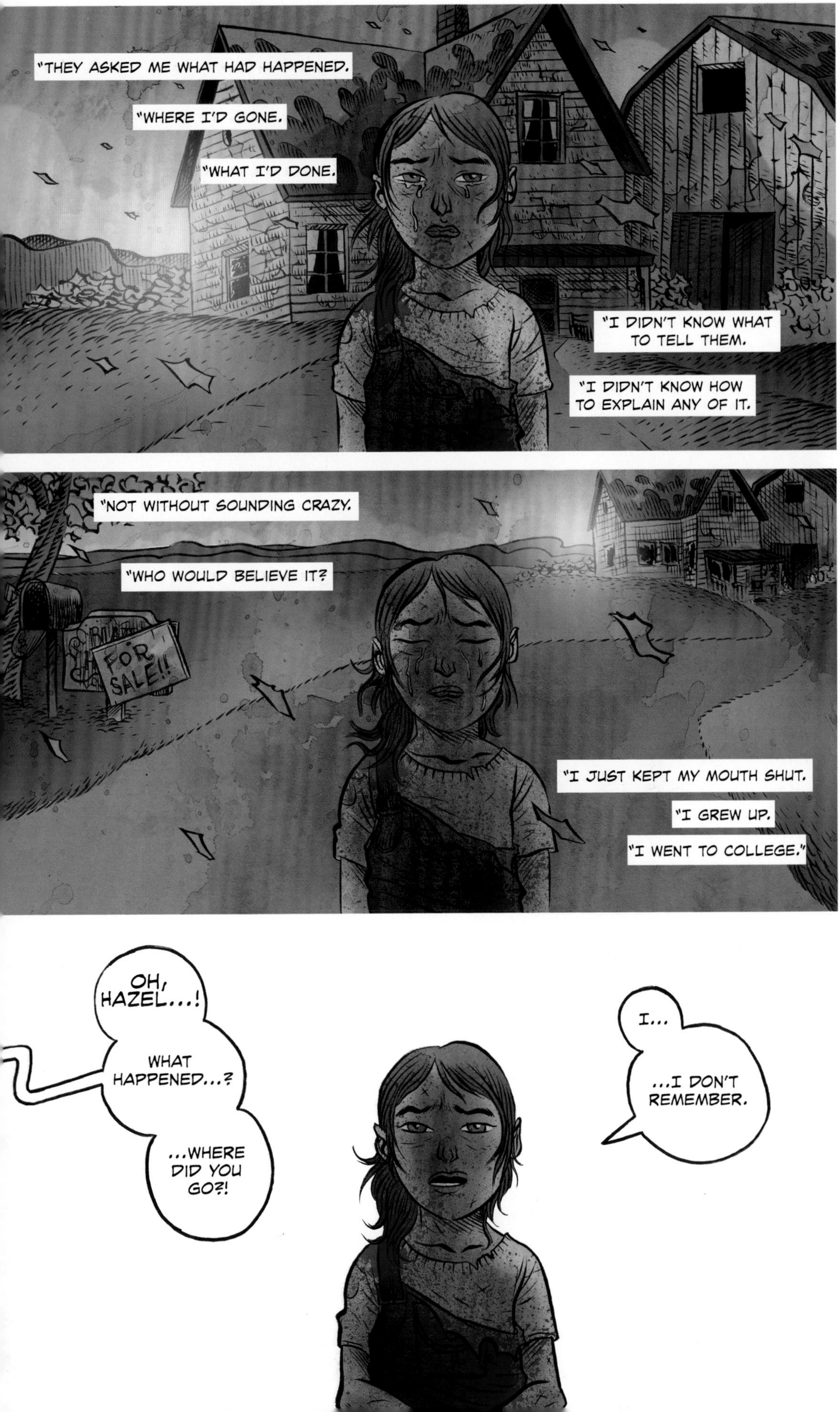
"THEY ASKED ME WHAT HAD HAPPENED.
"WHERE I'D GONE.
"WHAT I'D DONE.
"I DIDN'T KNOW WHAT TO TELL THEM.
"I DIDN'T KNOW HOW TO EXPLAIN ANY OF IT.
"NOT WITHOUT SOUNDING CRAZY.
"WHO WOULD BELIEVE IT?
FOR SALE!!
"I JUST KEPT MY MOUTH SHUT.
"I GREW UP.
"I WENT TO COLLEGE."
OH, HAZEL...!
WHAT HAPPENED...?
...WHERE DID YOU GO?!
I...
...I DON'T REMEMBER.

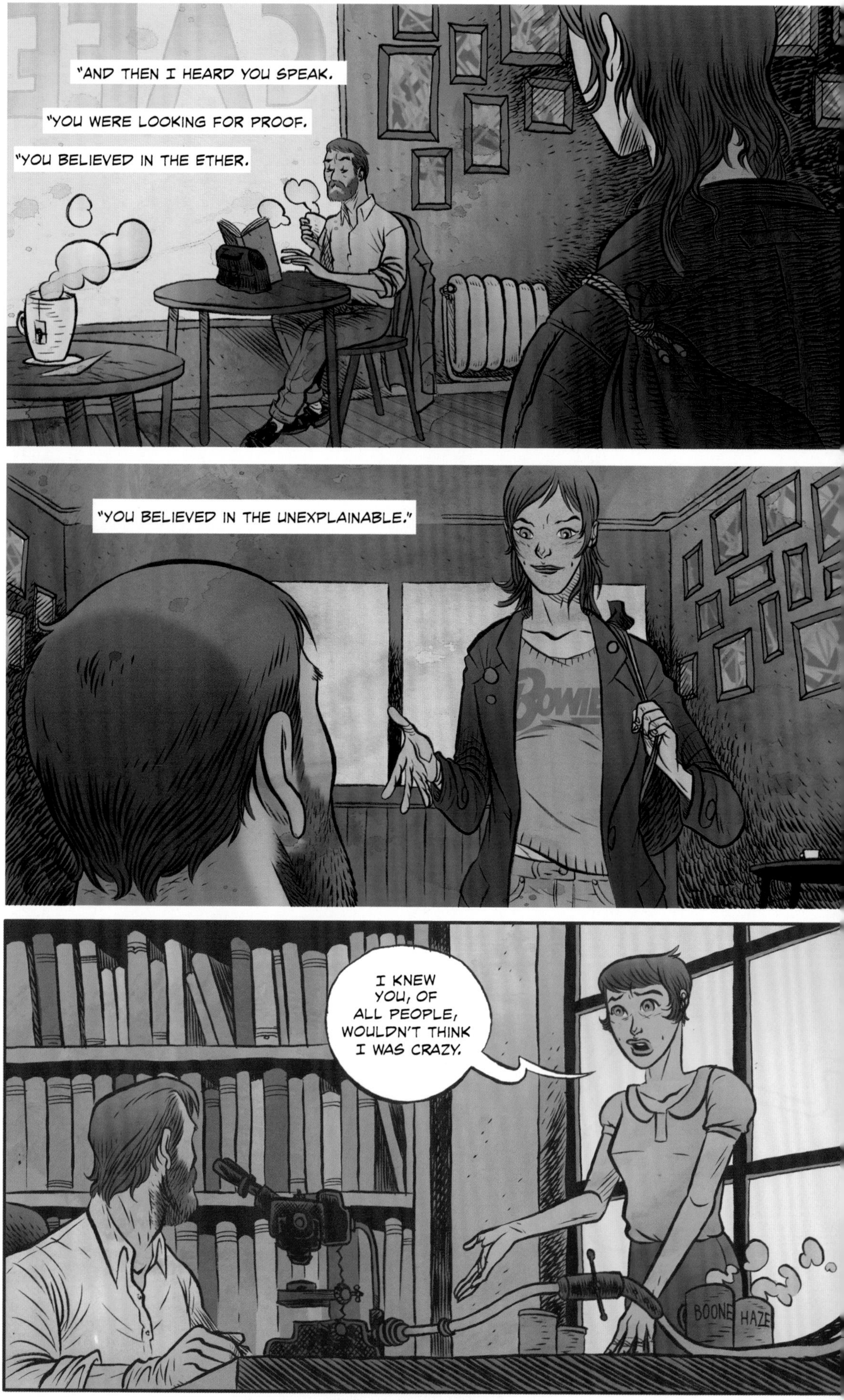
"AND THEN I HEARD YOU SPEAK.
"YOU WERE LOOKING FOR PROOF.
"YOU BELIEVED IN THE ETHER.
"YOU BELIEVED IN THE UNEXPLAINABLE."
I KNEW YOU, OF ALL PEOPLE, WOULDN'T THINK I WAS CRAZY.
BOONE
HAZE

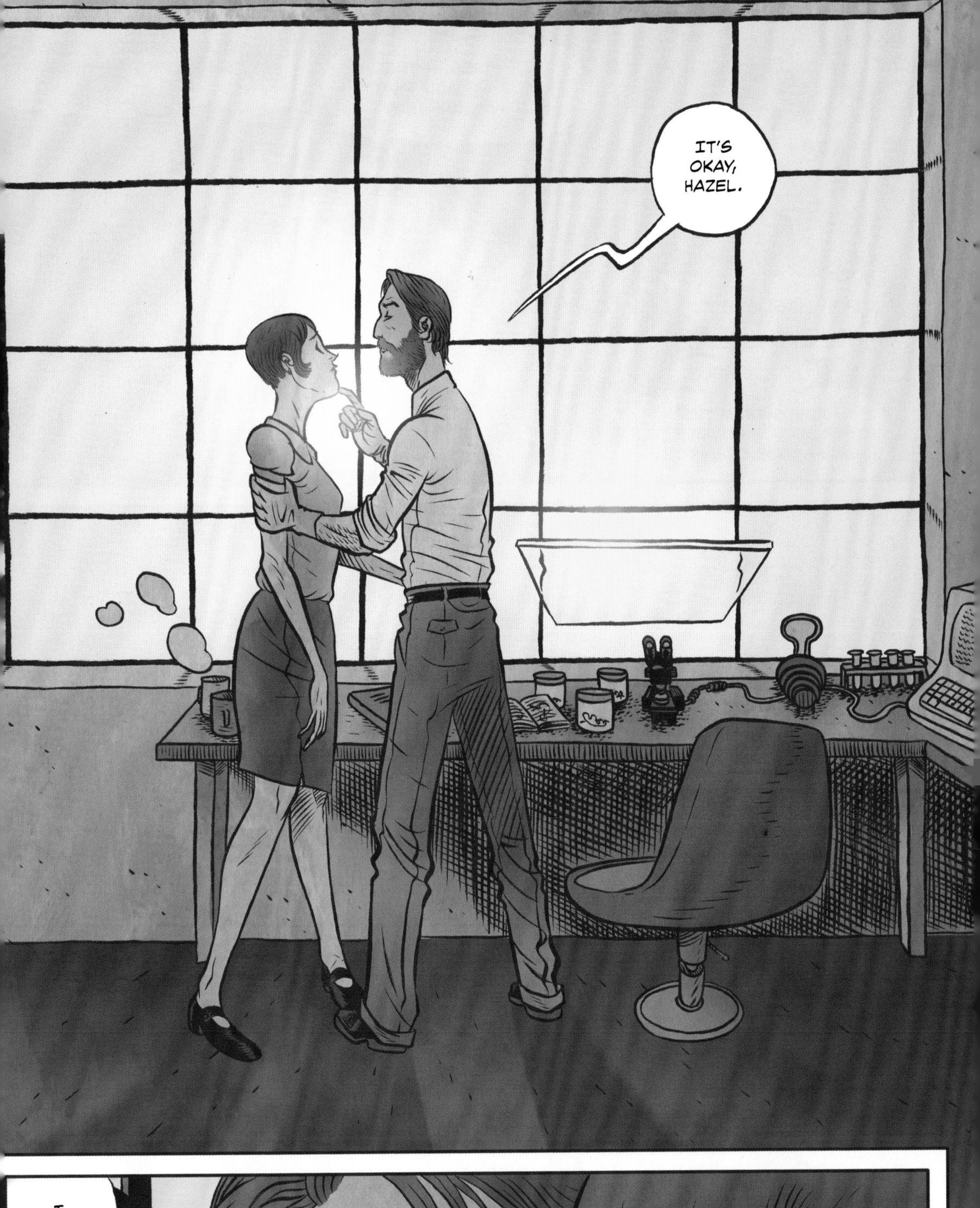
IT'S OKAY, HAZEL.

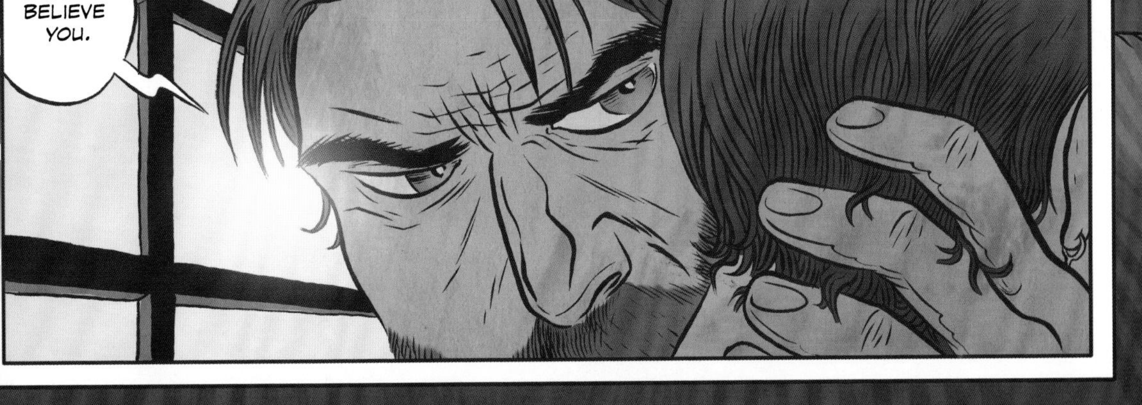
I BELIEVE YOU.

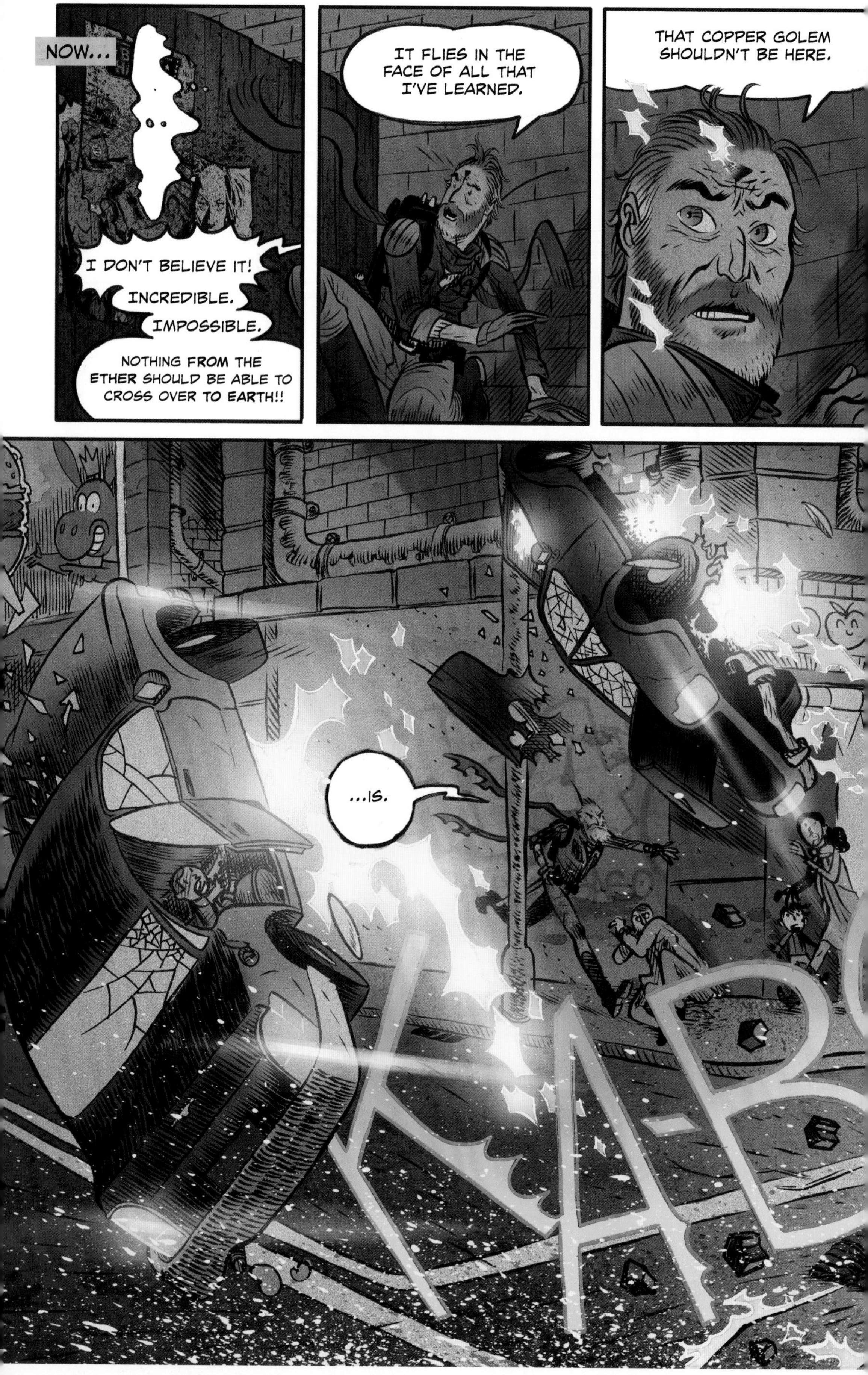
NOW...
I DON'T BELIEVE IT!
INCREDIBLE.
IMPOSSIBLE.
NOTHING FROM THE ETHER SHOULD BE ABLE TO CROSS OVER TO EARTH!!
IT FLIES IN THE FACE OF ALL THAT I'VE LEARNED.
THAT COPPER GOLEM SHOULDN'T BE HERE.
...IS.

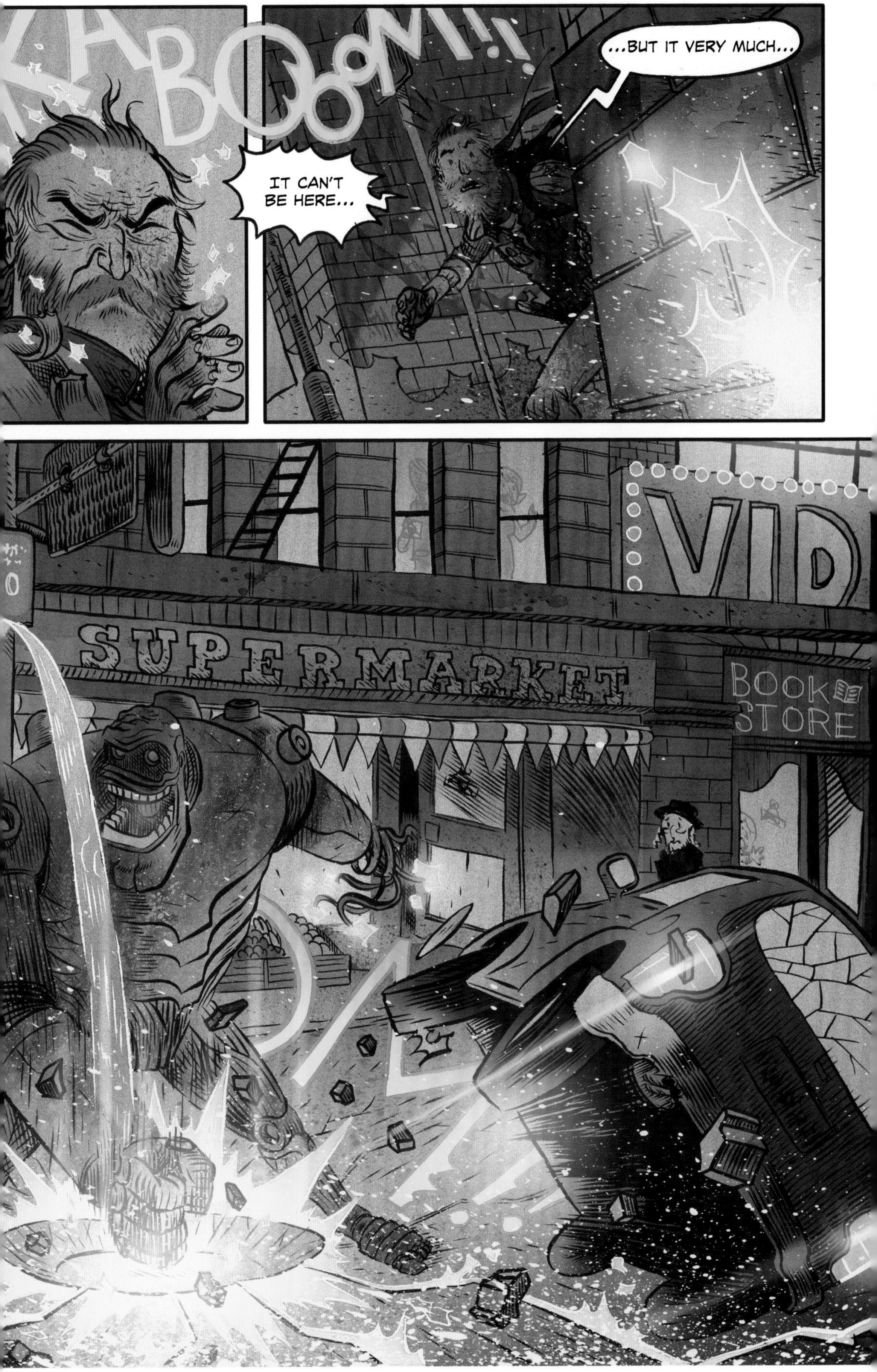
KABOOM!!
IT CAN'T BE HERE...
...BUT IT VERY MUCH...
VID
SUPERMARKET
BOOK STORE

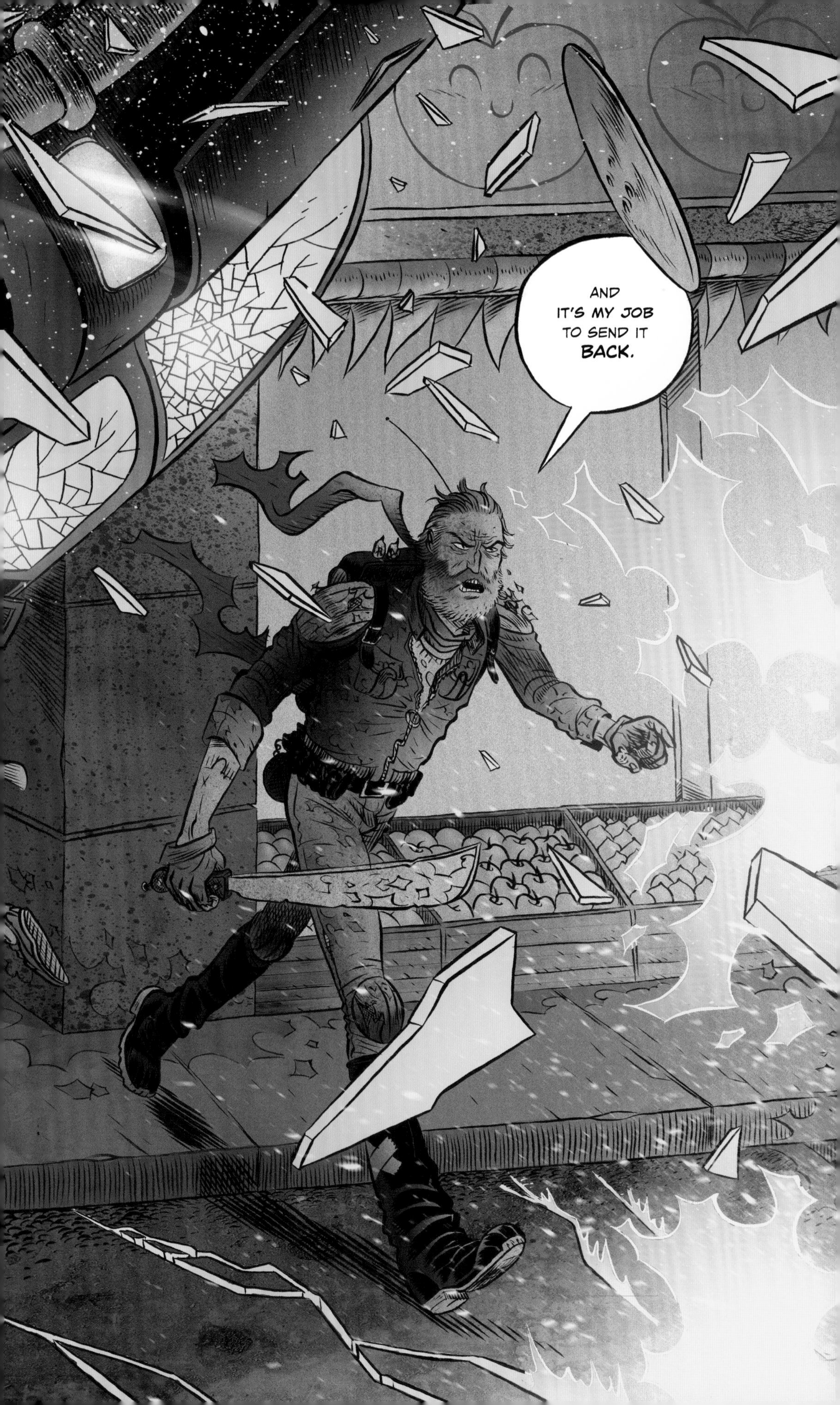
AND IT'S MY JOB TO SEND IT BACK.

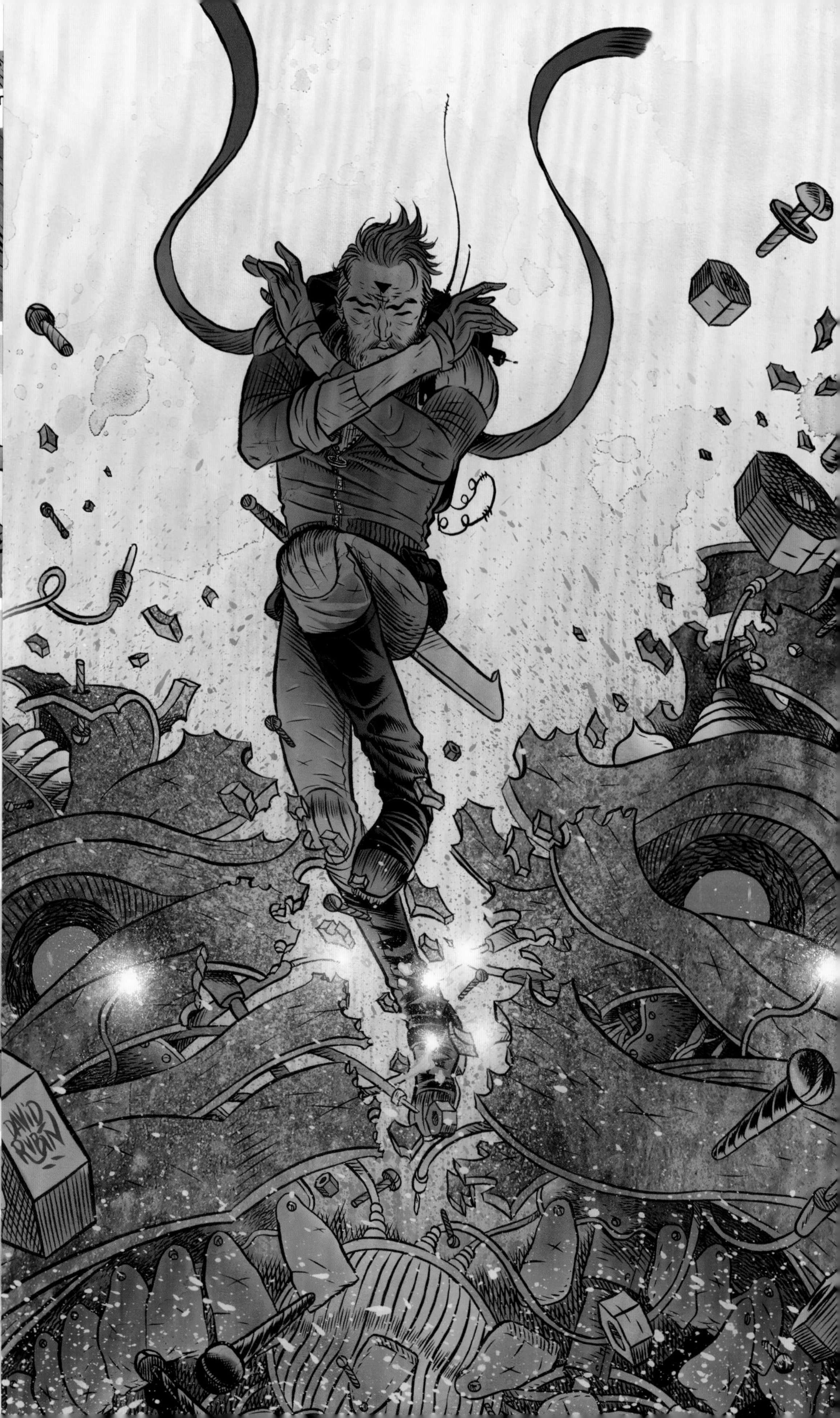
DAVID RUBIN

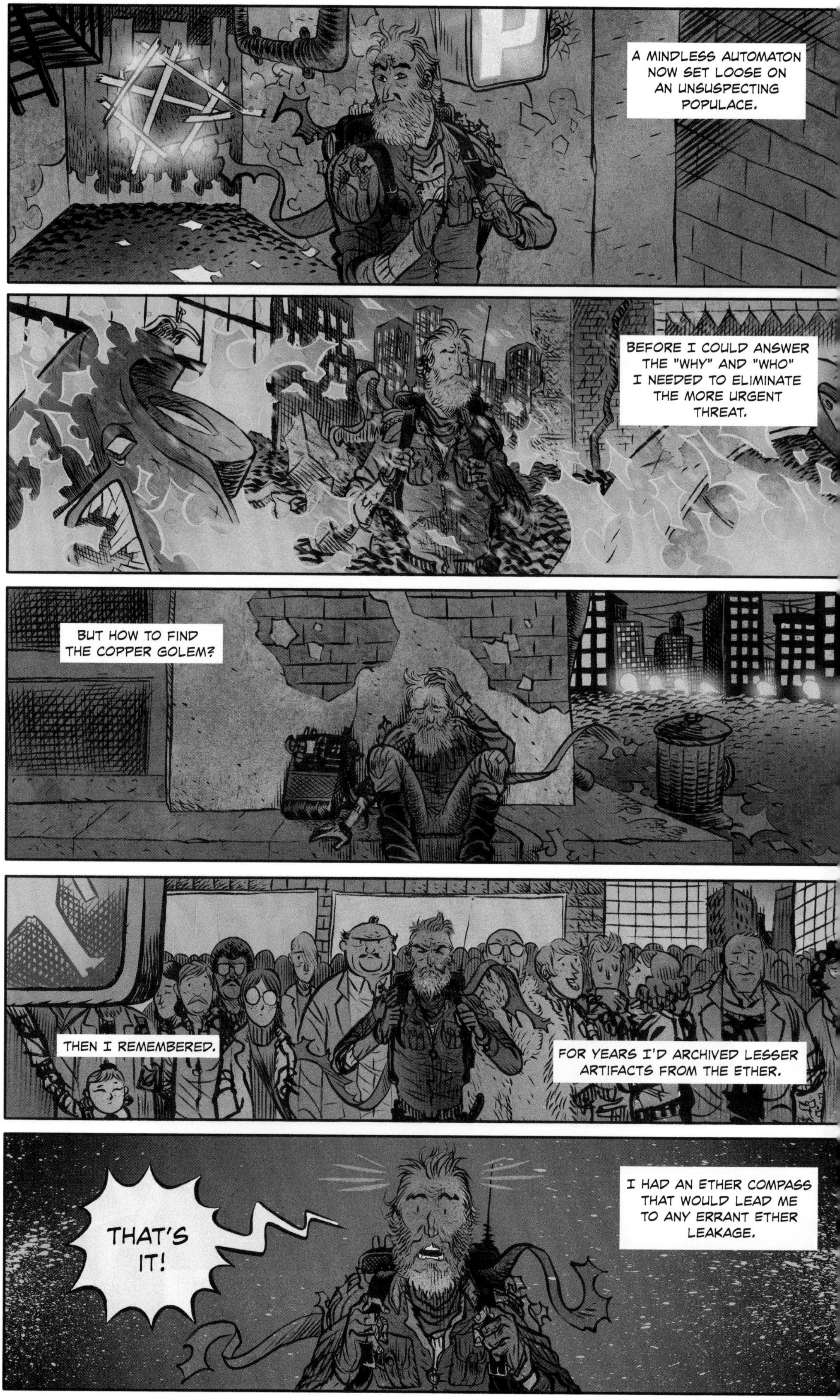
A MINDLESS AUTOMATON NOW SET LOOSE ON AN UNSUSPECTING POPULACE.
BEFORE I COULD ANSWER THE "WHY" AND "WHO" I NEEDED TO ELIMINATE THE MORE URGENT THREAT.
BUT HOW TO FIND THE COPPER GOLEM?
THEN I REMEMBERED.
FOR YEARS I'D ARCHIVED LESSER ARTIFACTS FROM THE ETHER.
THAT'S IT!
I HAD AN ETHER COMPASS THAT WOULD LEAD ME TO ANY ERRANT ETHER LEAKAGE.

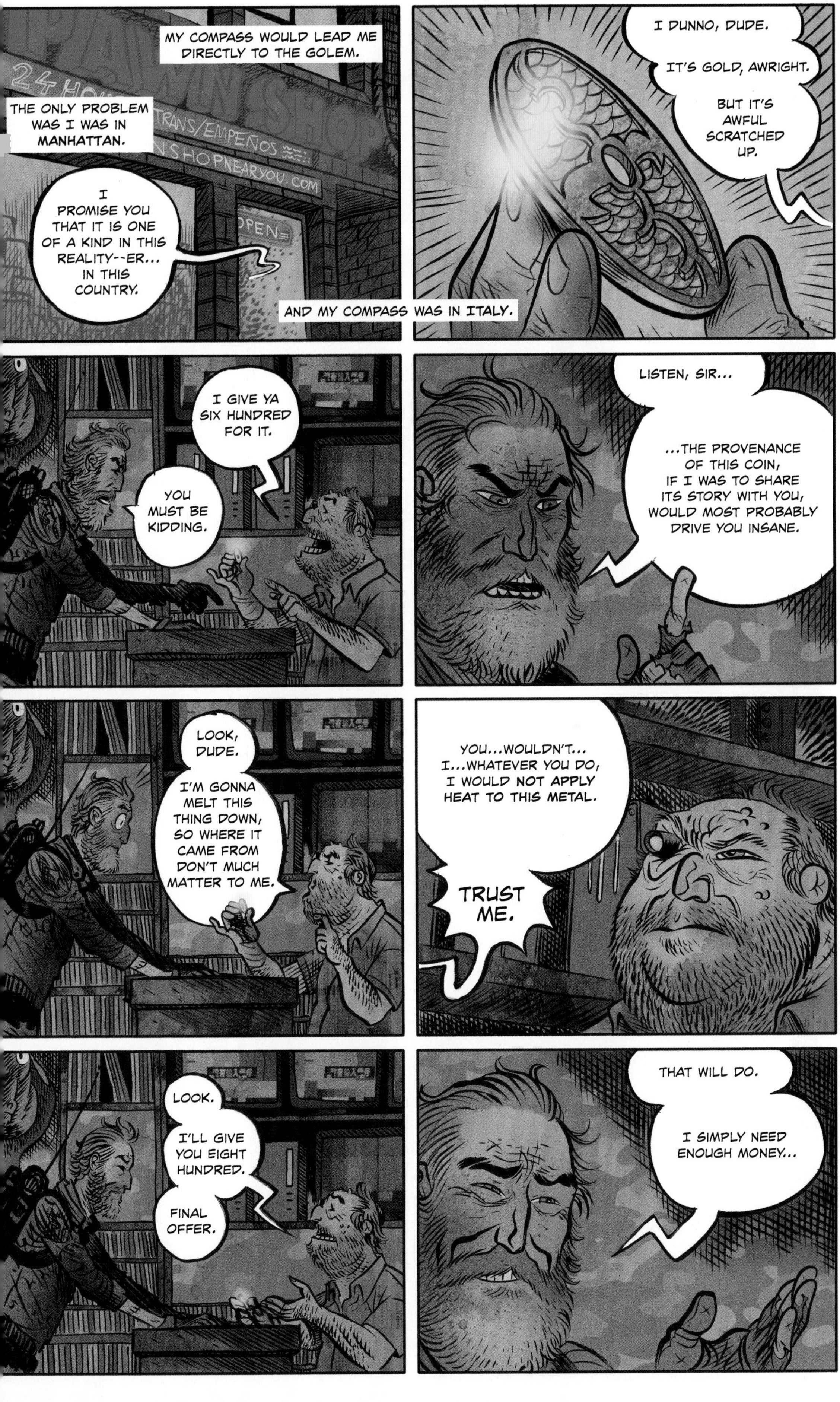
24 HOUR
PAWN SHOP
TRANS/EMPEÑOS
PAWNSHOPNEARYOU.COM
OPEN
MY COMPASS WOULD LEAD ME DIRECTLY TO THE GOLEM.
THE ONLY PROBLEM WAS I WAS IN MANHATTAN.
I PROMISE YOU THAT IT IS ONE OF A KIND IN THIS REALITY--ER... IN THIS COUNTRY.
AND MY COMPASS WAS IN ITALY.
I DUNNO, DUDE.
IT'S GOLD, AWRIGHT.
BUT IT'S AWFUL SCRATCHED UP.
I GIVE YA SIX HUNDRED FOR IT.
YOU MUST BE KIDDING.
LISTEN, SIR...
...THE PROVENANCE OF THIS COIN, IF I WAS TO SHARE ITS STORY WITH YOU, WOULD MOST PROBABLY DRIVE YOU INSANE.
LOOK, DUDE.
I'M GONNA MELT THIS THING DOWN, SO WHERE IT CAME FROM DON'T MUCH MATTER TO ME.
YOU...WOULDN'T... I...WHATEVER YOU DO, I WOULD NOT APPLY HEAT TO THIS METAL.
TRUST ME.
LOOK.
I'LL GIVE YOU EIGHT HUNDRED.
FINAL OFFER.
THAT WILL DO.
I SIMPLY NEED ENOUGH MONEY...

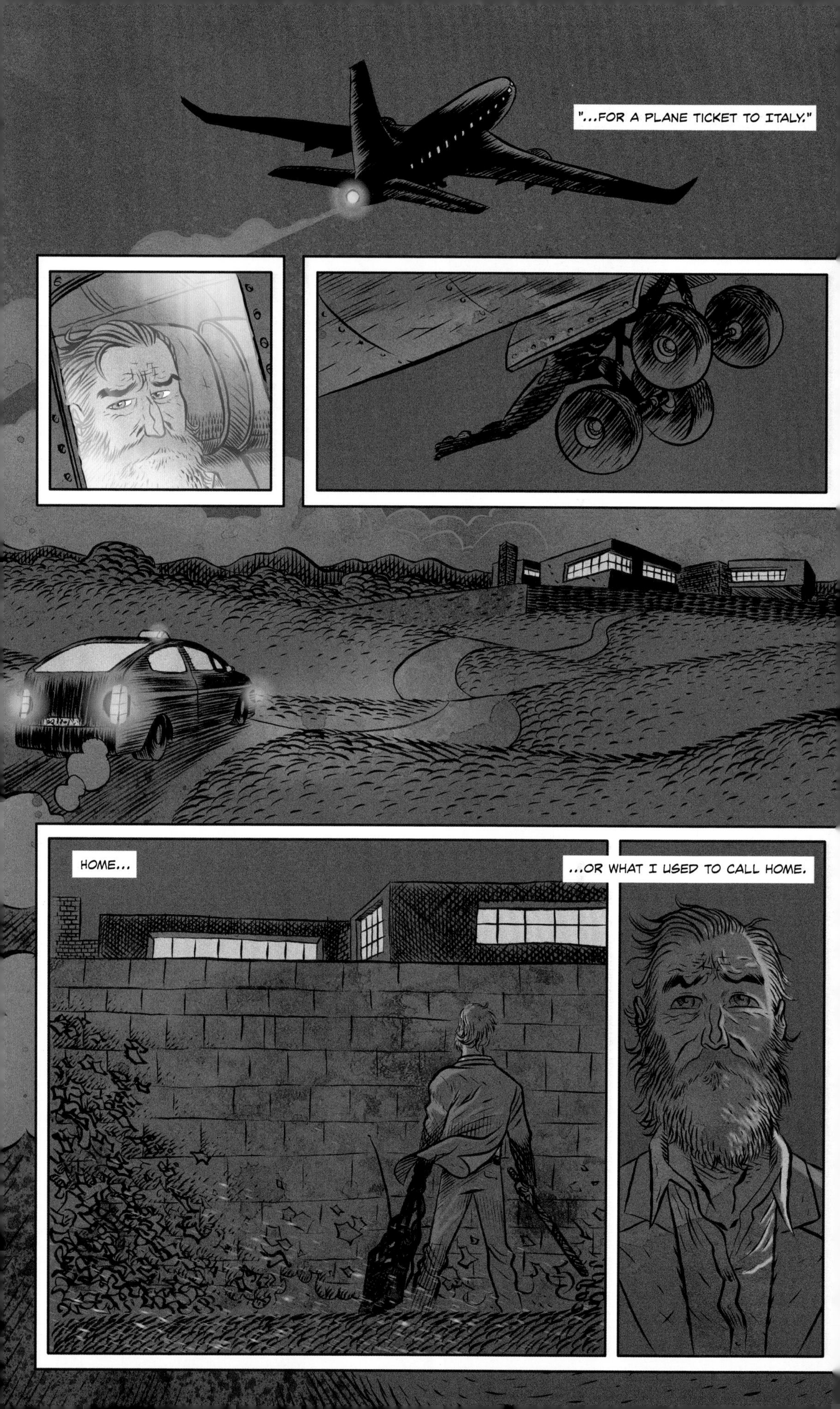
"...FOR A PLANE TICKET TO ITALY."
HOME...
...OR WHAT I USED TO CALL HOME.

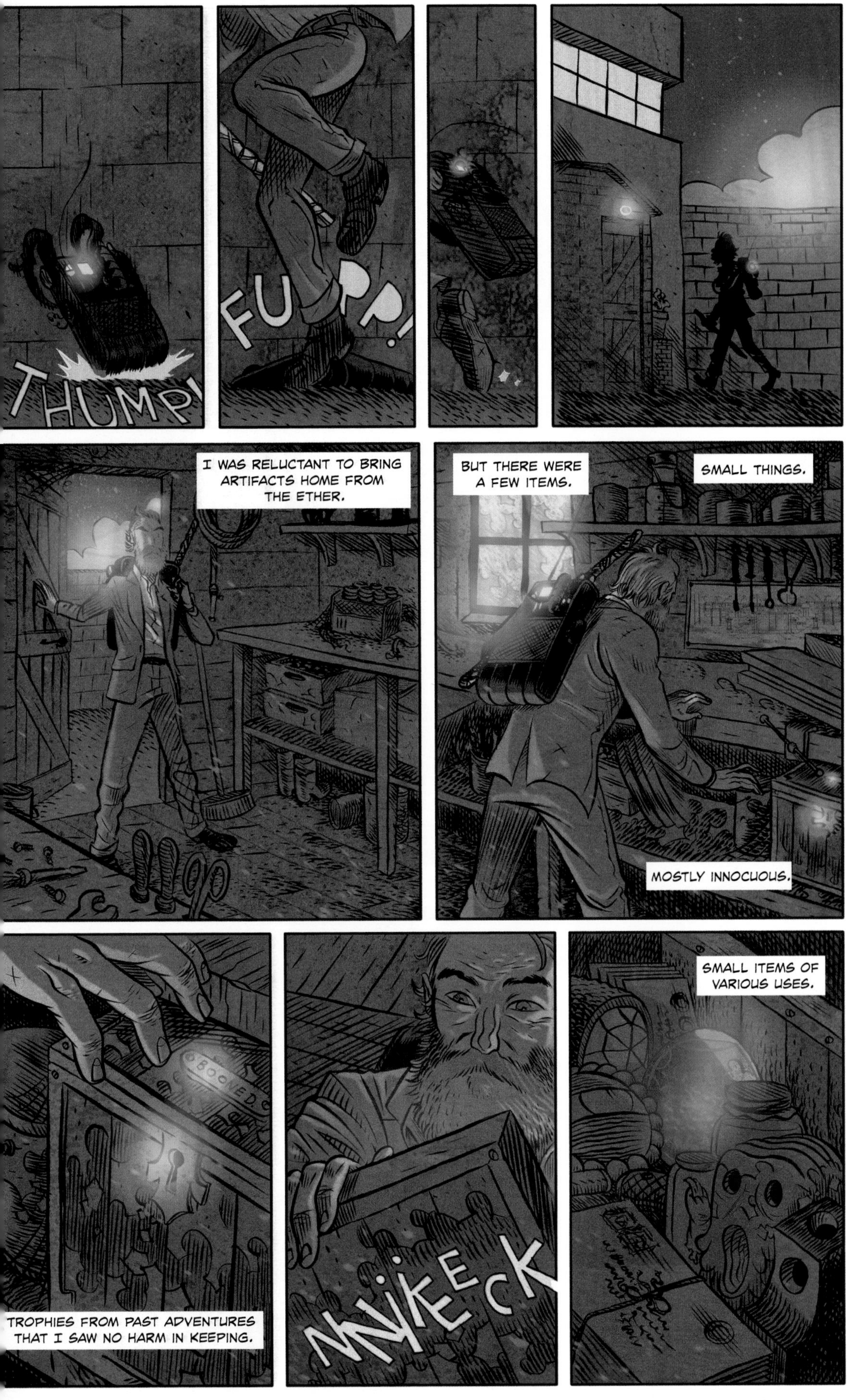
THUMP!
FUPP!
I WAS RELUCTANT TO BRING ARTIFACTS HOME FROM THE ETHER.
BUT THERE WERE A FEW ITEMS.
SMALL THINGS.
MOSTLY INNOCUOUS.
BOONED
TROPHIES FROM PAST ADVENTURES THAT I SAW NO HARM IN KEEPING.
MKEECK
SMALL ITEMS OF VARIOUS USES.

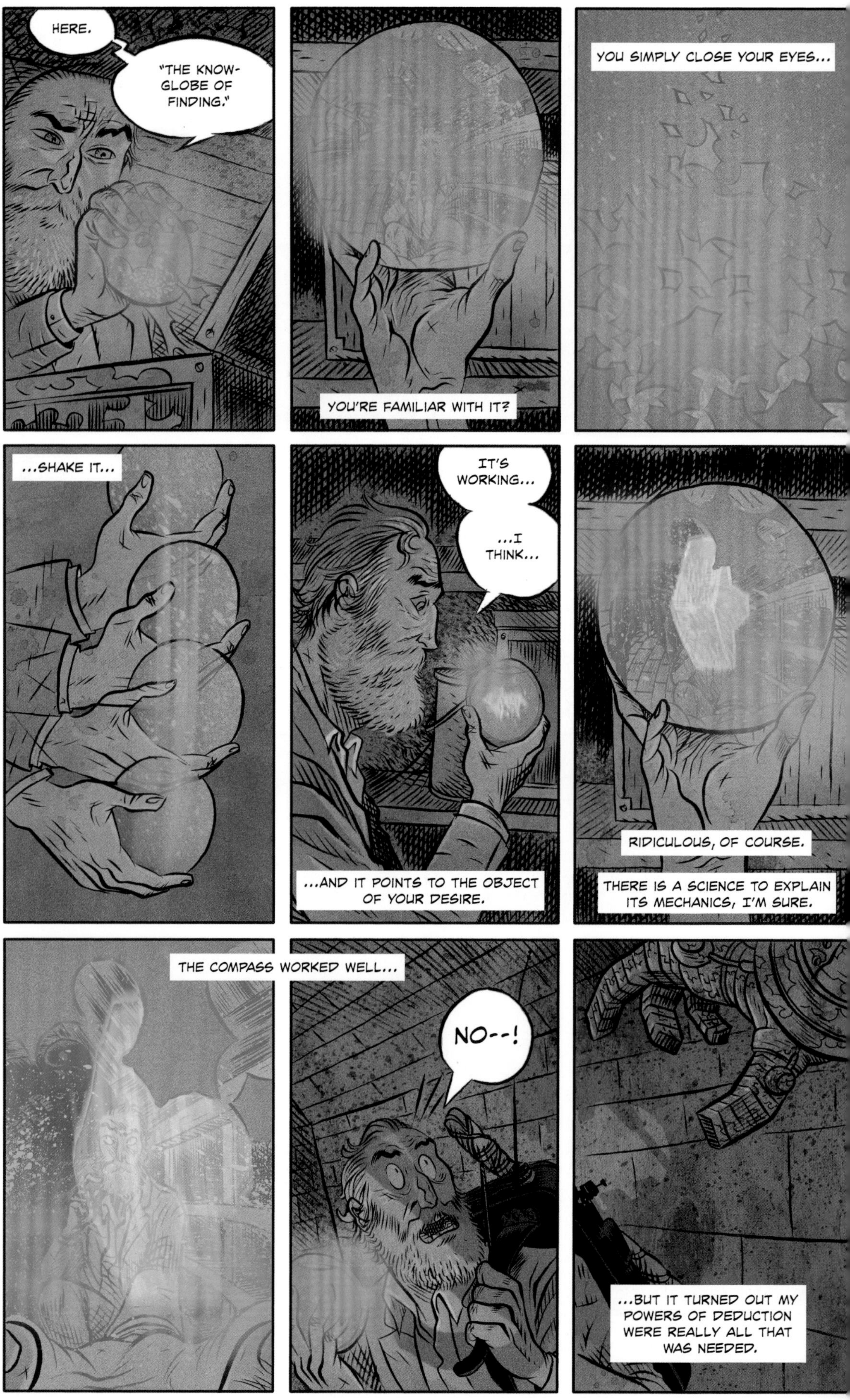
HERE.
"THE KNOW-GLOBE OF FINDING."
YOU'RE FAMILIAR WITH IT?
YOU SIMPLY CLOSE YOUR EYES...
...SHAKE IT...
IT'S WORKING...
...I THINK...
...AND IT POINTS TO THE OBJECT OF YOUR DESIRE.
RIDICULOUS, OF COURSE.
THERE IS A SCIENCE TO EXPLAIN ITS MECHANICS, I'M SURE.
THE COMPASS WORKED WELL...
NO--!
...BUT IT TURNED OUT MY POWERS OF DEDUCTION WERE REALLY ALL THAT WAS NEEDED.

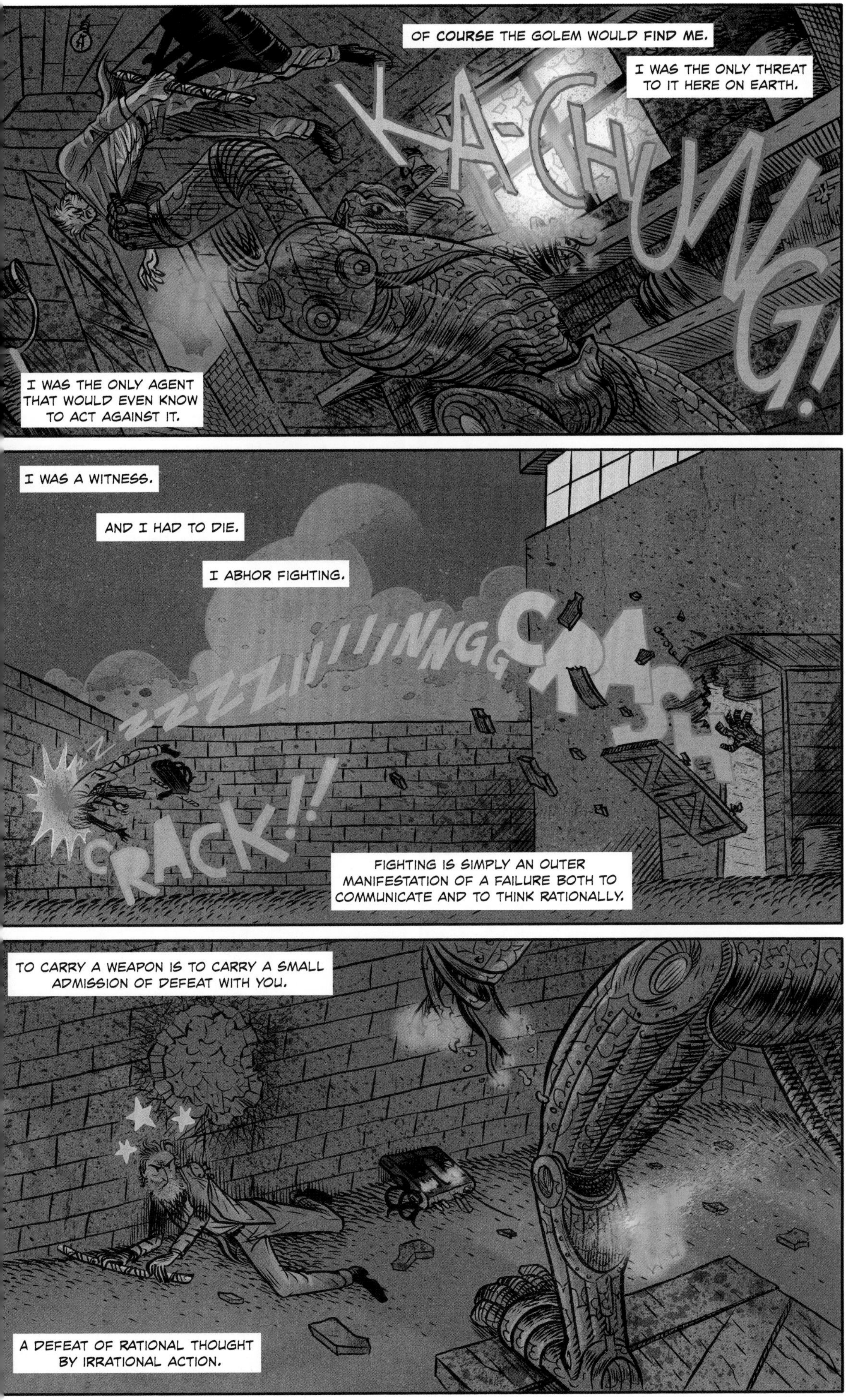
OF COURSE THE GOLEM WOULD FIND ME.
I WAS THE ONLY THREAT TO IT HERE ON EARTH.
KA-CHUNG!
I WAS THE ONLY AGENT THAT WOULD EVEN KNOW TO ACT AGAINST IT.
I WAS A WITNESS.
AND I HAD TO DIE.
I ABHOR FIGHTING.
ZZZZZIIIIINNGG
CRASH
CRACK!!
FIGHTING IS SIMPLY AN OUTER MANIFESTATION OF A FAILURE BOTH TO COMMUNICATE AND TO THINK RATIONALLY.
TO CARRY A WEAPON IS TO CARRY A SMALL ADMISSION OF DEFEAT WITH YOU.
A DEFEAT OF RATIONAL THOUGHT BY IRRATIONAL ACTION.

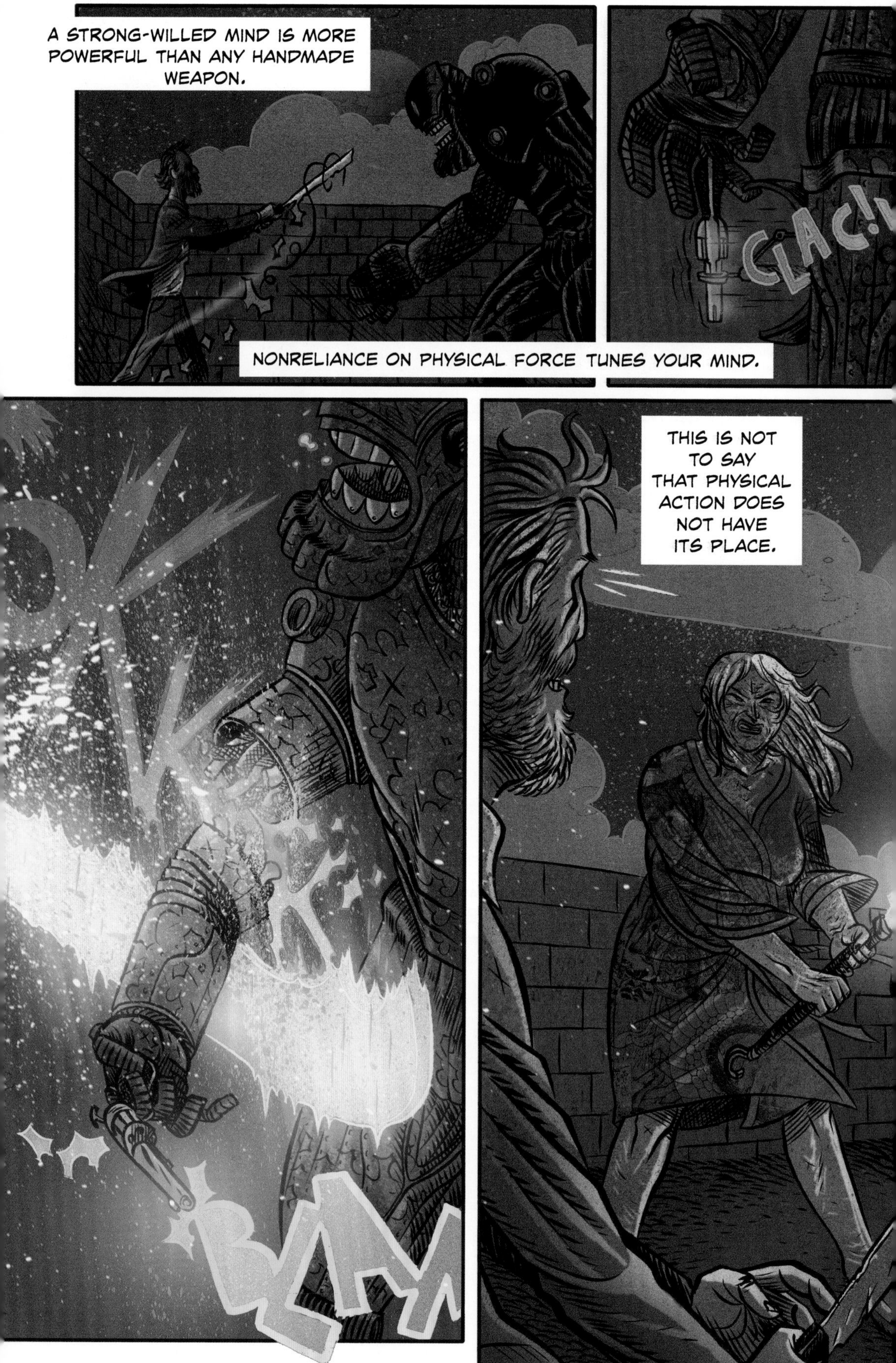
A STRONG-WILLED MIND IS MORE POWERFUL THAN ANY HANDMADE WEAPON.
CLAC!
NONRELIANCE ON PHYSICAL FORCE TUNES YOUR MIND.
THIS IS NOT TO SAY THAT PHYSICAL ACTION DOES NOT HAVE ITS PLACE.

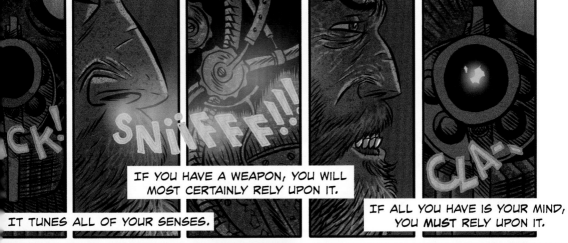

SNiFFFF!!!

IF YOU HAVE A WEAPON, YOU WILL MOST CERTAINLY RELY UPON IT.

IT TUNES ALL OF YOUR SENSES.

CLA-

IF ALL YOU HAVE IS YOUR MIND, YOU *MUST* RELY UPON IT.

GRRzzz whooezzz

SCREAM

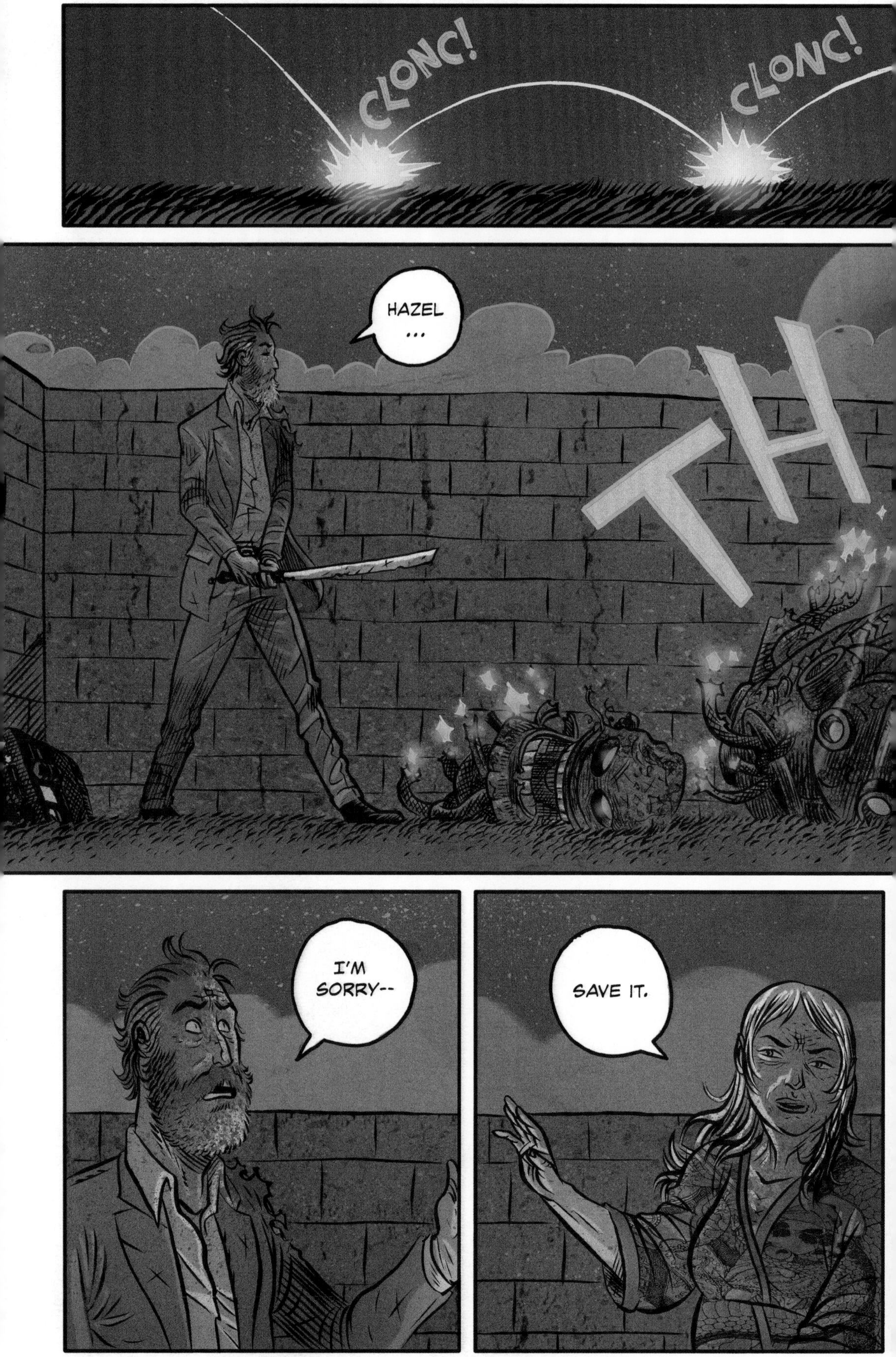
CLONC!
CLONC!
HAZEL ...
TH
I'M SORRY--
SAVE IT.

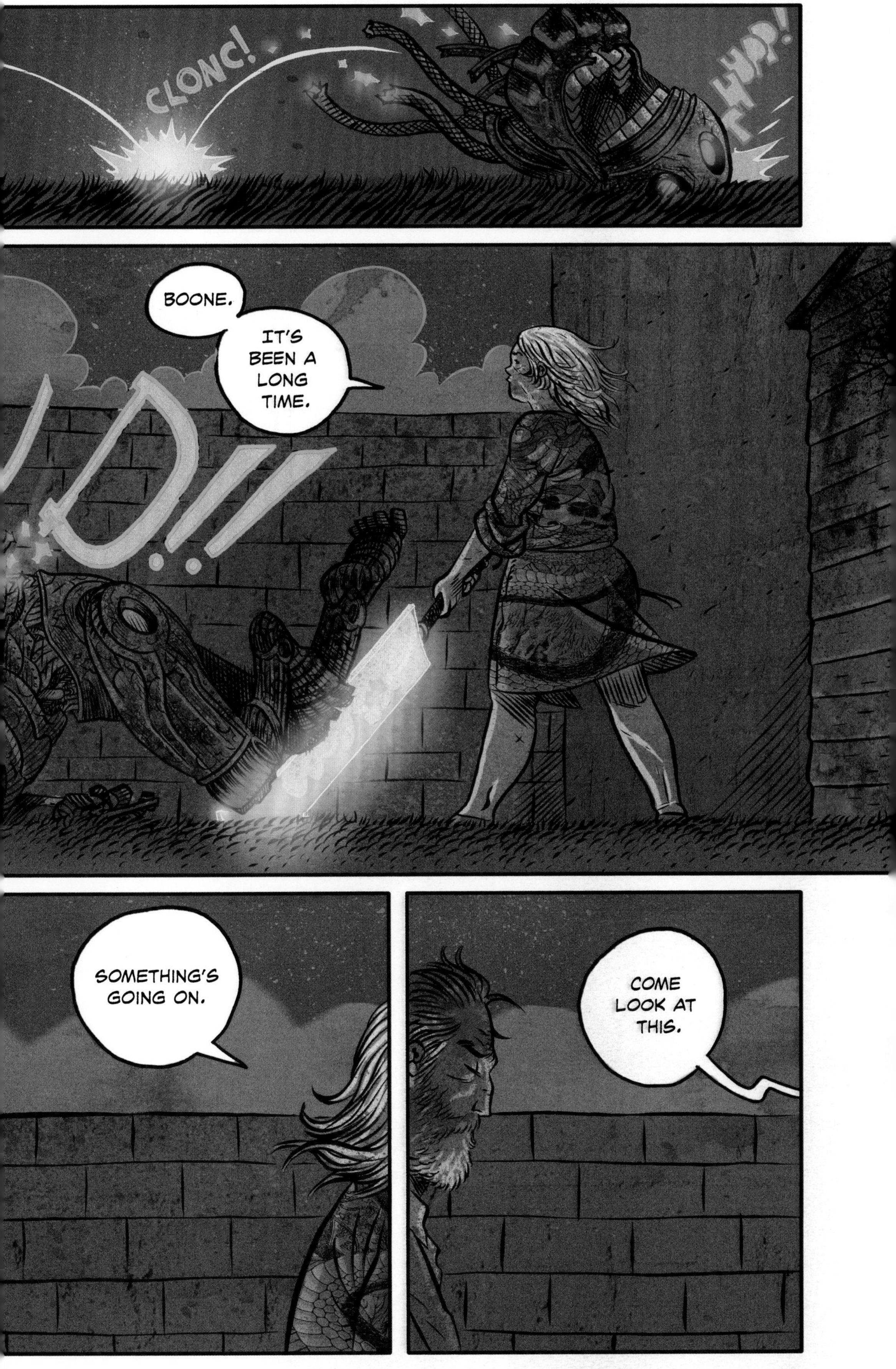
CLONC!
THUPP!
BOONE.
IT'S BEEN A LONG TIME.
SOMETHING'S GOING ON.
COME LOOK AT THIS.

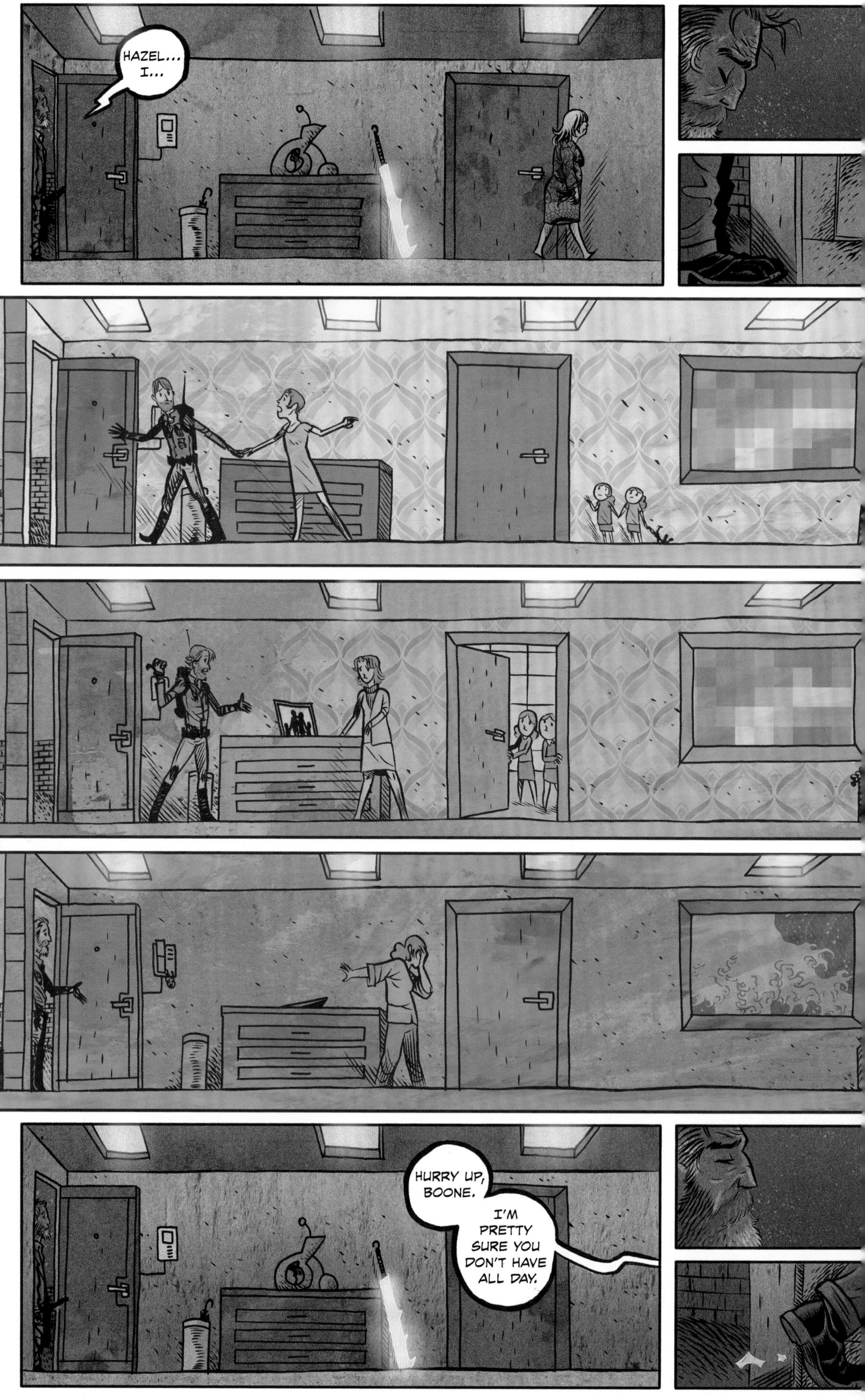
HAZEL... I...
HURRY UP, BOONE.
I'M PRETTY SURE YOU DON'T HAVE ALL DAY.

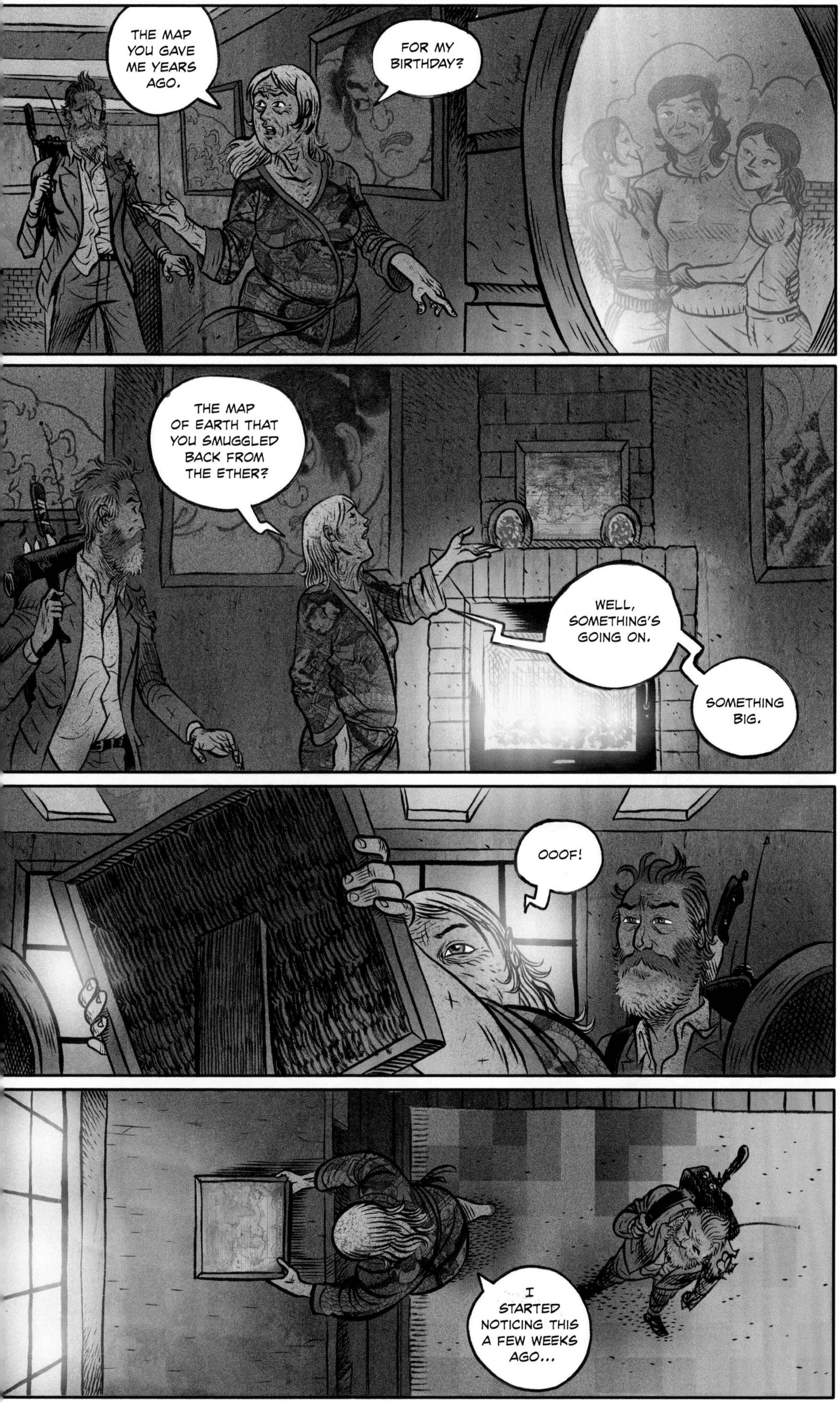
THE MAP YOU GAVE ME YEARS AGO.
FOR MY BIRTHDAY?
THE MAP OF EARTH THAT YOU SMUGGLED BACK FROM THE ETHER?
WELL, SOMETHING'S GOING ON.
SOMETHING BIG.
OOOF!
I STARTED NOTICING THIS A FEW WEEKS AGO...

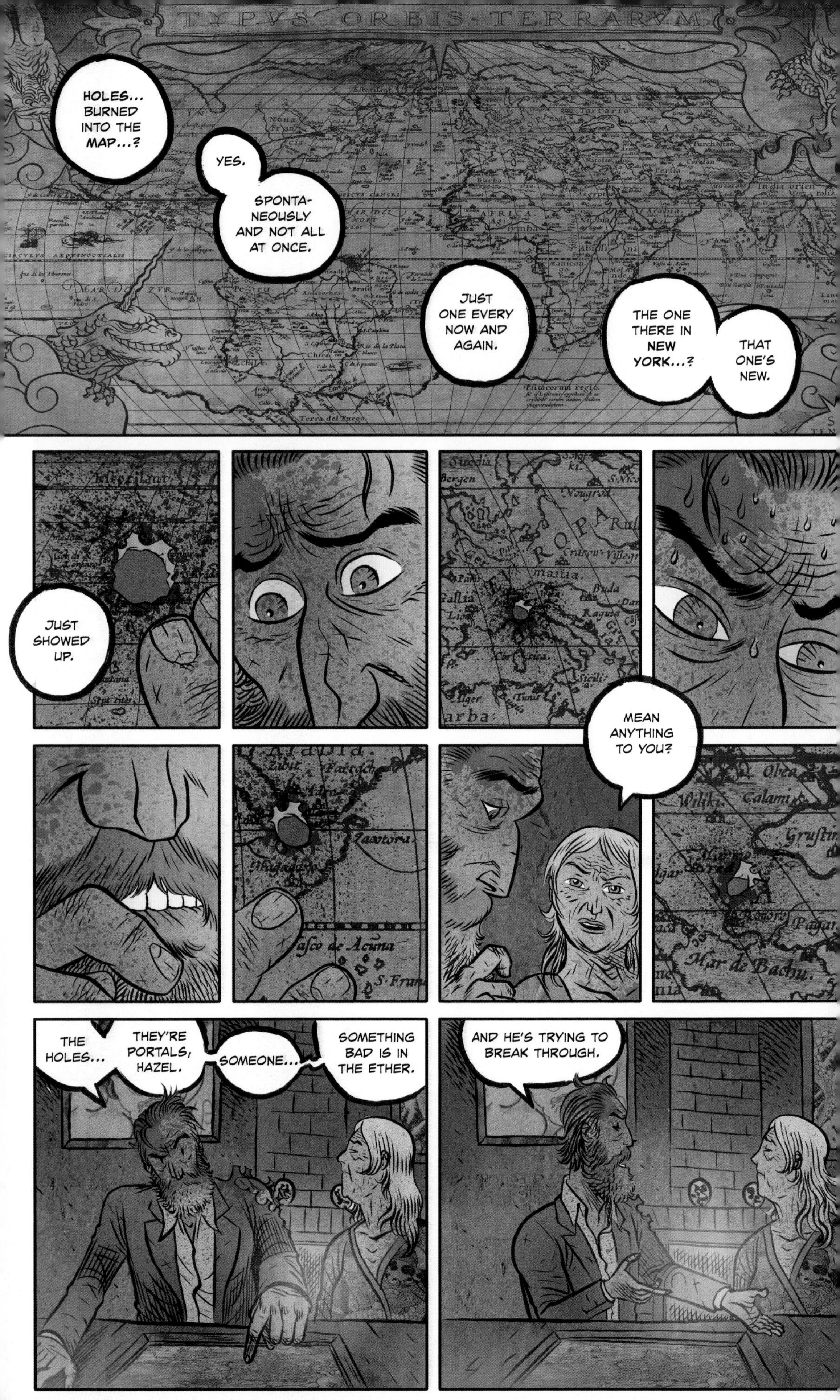
TYPVS ORBIS TERRARVM
HOLES... BURNED INTO THE MAP...?
YES.
SPONTANEOUSLY AND NOT ALL AT ONCE.
JUST ONE EVERY NOW AND AGAIN.
THE ONE THERE IN NEW YORK...?
THAT ONE'S NEW.
JUST SHOWED UP.
MEAN ANYTHING TO YOU?
THE HOLES...
THEY'RE PORTALS, HAZEL.
SOMEONE...
SOMETHING BAD IS IN THE ETHER.
AND HE'S TRYING TO BREAK THROUGH.

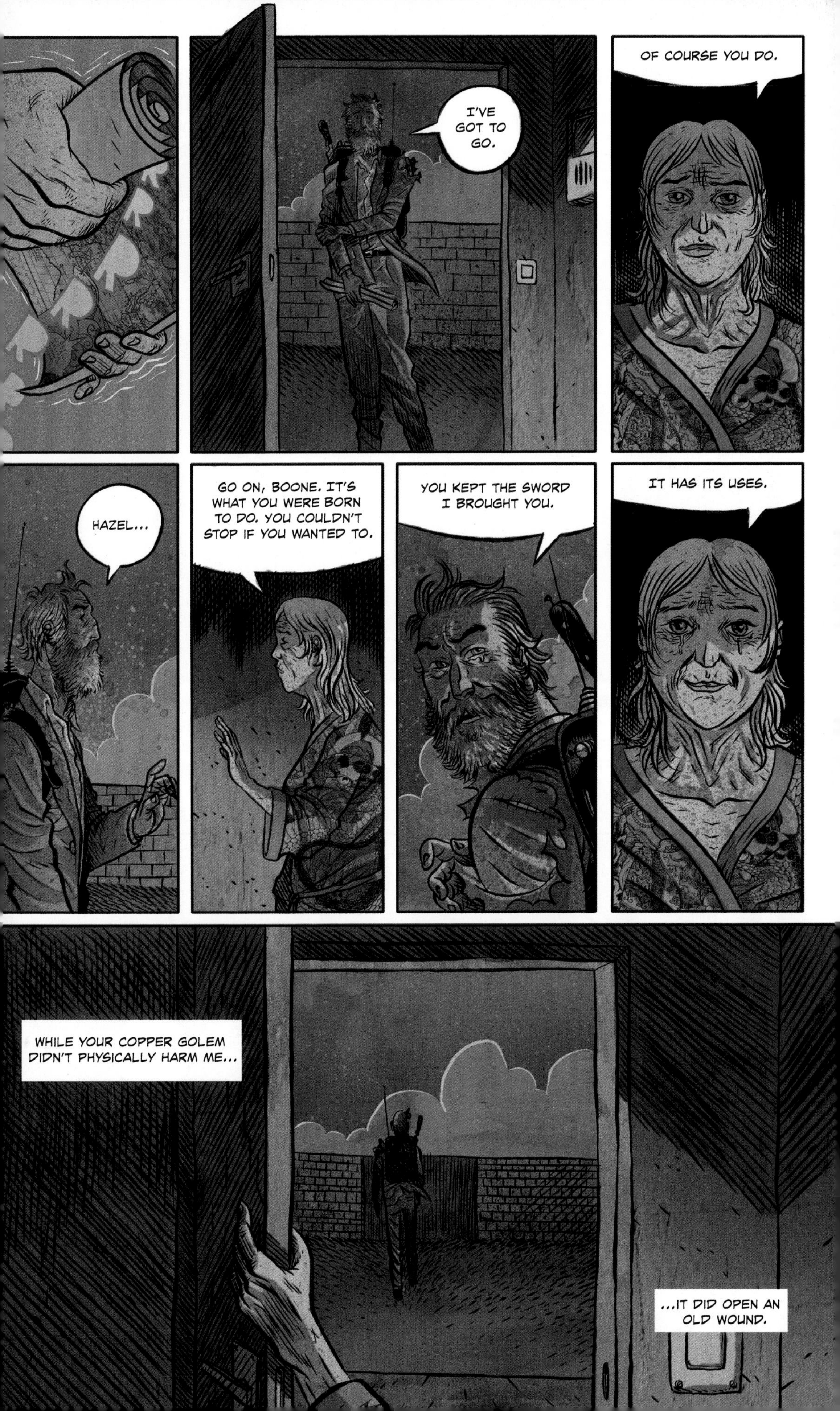
I'VE GOT TO GO.
OF COURSE YOU DO.
HAZEL...
GO ON, BOONE. IT'S WHAT YOU WERE BORN TO DO. YOU COULDN'T STOP IF YOU WANTED TO.
YOU KEPT THE SWORD I BROUGHT YOU.
IT HAS ITS USES.
WHILE YOUR COPPER GOLEM DIDN'T PHYSICALLY HARM ME...
...IT DID OPEN AN OLD WOUND.

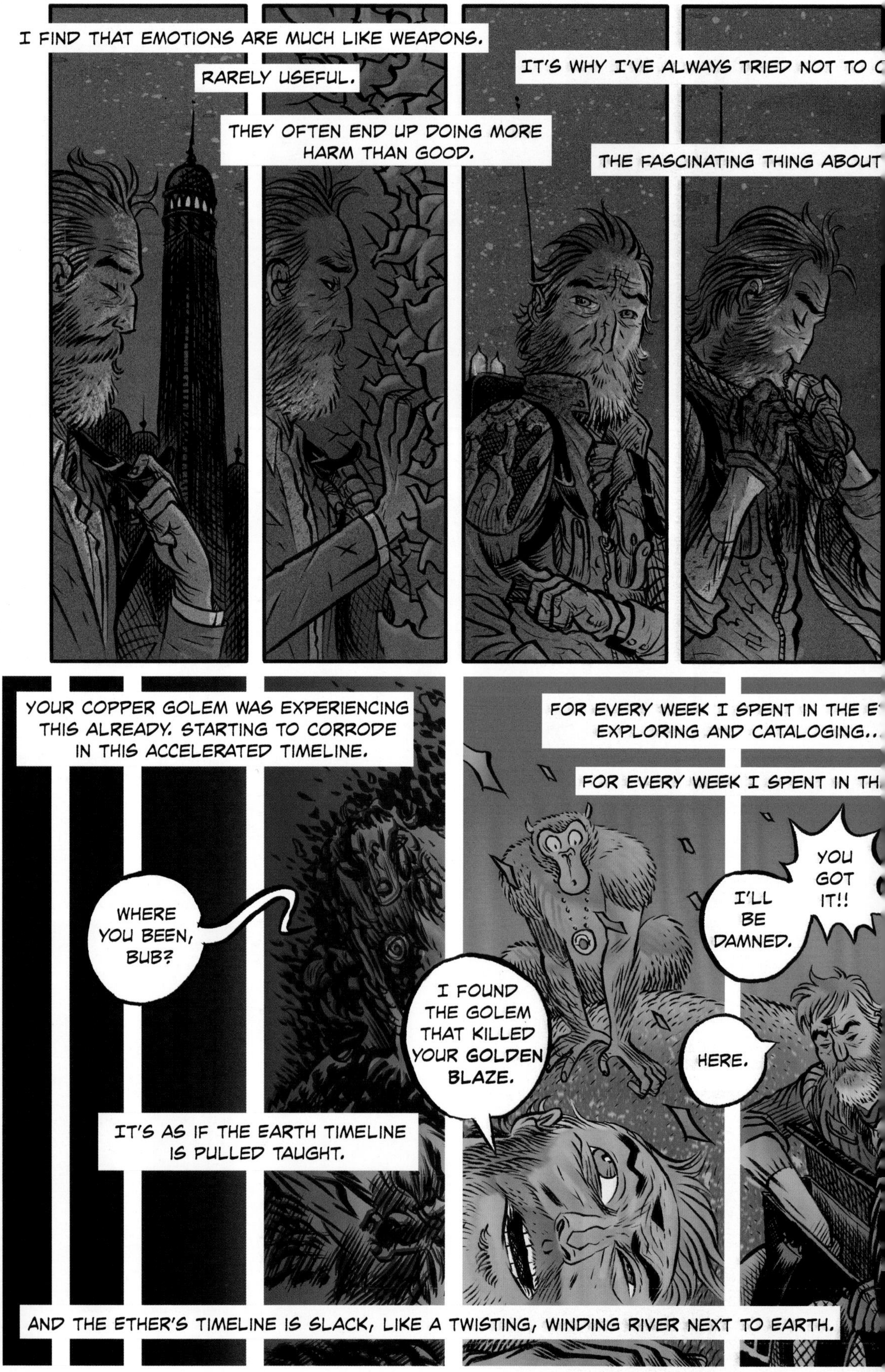
I FIND THAT EMOTIONS ARE MUCH LIKE WEAPONS.
RARELY USEFUL.
THEY OFTEN END UP DOING MORE HARM THAN GOOD.
IT'S WHY I'VE ALWAYS TRIED NOT TO
THE FASCINATING THING ABOUT
YOUR COPPER GOLEM WAS EXPERIENCING THIS ALREADY. STARTING TO CORRODE IN THIS ACCELERATED TIMELINE.
WHERE YOU BEEN, BUB?
IT'S AS IF THE EARTH TIMELINE IS PULLED TAUGHT.
FOR EVERY WEEK I SPENT IN THE
EXPLORING AND CATALOGING...
FOR EVERY WEEK I SPENT IN TH
I FOUND THE GOLEM THAT KILLED YOUR GOLDEN BLAZE.
I'LL BE DAMNED.
YOU GOT IT!!
HERE.
AND THE ETHER'S TIMELINE IS SLACK, LIKE A TWISTING, WINDING RIVER NEXT TO EARTH.

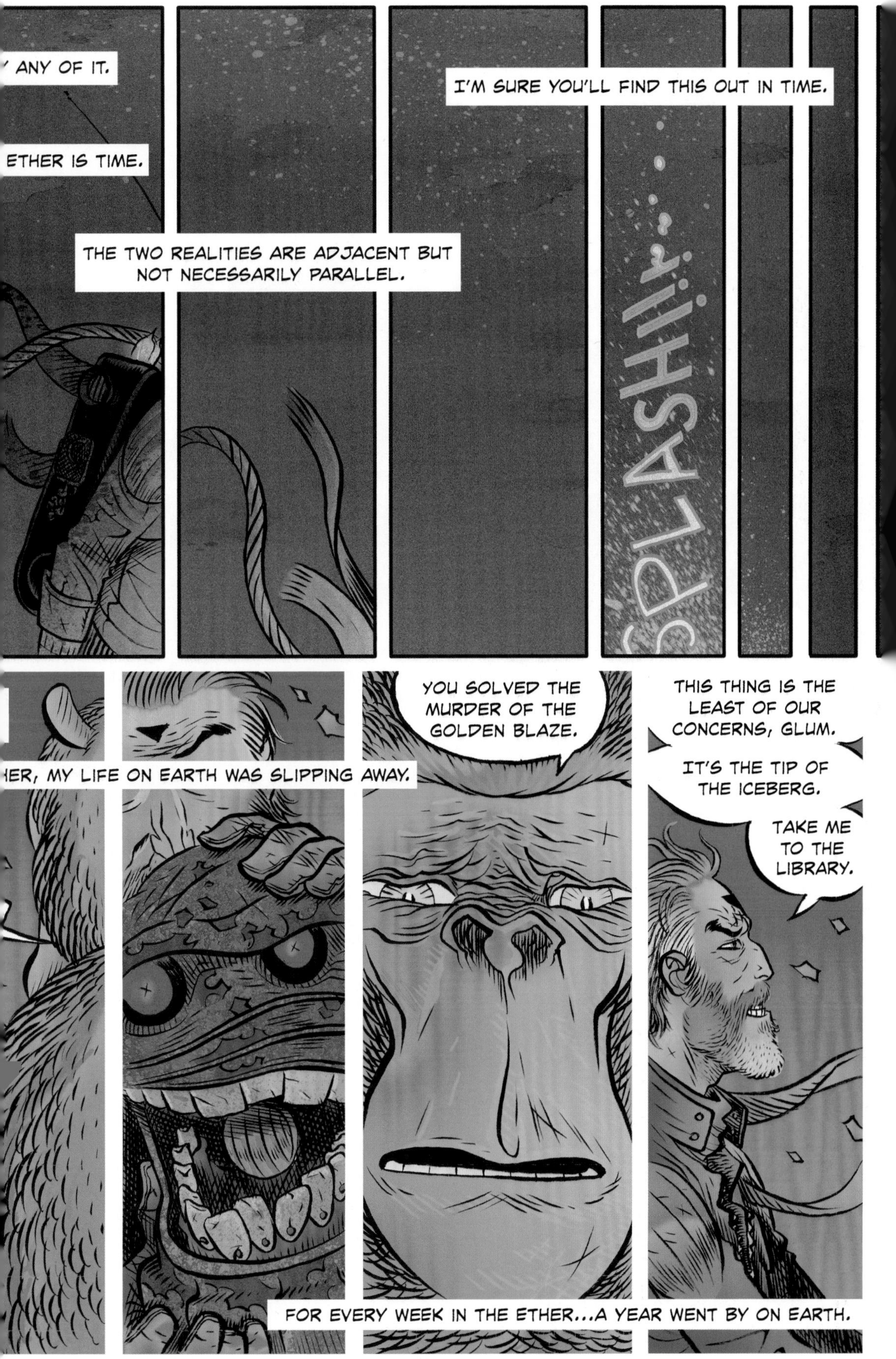

' ANY OF IT.
ETHER IS TIME.
THE TWO REALITIES ARE ADJACENT BUT NOT NECESSARILY PARALLEL.
I'M SURE YOU'LL FIND THIS OUT IN TIME.
SPLASH!!
HER, MY LIFE ON EARTH WAS SLIPPING AWAY.
YOU SOLVED THE MURDER OF THE GOLDEN BLAZE.
THIS THING IS THE LEAST OF OUR CONCERNS, GLUM.
IT'S THE TIP OF THE ICEBERG.
TAKE ME TO THE LIBRARY.
FOR EVERY WEEK IN THE ETHER...A YEAR WENT BY ON EARTH.

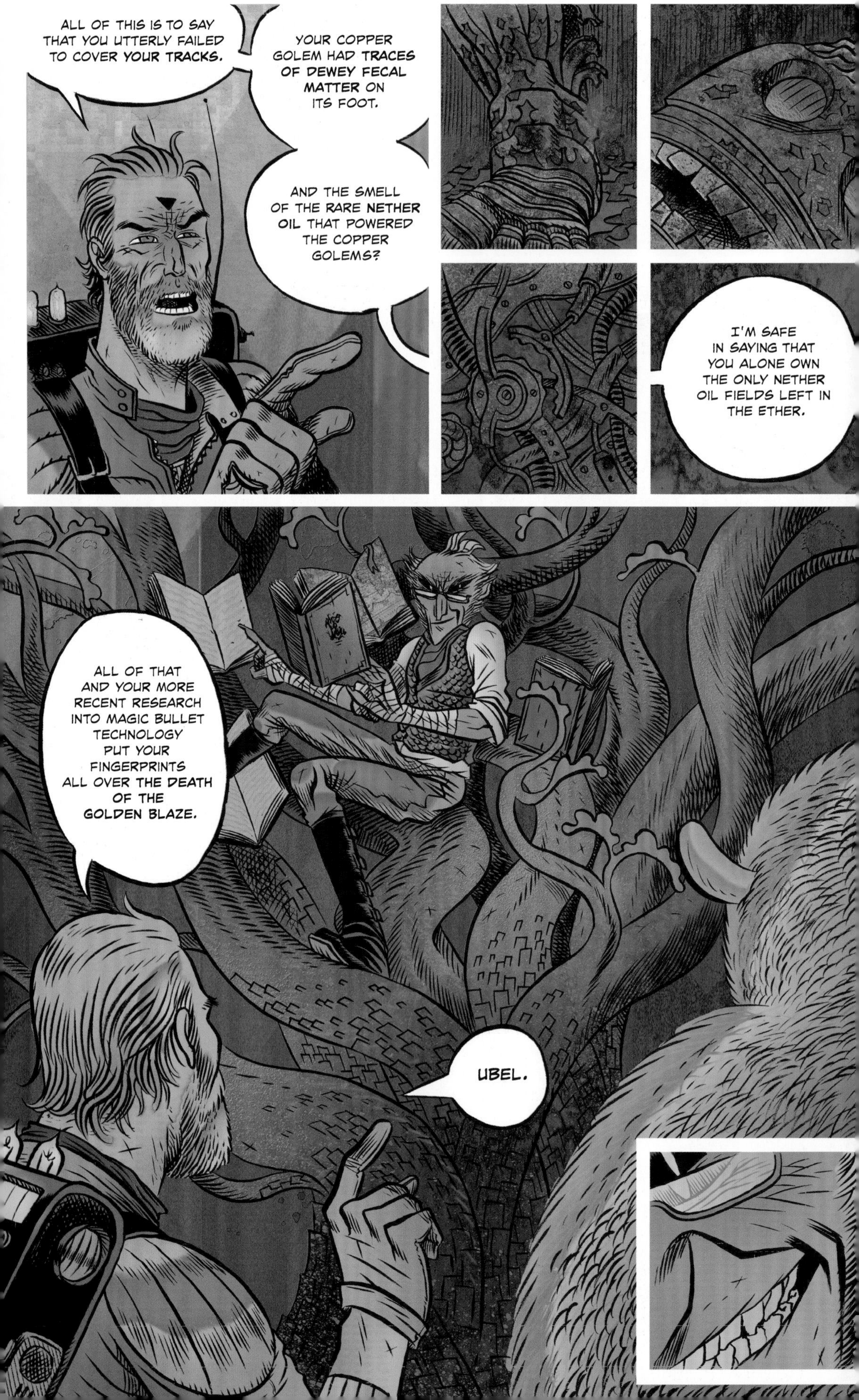

ALL OF THIS IS TO SAY THAT YOU UTTERLY FAILED TO COVER YOUR TRACKS.
YOUR COPPER GOLEM HAD TRACES OF DEWEY FECAL MATTER ON ITS FOOT.
AND THE SMELL OF THE RARE NETHER OIL THAT POWERED THE COPPER GOLEMS?
I'M SAFE IN SAYING THAT YOU ALONE OWN THE ONLY NETHER OIL FIELDS LEFT IN THE ETHER.
ALL OF THAT AND YOUR MORE RECENT RESEARCH INTO MAGIC BULLET TECHNOLOGY PUT YOUR FINGERPRINTS ALL OVER THE DEATH OF THE GOLDEN BLAZE.
UBEL.

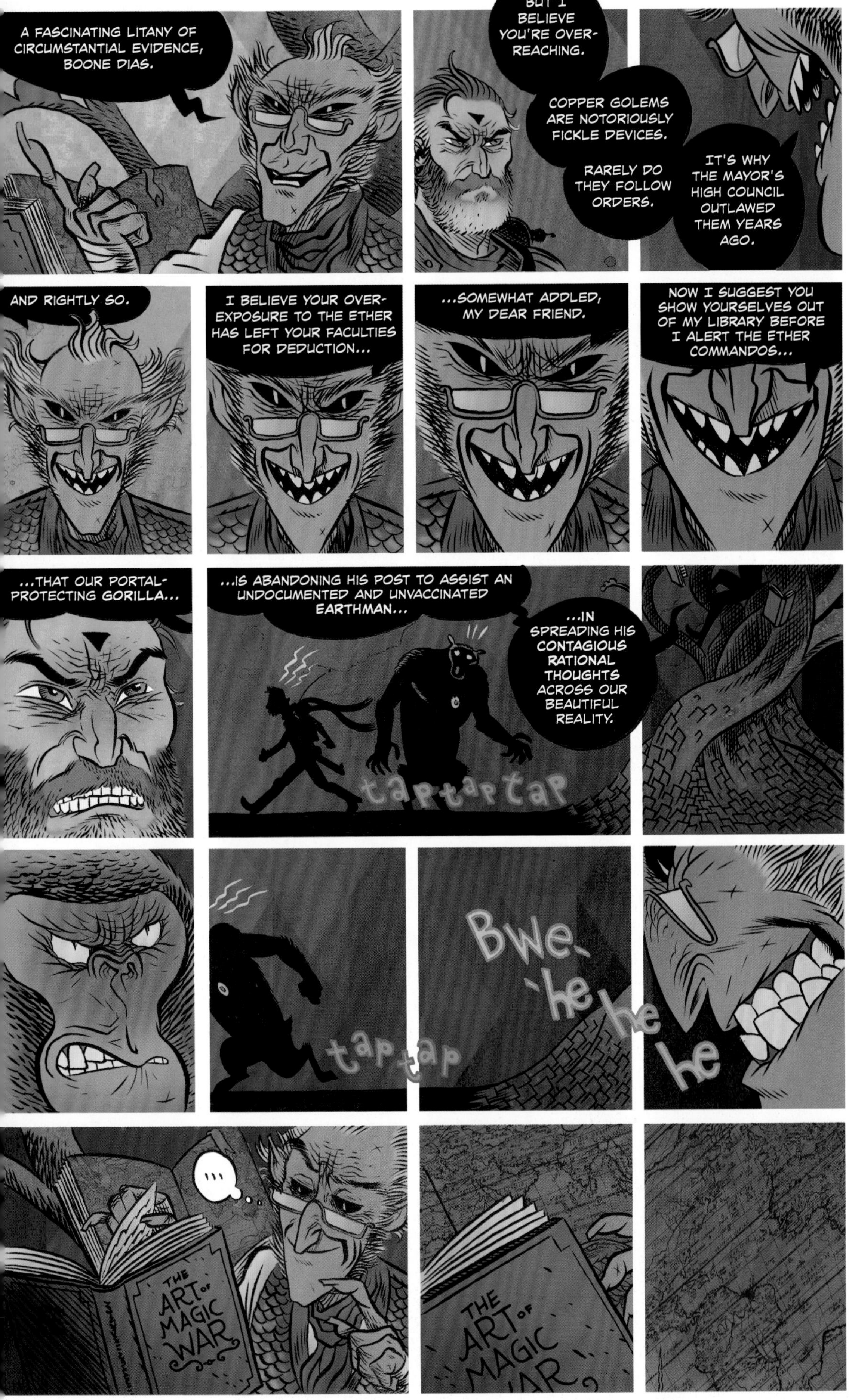

A FASCINATING LITANY OF CIRCUMSTANTIAL EVIDENCE, BOONE DIAS.
BUT I BELIEVE YOU'RE OVER-REACHING.
COPPER GOLEMS ARE NOTORIOUSLY FICKLE DEVICES.
RARELY DO THEY FOLLOW ORDERS.
IT'S WHY THE MAYOR'S HIGH COUNCIL OUTLAWED THEM YEARS AGO.
AND RIGHTLY SO.
I BELIEVE YOUR OVER-EXPOSURE TO THE ETHER HAS LEFT YOUR FACULTIES FOR DEDUCTION...
...SOMEWHAT ADDLED, MY DEAR FRIEND.
NOW I SUGGEST YOU SHOW YOURSELVES OUT OF MY LIBRARY BEFORE I ALERT THE ETHER COMMANDOS...
...THAT OUR PORTAL-PROTECTING GORILLA...
...IS ABANDONING HIS POST TO ASSIST AN UNDOCUMENTED AND UNVACCINATED EARTHMAN...
...IN SPREADING HIS CONTAGIOUS RATIONAL THOUGHTS ACROSS OUR BEAUTIFUL REALITY.
taptaptap
taptap
Bwe-he he he
...
THE ART OF MAGIC WAR
THE ART OF MAGIC WAR

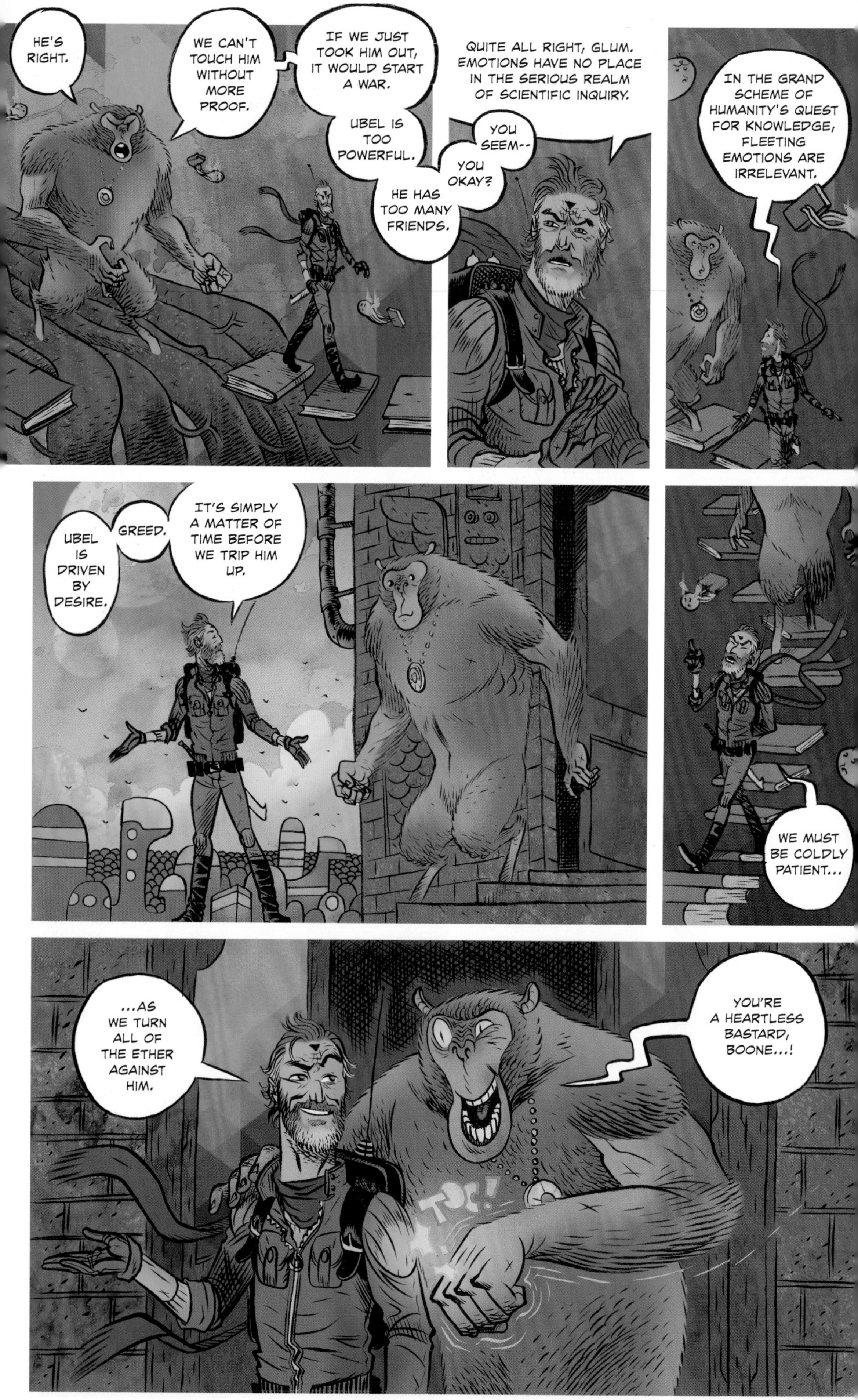
HE'S RIGHT.
WE CAN'T TOUCH HIM WITHOUT MORE PROOF.
IF WE JUST TOOK HIM OUT, IT WOULD START A WAR.
UBEL IS TOO POWERFUL.
HE HAS TOO MANY FRIENDS.
YOU SEEM--
YOU OKAY?
QUITE ALL RIGHT, GLUM. EMOTIONS HAVE NO PLACE IN THE SERIOUS REALM OF SCIENTIFIC INQUIRY.
IN THE GRAND SCHEME OF HUMANITY'S QUEST FOR KNOWLEDGE, FLEETING EMOTIONS ARE IRRELEVANT.
UBEL IS DRIVEN BY DESIRE.
GREED.
IT'S SIMPLY A MATTER OF TIME BEFORE WE TRIP HIM UP.
WE MUST BE COLDLY PATIENT...
...AS WE TURN ALL OF THE ETHER AGAINST HIM.
YOU'RE A HEARTLESS BASTARD, BOONE...!
TOC!

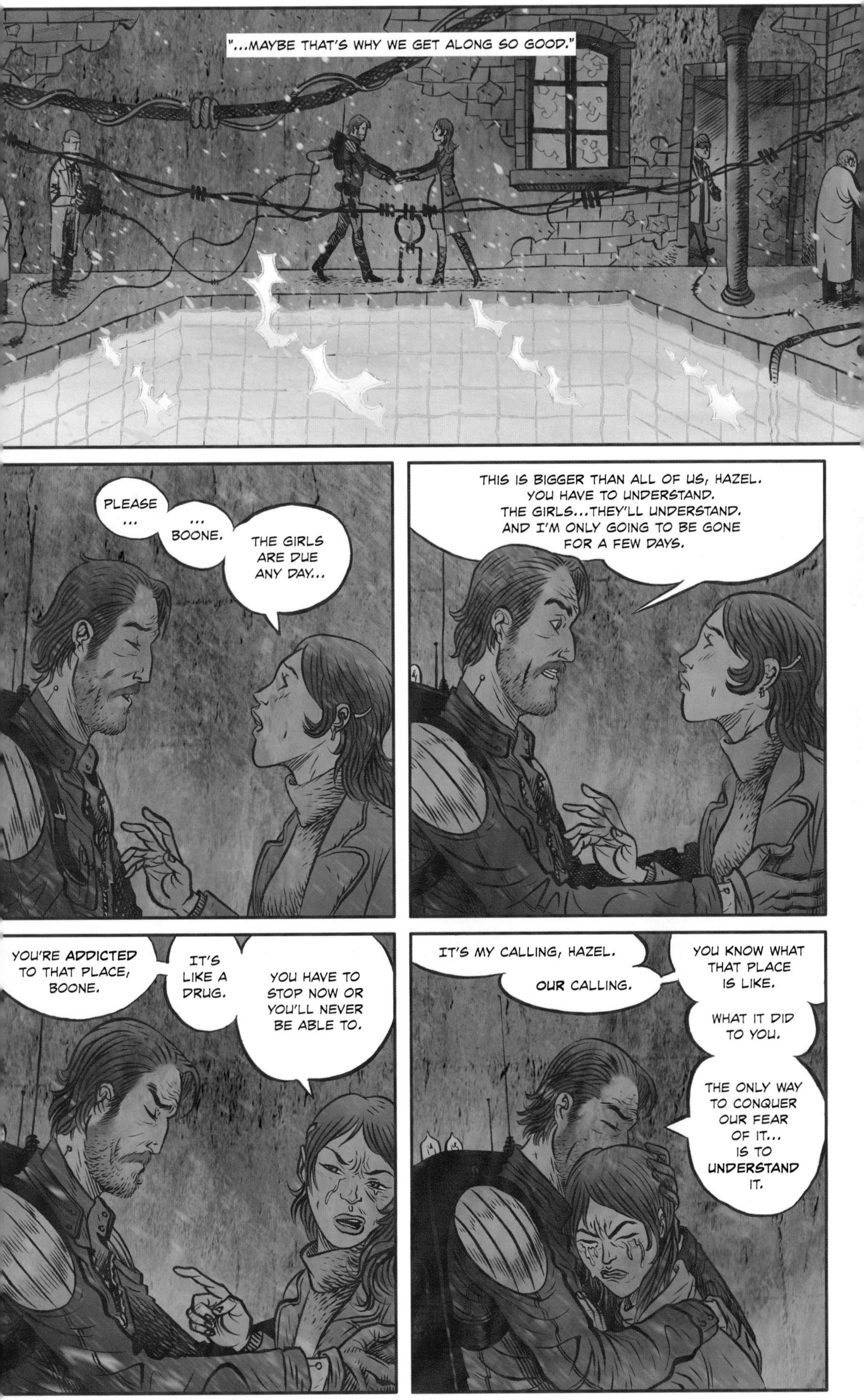
"...MAYBE THAT'S WHY WE GET ALONG SO GOOD."
PLEASE ...
... BOONE.
THE GIRLS ARE DUE ANY DAY...
THIS IS BIGGER THAN ALL OF US, HAZEL. YOU HAVE TO UNDERSTAND. THE GIRLS...THEY'LL UNDERSTAND. AND I'M ONLY GOING TO BE GONE FOR A FEW DAYS.
YOU'RE **ADDICTED** TO THAT PLACE, BOONE.
IT'S LIKE A DRUG.
YOU HAVE TO STOP NOW OR YOU'LL NEVER BE ABLE TO.
IT'S MY CALLING, HAZEL.
OUR CALLING.
YOU KNOW WHAT THAT PLACE IS LIKE.
WHAT IT DID TO YOU.
THE ONLY WAY TO CONQUER OUR FEAR OF IT... IS TO **UNDERSTAND** IT.

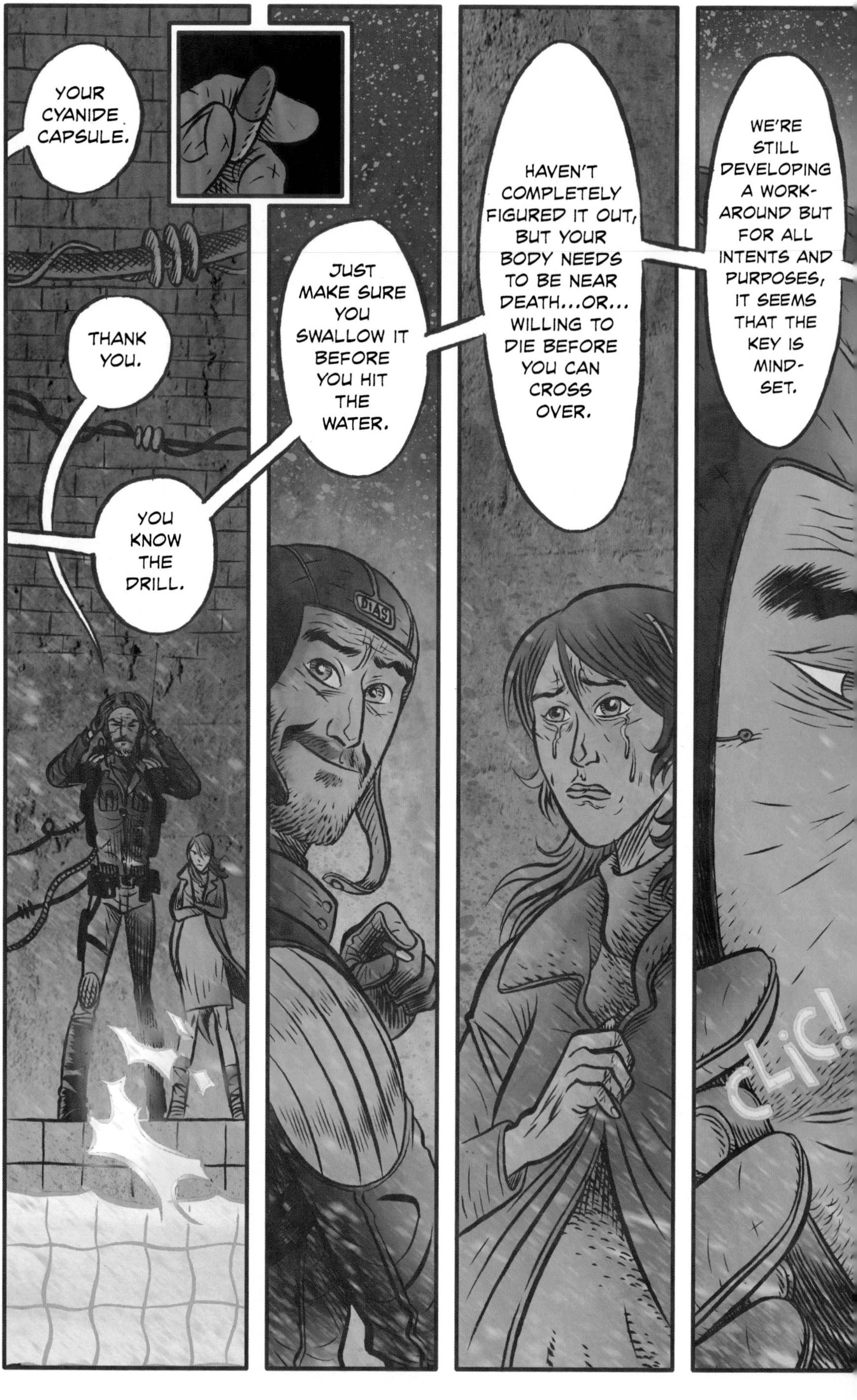
YOUR CYANIDE CAPSULE.
THANK YOU.
YOU KNOW THE DRILL.
JUST MAKE SURE YOU SWALLOW IT BEFORE YOU HIT THE WATER.
HAVEN'T COMPLETELY FIGURED IT OUT, BUT YOUR BODY NEEDS TO BE NEAR DEATH...OR... WILLING TO DIE BEFORE YOU CAN CROSS OVER.
WE'RE STILL DEVELOPING A WORK-AROUND BUT FOR ALL INTENTS AND PURPOSES, IT SEEMS THAT THE KEY IS MIND-SET.
CLIC!

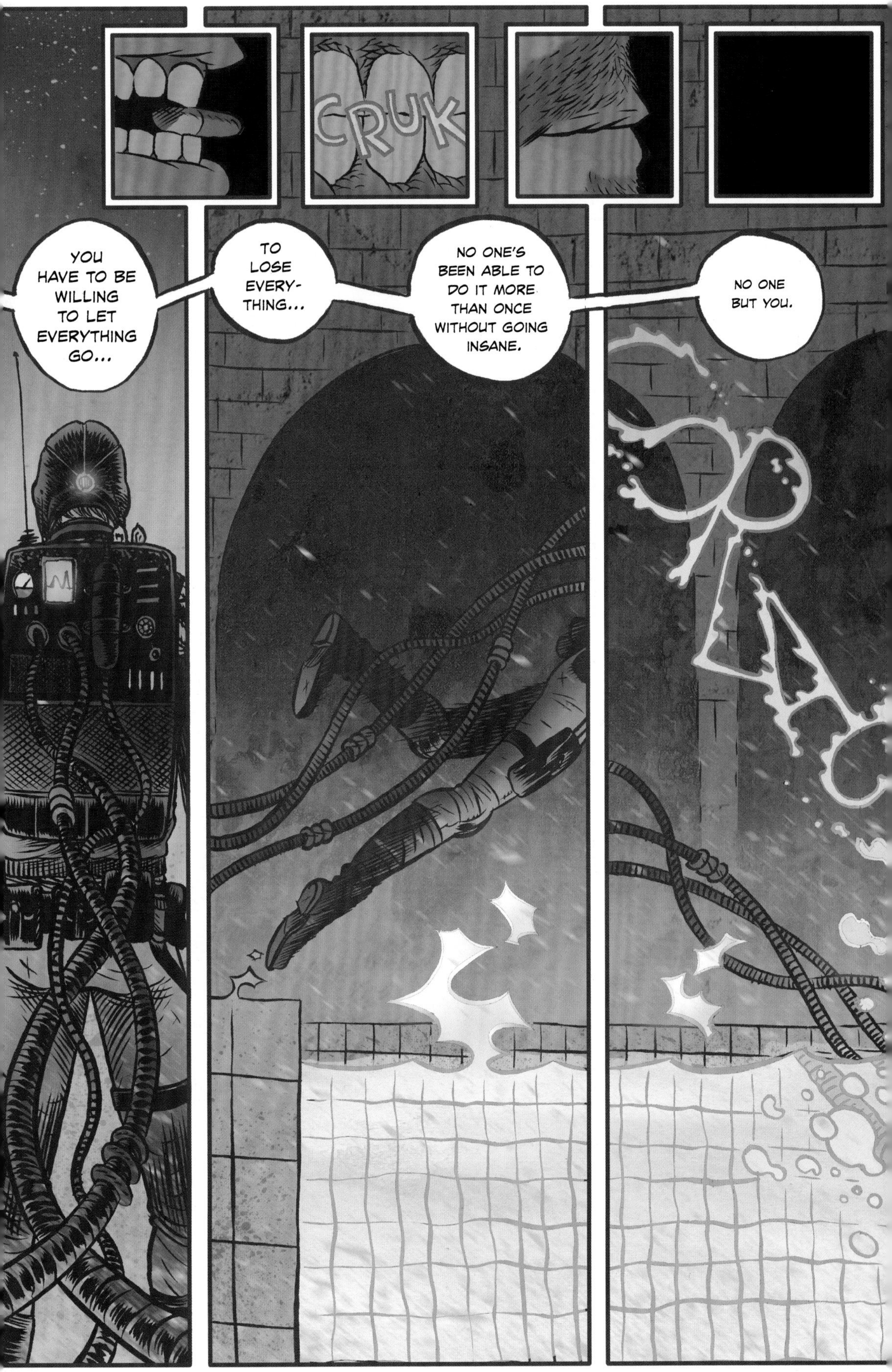

CRUK
YOU HAVE TO BE WILLING TO LET EVERYTHING GO...
TO LOSE EVERY-THING...
NO ONE'S BEEN ABLE TO DO IT MORE THAN ONCE WITHOUT GOING INSANE.
NO ONE BUT YOU.

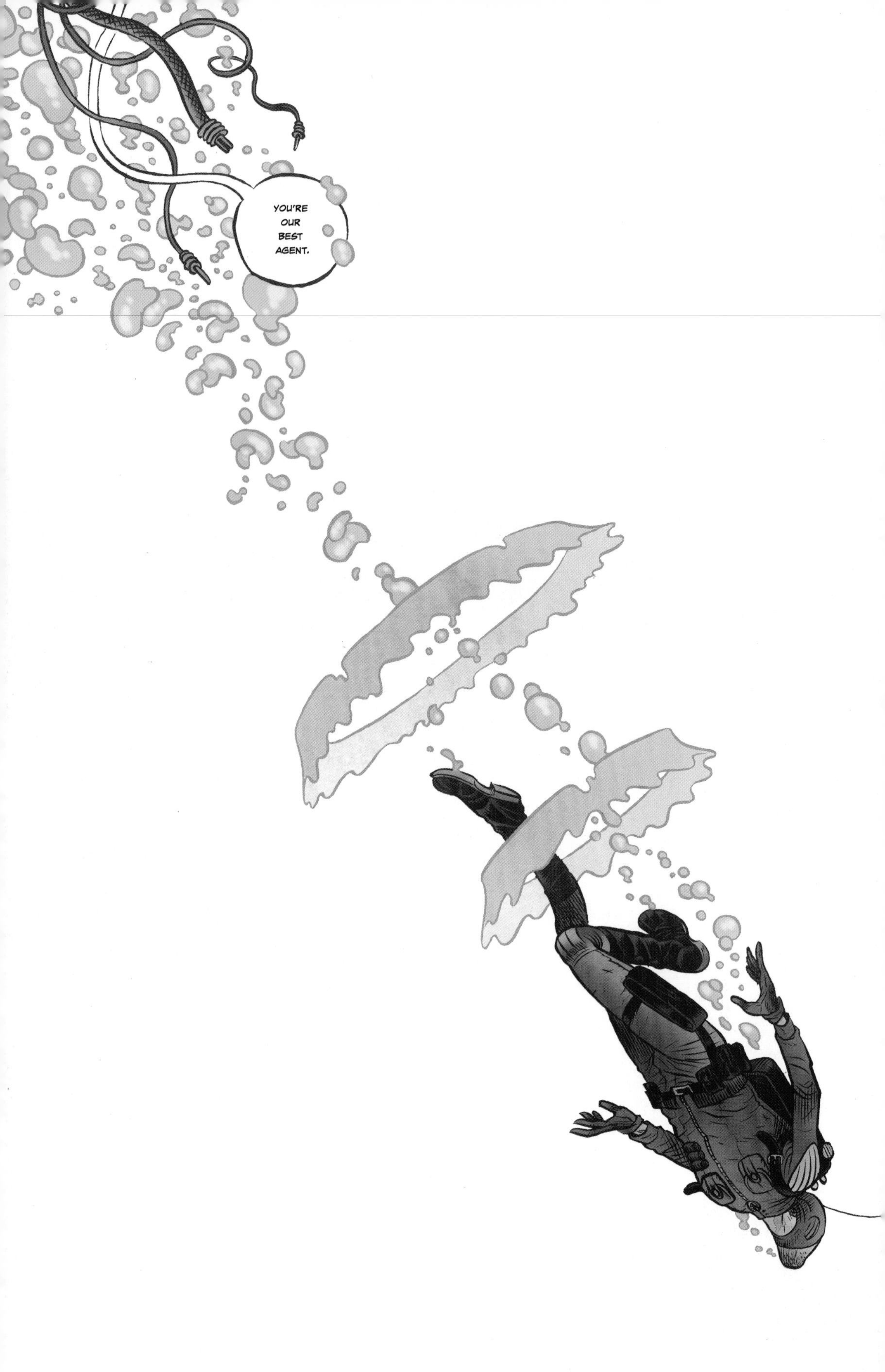
YOU'RE OUR BEST AGENT.

END OF VOLUME ONE --MATT KINDT + DAVID RUBÍN--

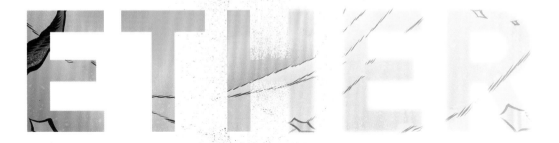

ETHER

SKETCHBOOK

notes by **MATT KINDT**

British art collector on his 10th expedition into the Deadworld
Magical spores with the potential to infect humans, or sometimes grant extra abilities
The Ether
Lyceum
Magic Corps
Team of magic characters used against
trav•e•logue
hand•book

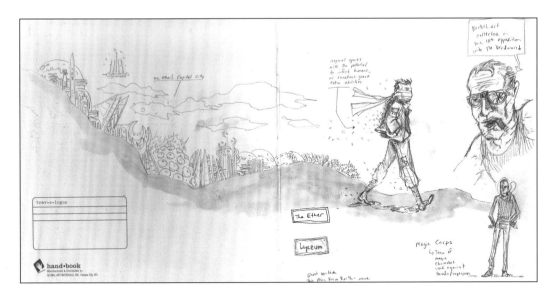

This is the opening spread of one of my sketchbooks. It's the origin of the idea for *Ether*. I was in a meeting and just doodling this crazy-looking city and thinking about magical realms and how, as a writer, I don't really like magic as a genre and mystical cities. I always felt like it was too easy to cheat with narrative and plot when magic is involved. But the more I doodled on this page, the more I thought about how much fun it would be to create a magical realm that we could populate and make "real." And to do that, I could send in a completely rational person to document and map and analyze how this place works, strip it of the magic, and explain it all with science. That's how Boone was born.

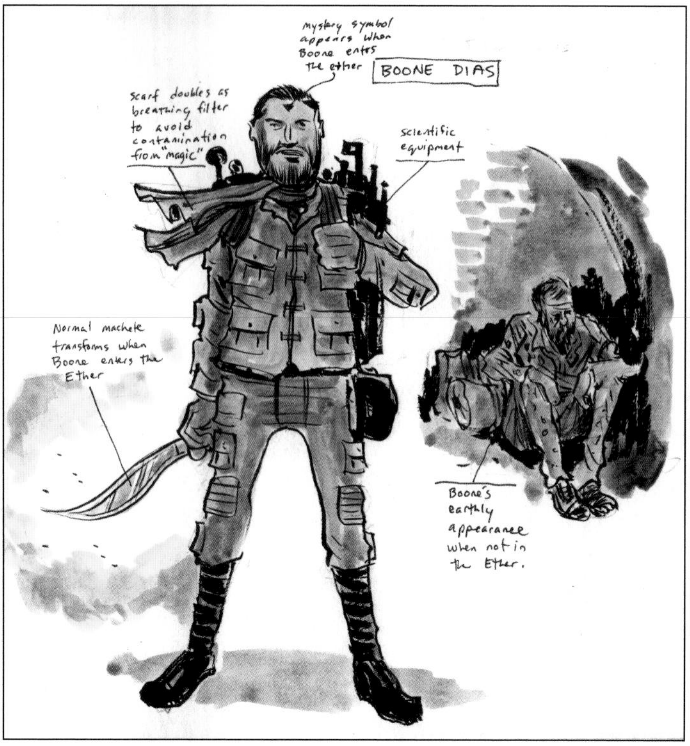
mystery symbol appears when Boone enters the ether
BOONE DIAS
scarf doubles as breathing filter to avoid contamination from "magic"
scientific equipment
Normal machete transforms when Boone enters the Ether
Boone's earthly appearance when not in the Ether.

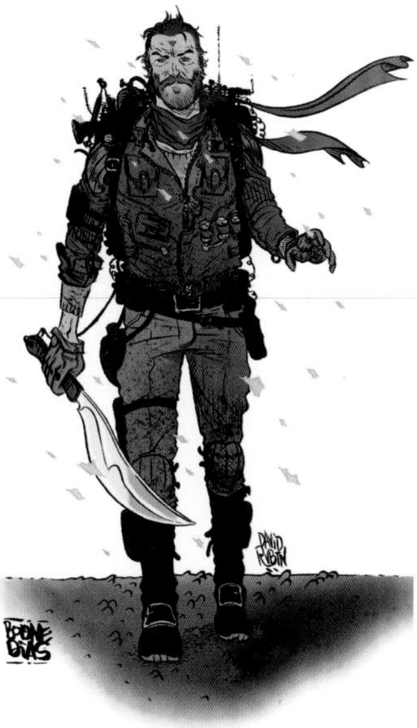
BOONE DIAS

Originally I was going to draw this series myself, so I did a bunch of sketches to help me figure out who the characters were and how they would look. When I found out David was available for this project, I immediately gave up any thought of drawing this, and I was hesitant to send him the work I'd already done. It was really fun to see him interpret the characters and filter them through his own eyes and aesthetic and refine it all.

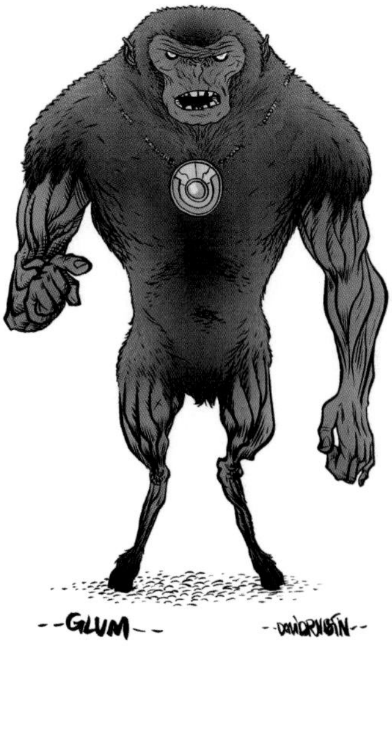
--GLUM--

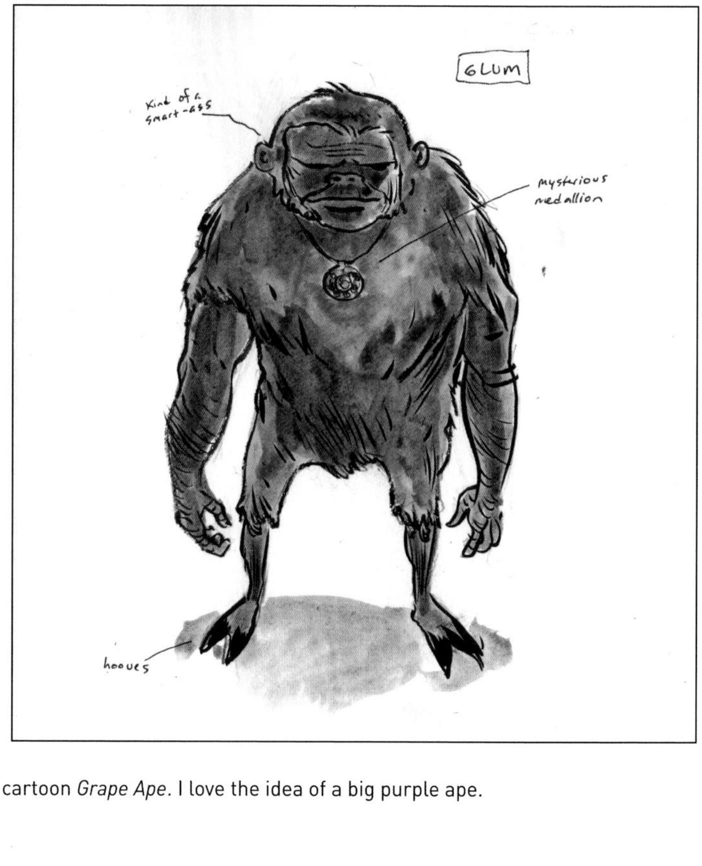
GLUM
Kind of a smart-ass
mysterious medallion
hooves

This character was inspired by the old cartoon *Grape Ape*. I love the idea of a big purple ape.

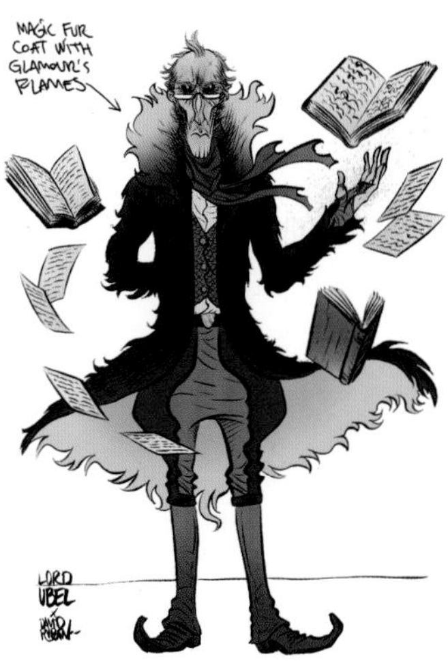
MAGIC FUR
COAT WITH
GLAMOUR'S
FLAMES
LORD
UBEL

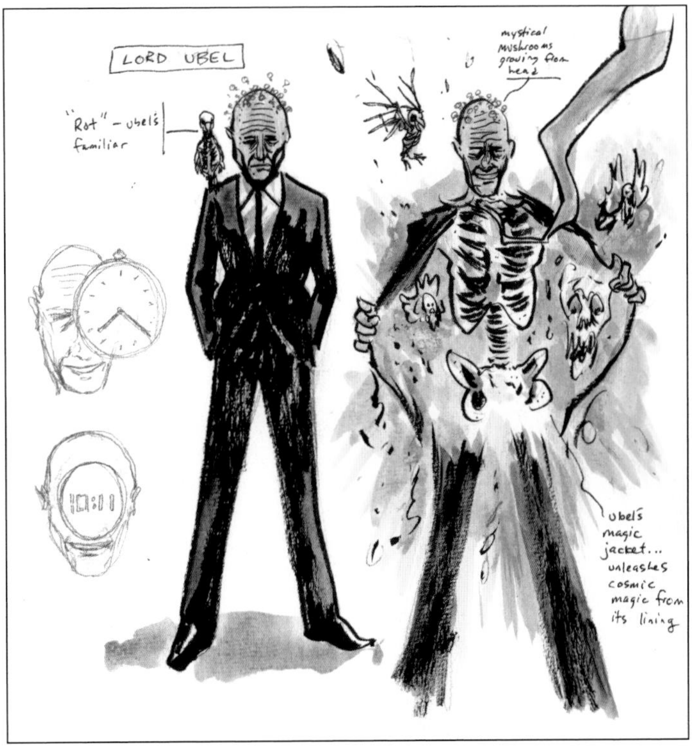
LORD UBEL
"Rot" - ubel's
familiar
mystical
mushrooms
growing from
head
ubel's
magic
jacket...
unleashes
cosmic
magic from
its lining

Ubel is our "Moriarty." David veered from my design the most on this character, and for the better. Getting rid of the suit was a good idea—and adding the curly-toed footwear made him more a part of the Ether world that we created.

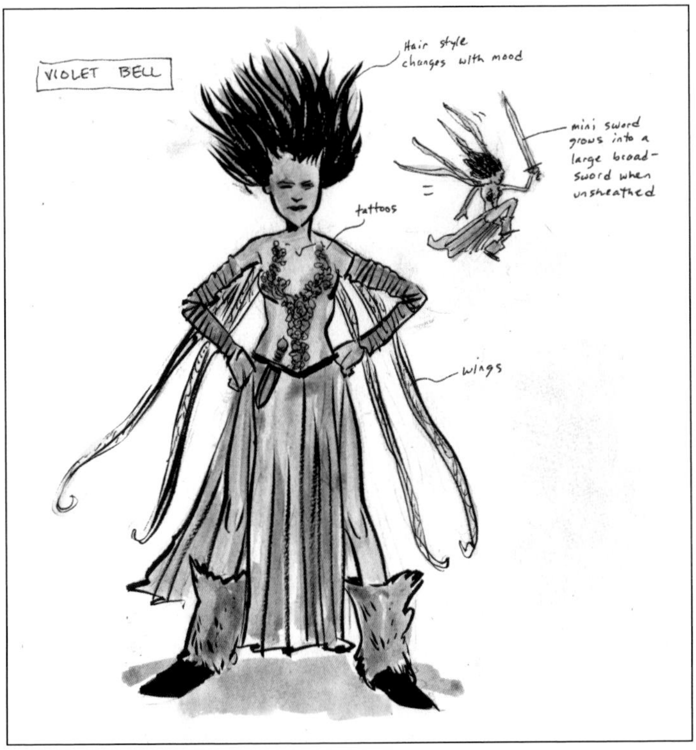
VIOLET BELL
Hair style
changes with mood
mini sword
grows into a
large broad-
sword when
unsheathed
tattoos
wings

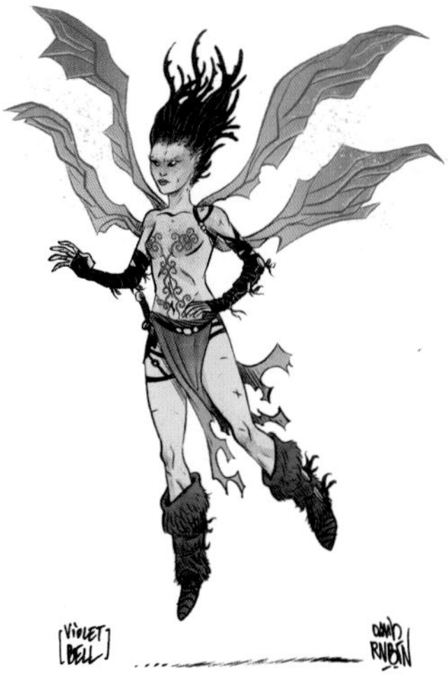
VIOLET
BELL

Violet is one letter shy of *violent*, which was the inspiration for her. I loved the idea of making a faerie that was street-wise and tough. She's going to be showing up a lot more in later chapters.

The murder victim in our first mystery. She has an entire backstory that we'll get to one day. She is supposed to be strong and feminine and not overly sexualized, and David strikes the perfect balance.

SHRINKS AND "SWORD"

EXTEND AND "LANCE"

BLAZE'S WEAPON CAN CHANGE THE FORM FROM LANCE TO SWORD OR VICE VERSA.

THE BLAZE
x DAVID RUBIN

SHIELD

NOTE: NEED A LOGO/ SYMBOL FOR THE ORDER??

ORDER OF THE GOLDEN DAWN'S ASSASSIN x DAVID RUBIN

These are the mysterious sentinels that we'll be seeing throughout the series. David went off of written descriptions here and created these from whole cloth. Once I knew David was involved, I stopped sketching because I didn't want to dilute his imagination with any of my preconceived visual ideas.

I love David's take on these golems. I loved the idea of these brass golems eventually getting rusty and turning green like the Statue of Liberty as they get older. You can tell a veteran golem by the color of its metal hide.

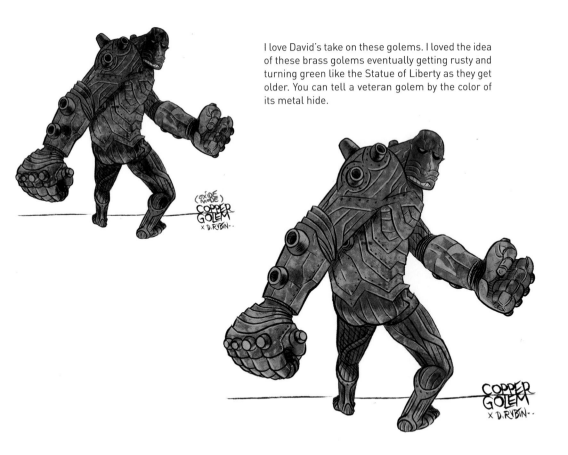

(OXIDE MODE)
COPPER GOLEM
X D. RUBIN

COPPER GOLEM
X D. RUBIN

This mayor cracks me up. I'm not sure I gave David any more description than a nervous-looking, cigar-chomping mayor. The feet with no shoes . . . the energy sphere over his head . . . all perfect.

ENERGY SPHERIC CROWN → CREDITED HIM AS THE MAYOR

THE MAYOR
X D. RUBIN

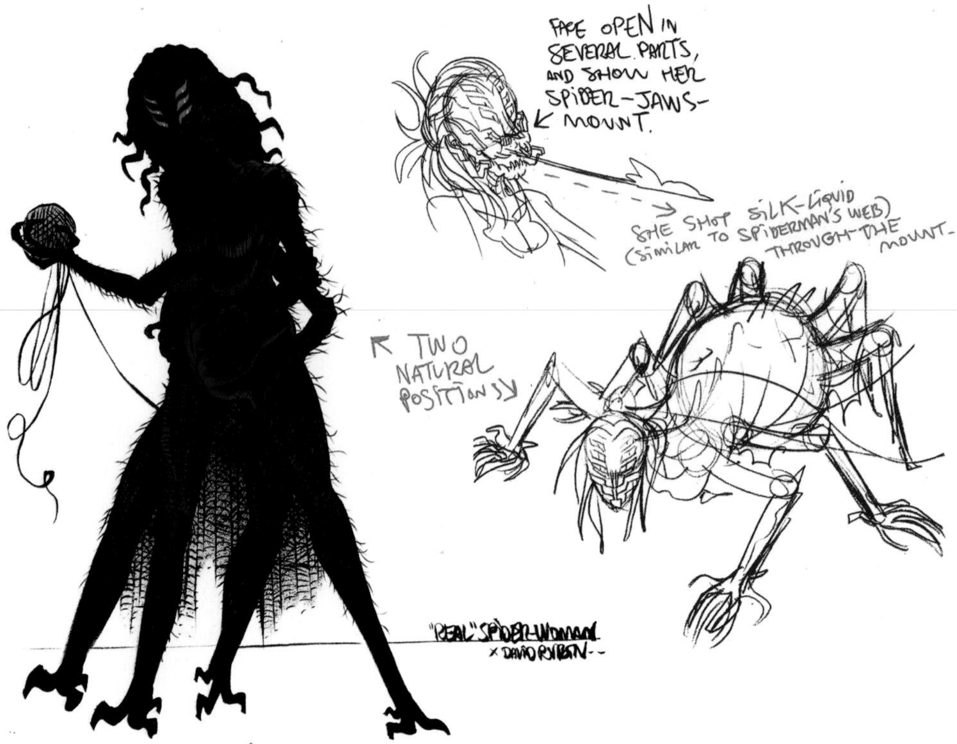
FACE OPEN IN SEVERAL PARTS, AND SHOW HER SPIDER-JAWS-MOUNT.
SHE SHOT SILK-LIQUID (SIMILAR TO SPIDERMAN'S WEB) THROUGH THE MOUNT.
TWO NATURAL POSITIONS
"REAL" SPIDER-WOMAN
x DAVID RUBIN --

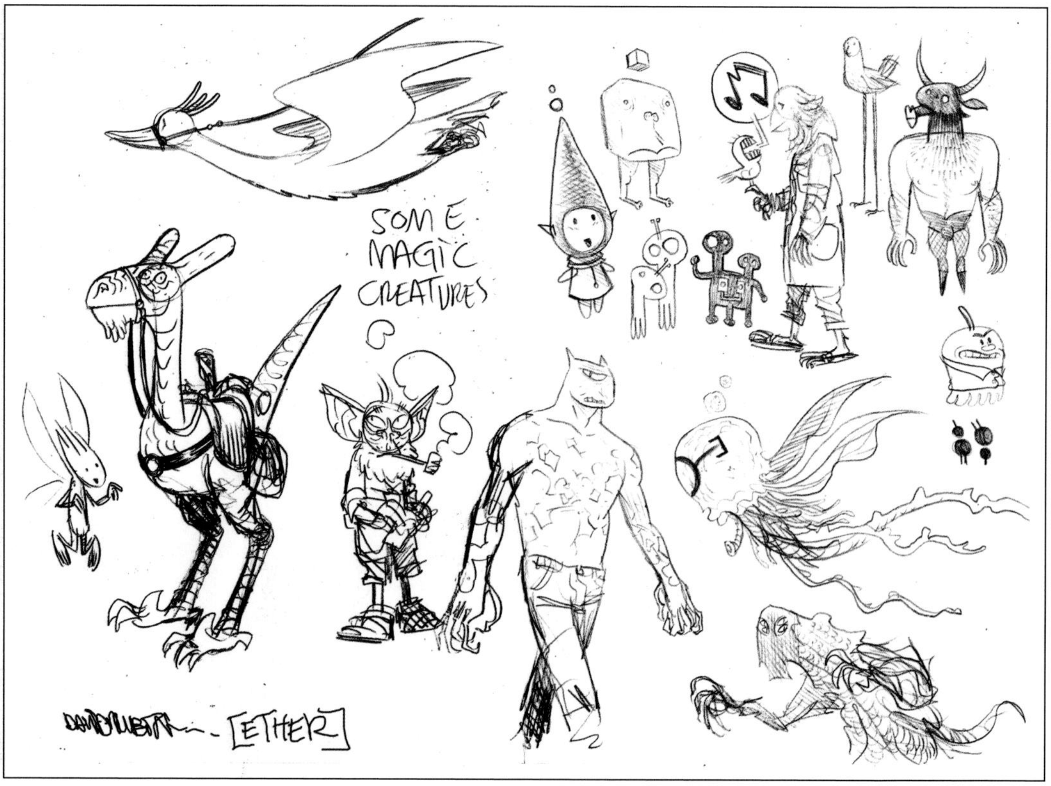
SOME MAGIC CREATURES
[ETHER]

Above and below, we see a lot of characters that weren't in the scripts. When I sent David the original pitch, he sent back pages and pages of designs for characters. I literally posted these over my writing table and used them as inspiration—and ended up writing a lot of these little doodles into the script. The big-toothed singing bird came out of one of these doodles, as did the bridge guard that speaks in strange symbols and bubbles. These are the pages where you can see our true collaboration starting to hum.

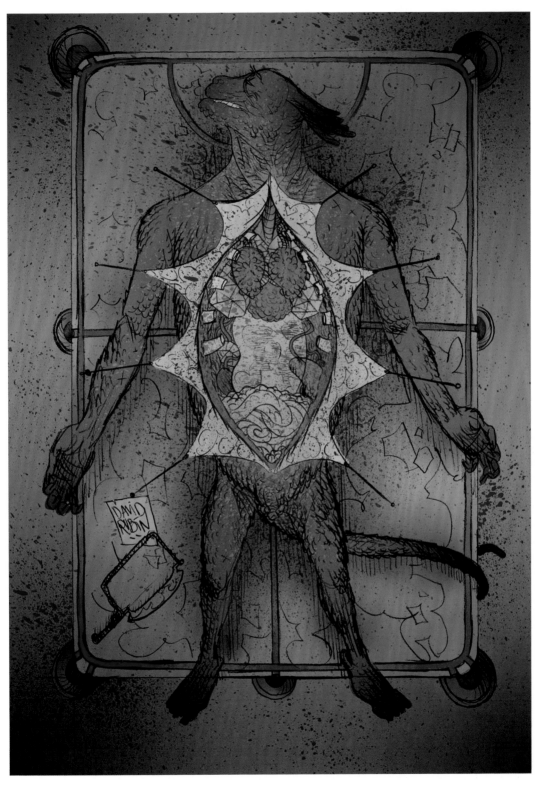

I love using the normally wasted pages of a comic (inside covers and back pages) to add content and build the world of the story. These autopsy images were some of the ideas we had to help make the Ether seem more grounded and real.

BIO-VEHICLES:

X DAVID RUBÍN--

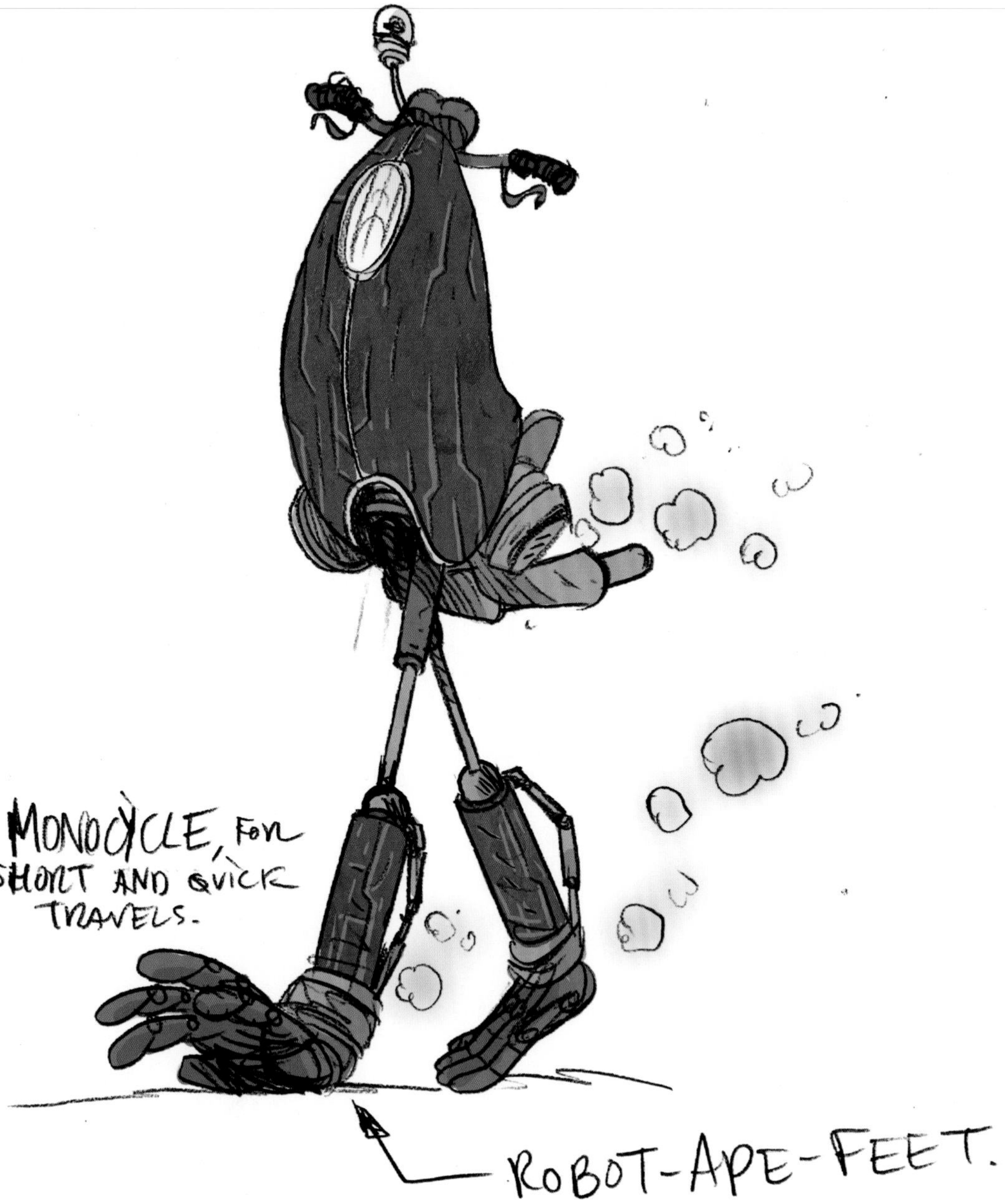
MONOCYCLE, FOR SHORT AND QUICK TRAVELS.
ROBOT-APE-FEET.

More designs that weren't in the script that I ended up writing scenes around. This stuff was too good not to use. And I'd never really thought of how the characters would get around in the Ether . . . until I saw these.

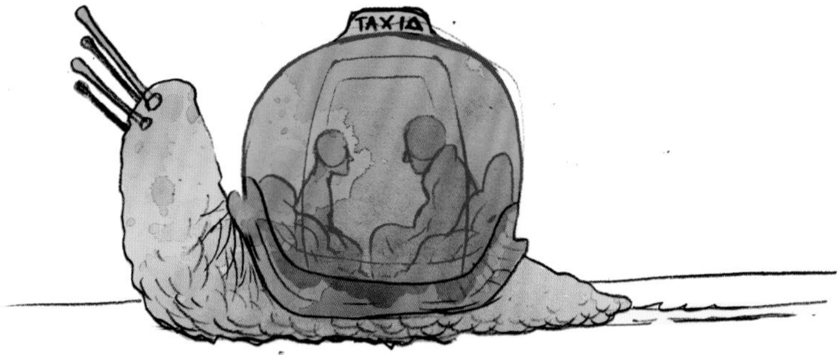

SNAIL-CAR ↗
(DESPITE ITS APPEARANCE IT CAN MOVE FAST.

BEETLE-TRUCK.

FOR TRANSPORT
OF MERCANCIES
OR PEOPLE.

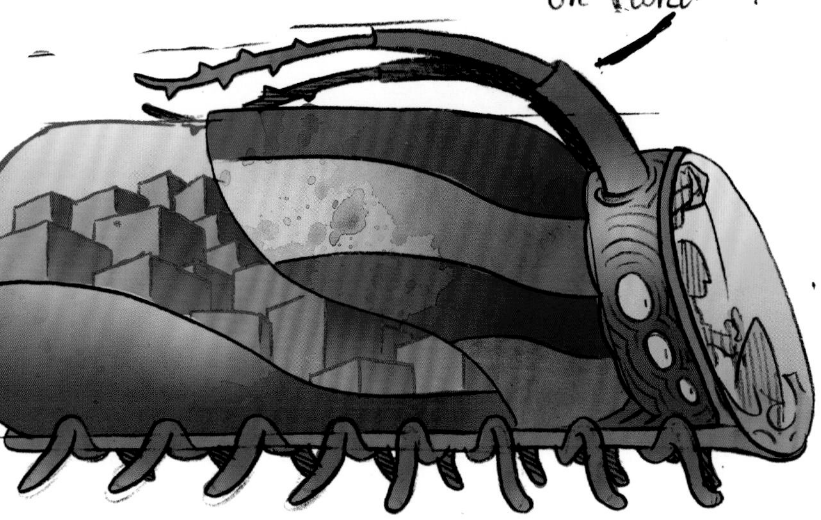

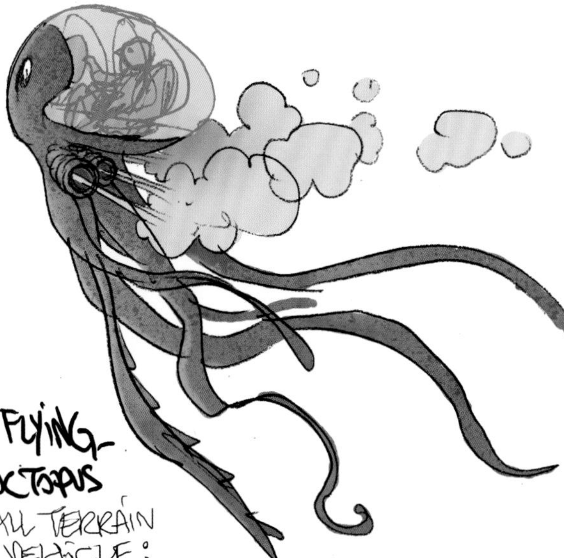

FLYING
OCTOPUS
(ALL TERRAIN
VEHICLE:
AIR/SEA/EARTH)

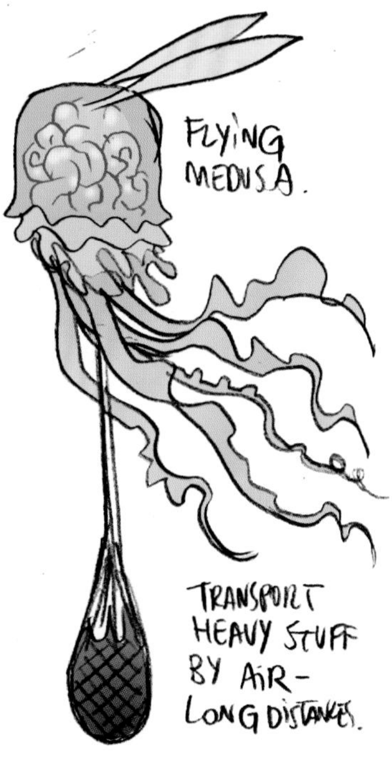

FLYING
MEDUSA.

TRANSPORT
HEAVY STUFF
BY AIR -
LONG DISTANCES.

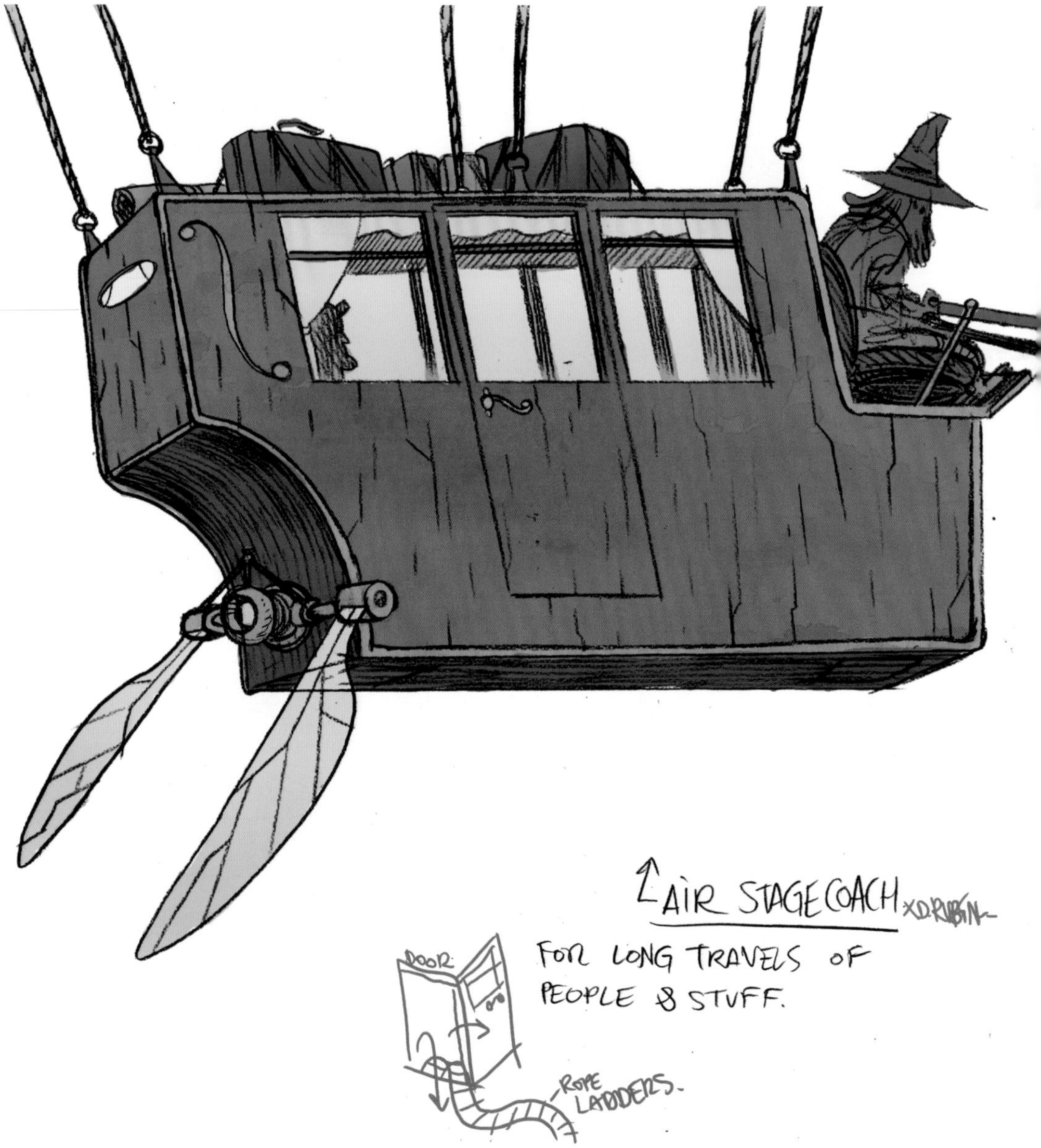

↑AIR STAGECOACH

FOR LONG TRAVELS OF PEOPLE & STUFF.

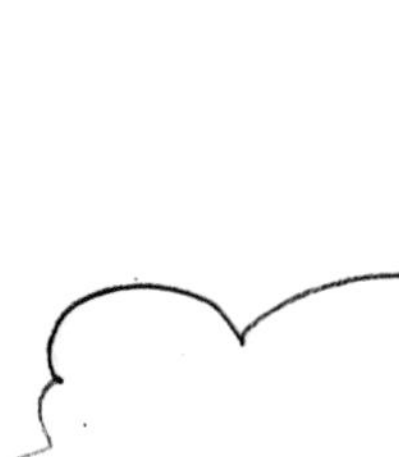
DOOR
ROPE LADDERS.

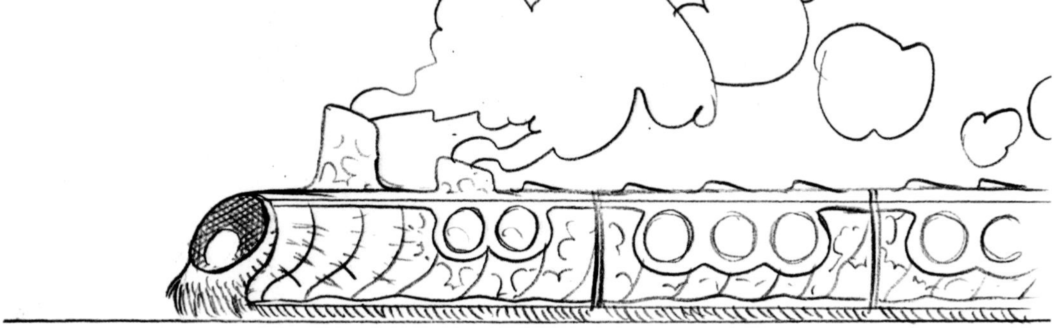

BUG-TRAIN

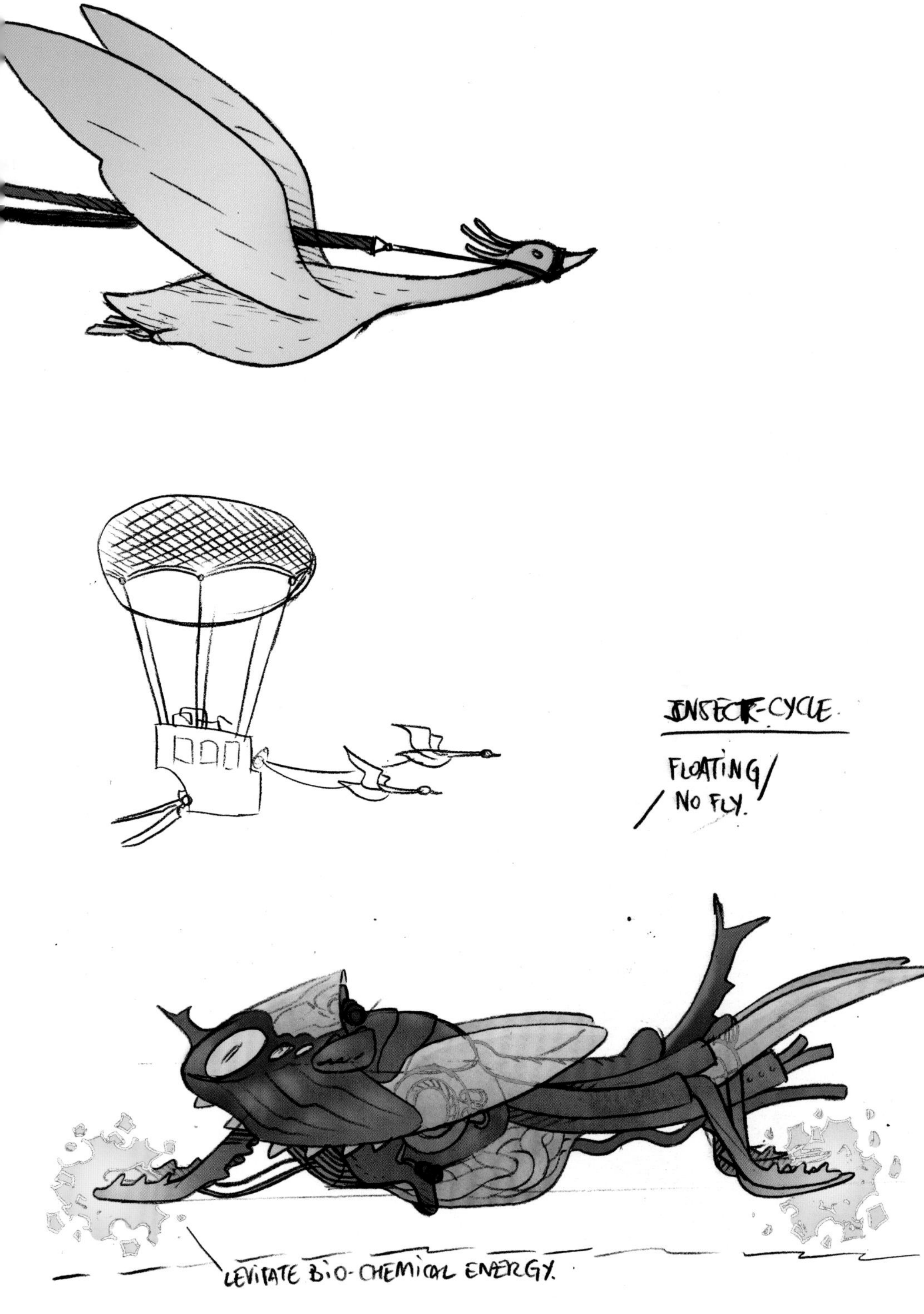
INSECT-CYCLE
FLOATING/
/NO FLY
LEVITATE BIO-CHEMICAL ENERGY

This motorcycle is definitely going to make it into one of the later stories. Too cool not to use.

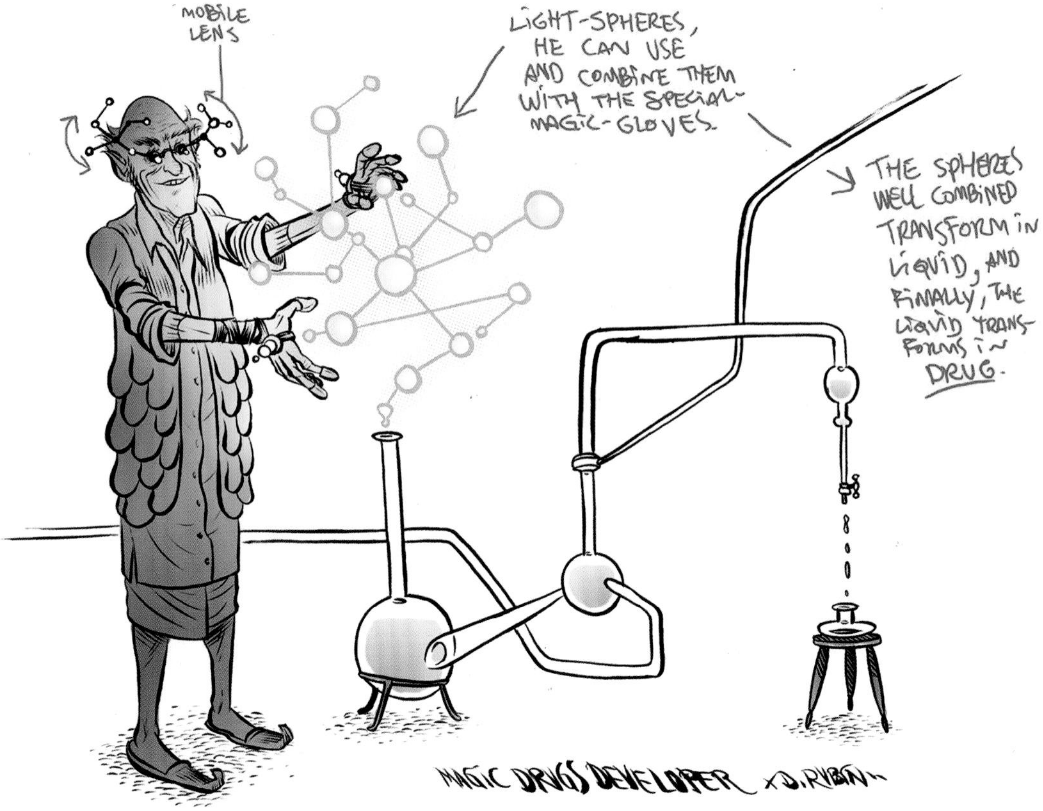
MOBILE LENS
LIGHT-SPHERES, HE CAN USE AND COMBINE THEM WITH THE SPECIAL-MAGIC-GLOVES.
THE SPHERES WELL COMBINED TRANSFORM IN LIQUID, AND FINALLY, THE LIQUID TRANS-FORMS IN DRUG.
MAGIC DRUGS DEVELOPER

This is David at his finest. Taking the characters and extrapolating what they do and figuring out visually how they will work.

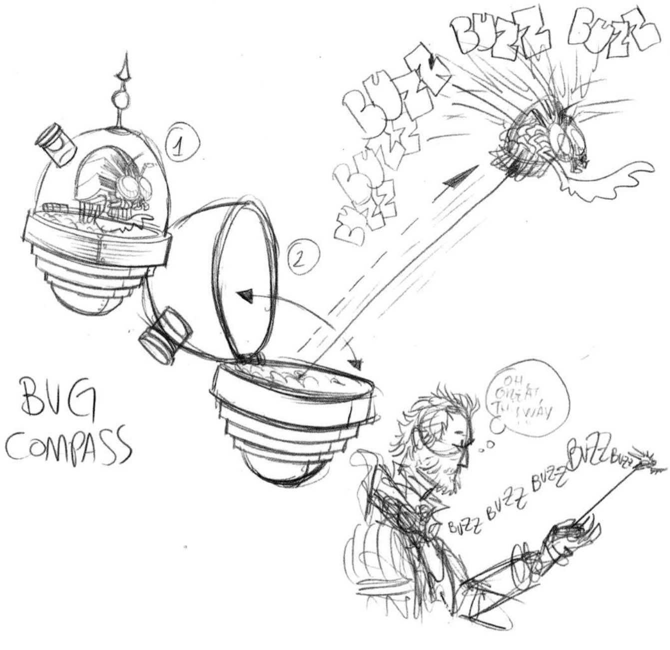
BUZZ BUZZ
1
2
BUG COMPASS

One of the weird ideas I had for Ether gadgets. I like the idea of the Ether using science and having established rules—they're just different from what we observe here on Earth.

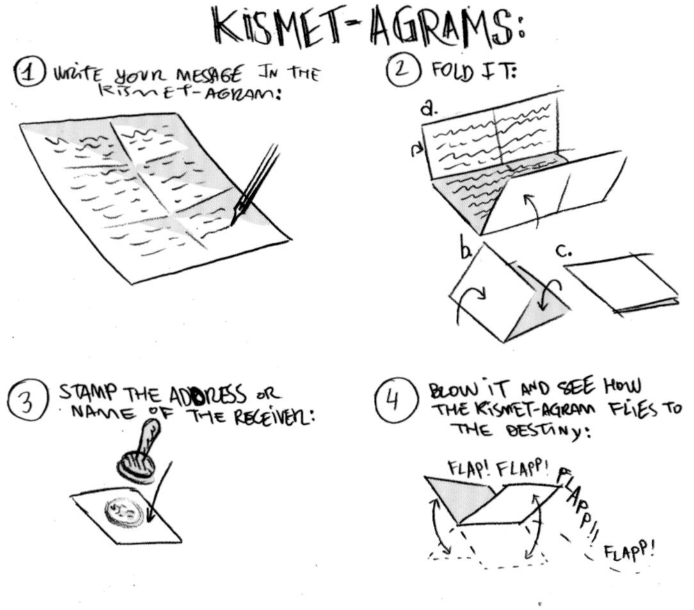
KISMET-AGRAMS:
1 WRITE YOUR MESSAGE IN THE KISMET-AGRAM:
2 FOLD IT:
a.
b.
c.
3 STAMP THE ADDRESS OR NAME OF THE RECEIVER:
4 BLOW IT AND SEE HOW THE KISMET-AGRAM FLIES TO THE DESTINY:
FLAP! FLAPP!
FLAPP!!
FLAPP!

I don't remember where this idea came from, but I love the word *kismet*. And "kismet-agram" is just fun to say out loud. Try it! Kismet-agram!

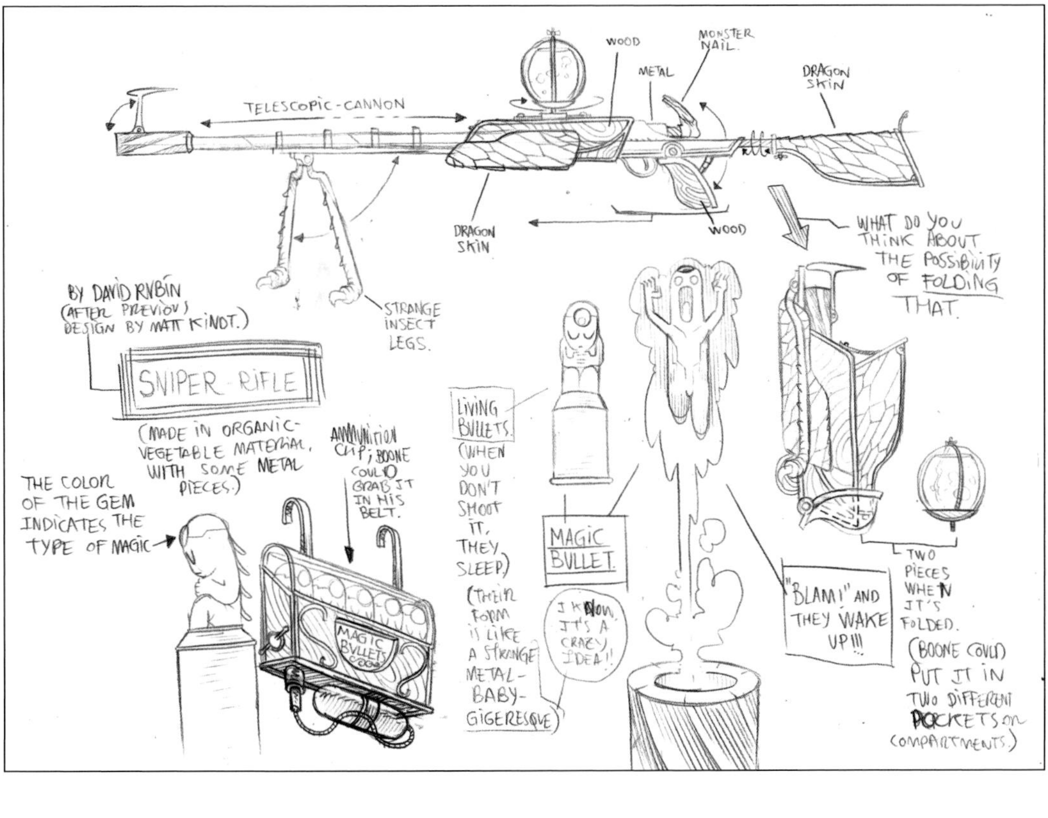
TELESCOPIC-CANNON
WOOD
MONSTER NAIL
METAL
DRAGON SKIN
DRAGON SKIN
WOOD
WHAT DO YOU THINK ABOUT THE POSSIBILITY OF FOLDING THAT.
BY DAVID RUBÍN (AFTER PREVIOUS DESIGN BY MATT KINDT.)
STRANGE INSECT LEGS.
SNIPER RIFLE
(MADE IN ORGANIC-VEGETABLE MATERIAL, WITH SOME METAL PIECES.)
AMMUNITION CLIP; BOONE COULD GRAB IT IN HIS BELT.
THE COLOR OF THE GEM INDICATES THE TYPE OF MAGIC
MAGIC BULLETS
LIVING BULLETS (WHEN YOU DON'T SHOOT IT, THEY SLEEP) (THEIR FORM IS LIKE A STRANGE METAL-BABY-GIGERESQUE)
I KNOW, IT'S A CRAZY IDEA!!
MAGIC BULLET
"BLAM!" AND THEY WAKE UP!!!
TWO PIECES WHEN IT'S FOLDED. (BOONE COULD PUT IT IN TWO DIFFERENT POCKETS or COMPARTMENTS.)

The murder was both central and incidental to the story we wanted to tell, but it was important for me that we illustrated the strangeness of this world via the murder. I've been a conspiracy nut since I was a teenager, and I've heard the "magic bullet" theory of the JFK assassination my entire life. Though it would be fun to literally have a magic bullet.

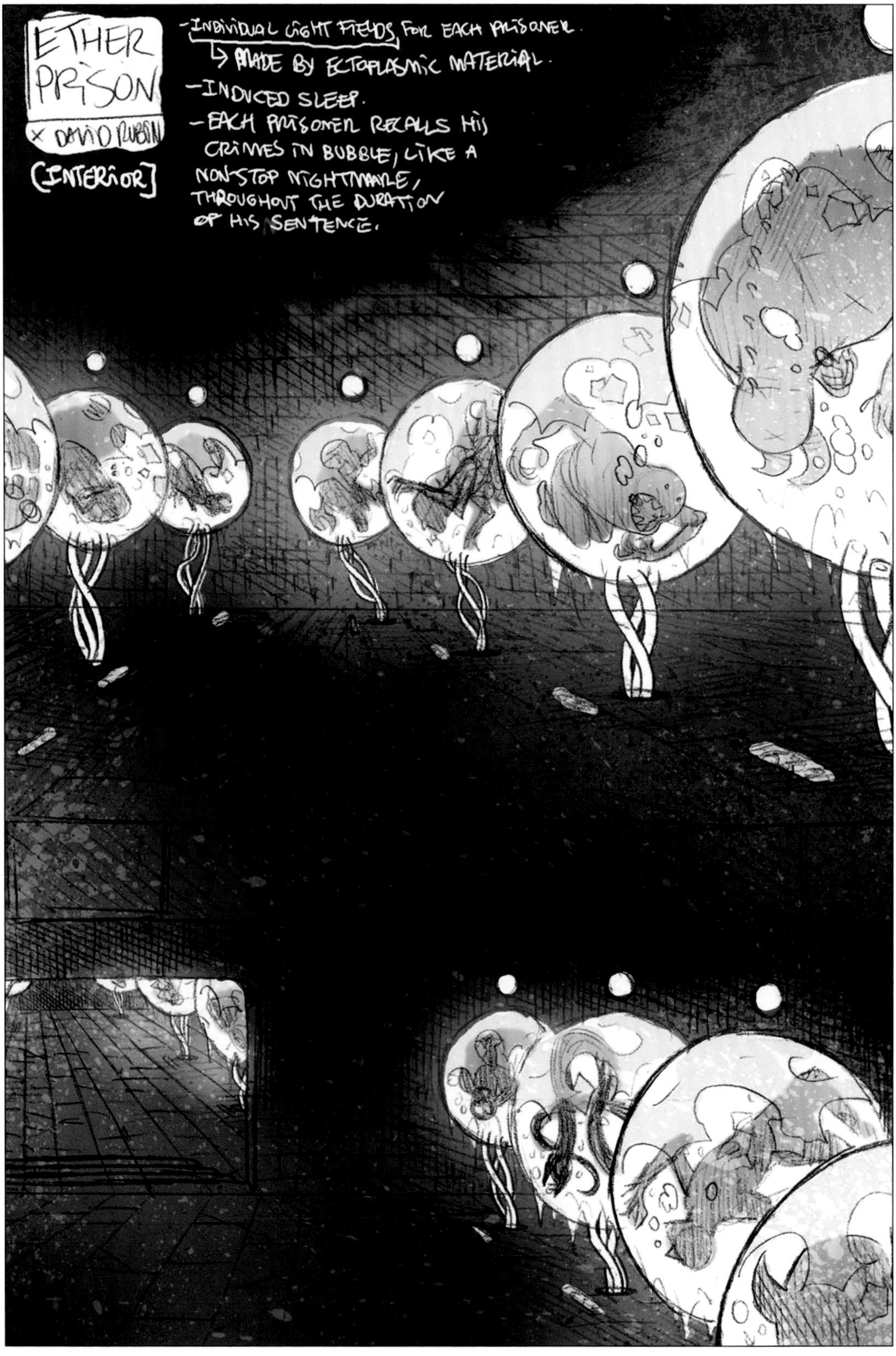
ETHER PRISON
× DAVID RUBIN
[INTERIOR]
- INDIVIDUAL LIGHT FIELDS FOR EACH PRISONER.
→ MADE BY ECTOPLASMIC MATERIAL.
- INDUCED SLEEP.
- EACH PRISONER RECALLS HIS CRIMES IN BUBBLE, LIKE A NON-STOP NIGHTMARE, THROUGHOUT THE DURATION OF HIS SENTENCE.

Some of my script and pitch just had questions in them for David. One of them was "What does a prison look like in the Ether?" This is what he came up with. We'll definitely be visiting this place in future stories.

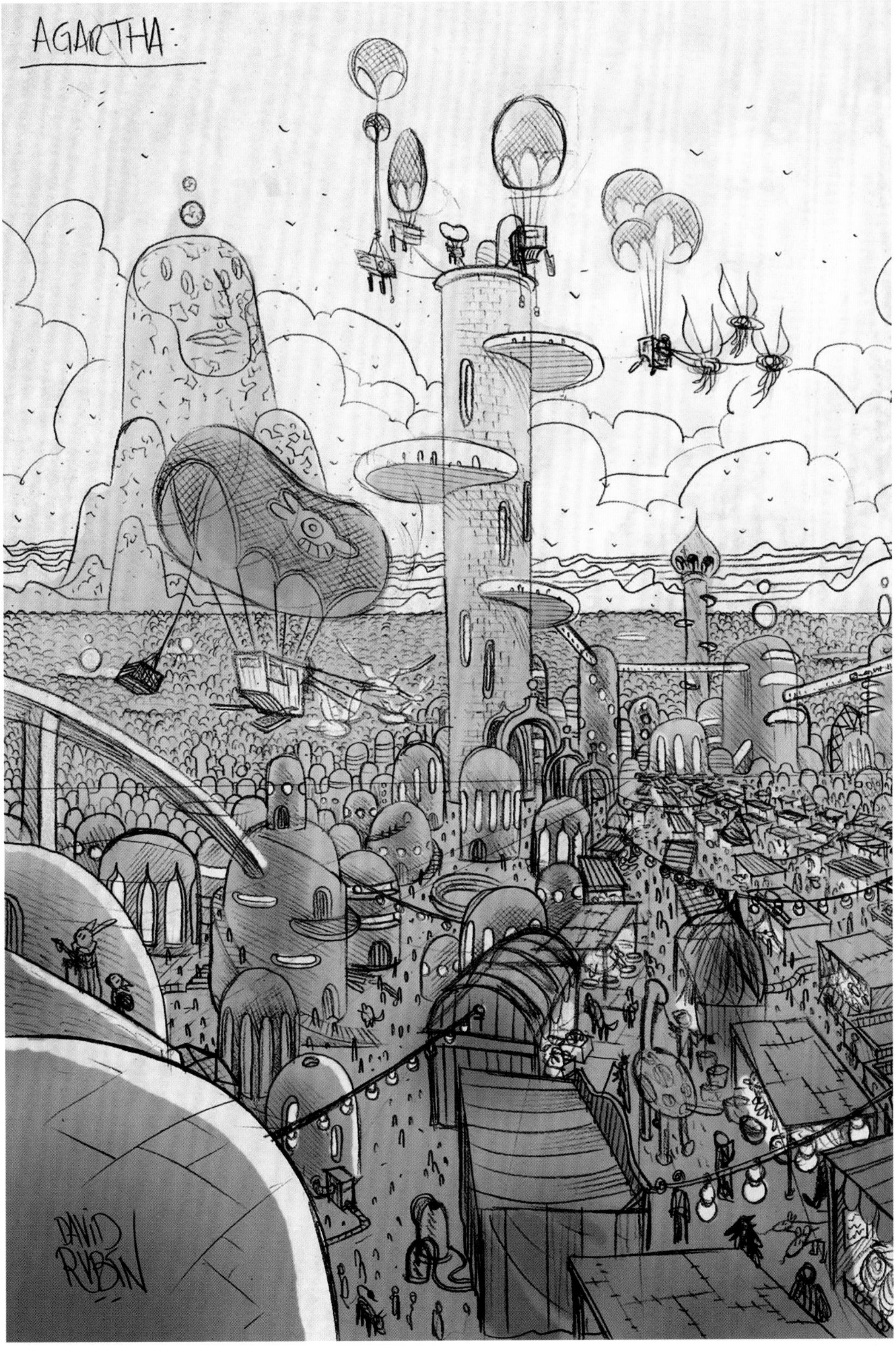
AGARTHA:
DAVID RUBIN

One of the strangely hard things to do when writing is to just get out of the way of the artist. In David's case, if you get out of his way—he will amaze you.

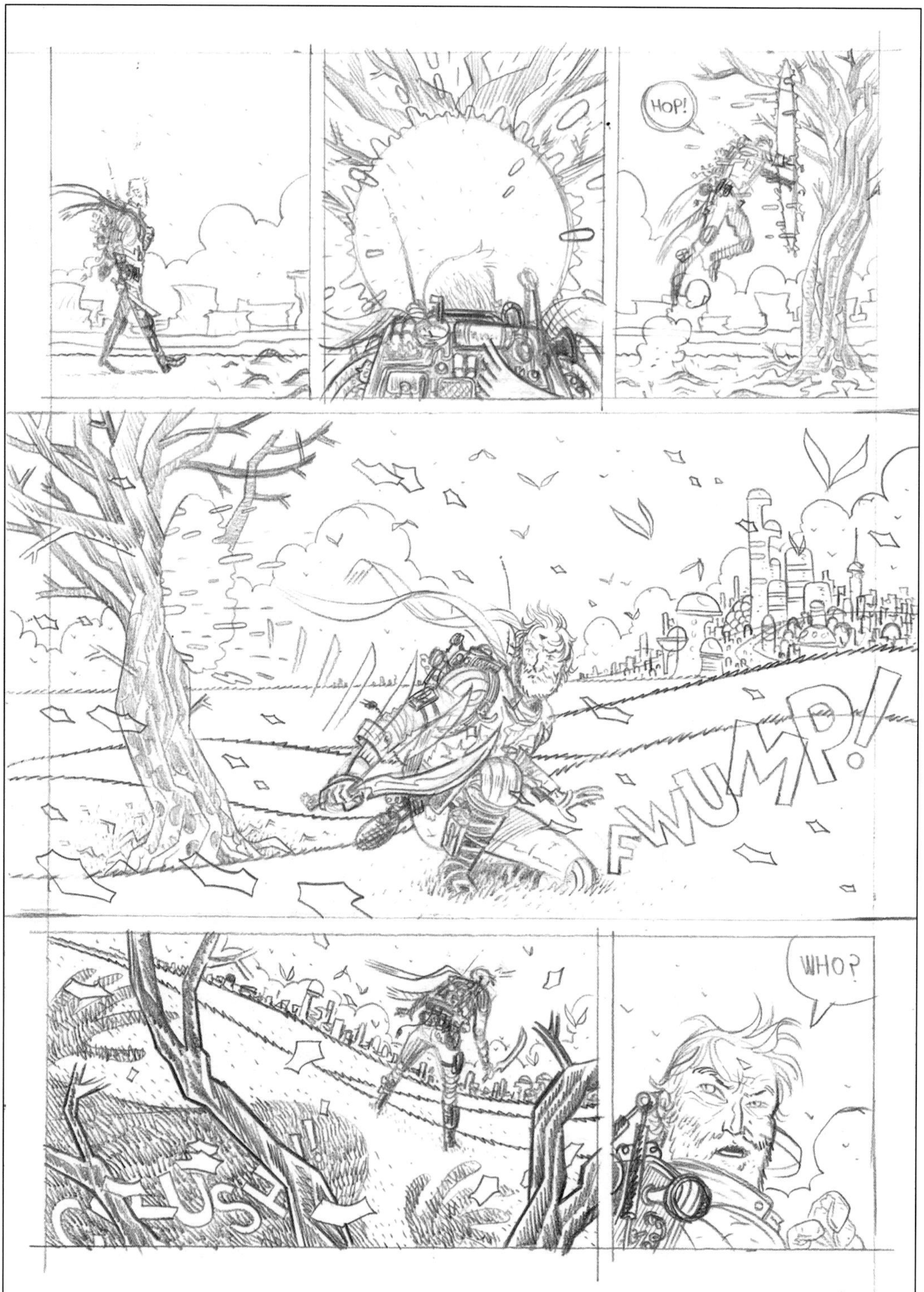
HOP!
FWUMP!
CLUSH!
WHO?
01.

David and I did this short story to sort of feel each other out and to establish a look for the book. Needless to say, I fell in love. The sound effects alone won me over.

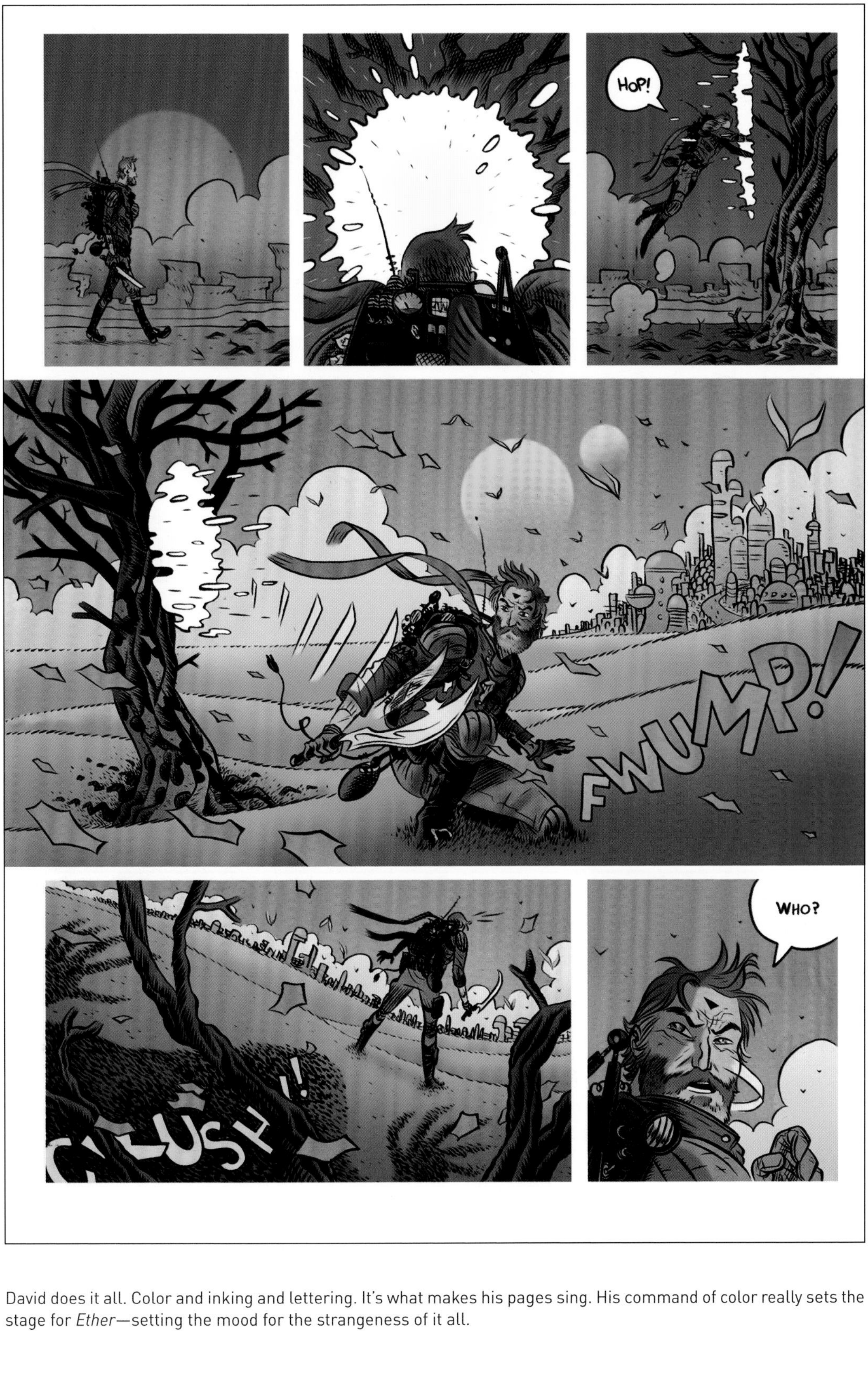
HOP!
FWUMP!
CHUSH!
WHO?

David does it all. Color and inking and lettering. It's what makes his pages sing. His command of color really sets the stage for *Ether*—setting the mood for the strangeness of it all.

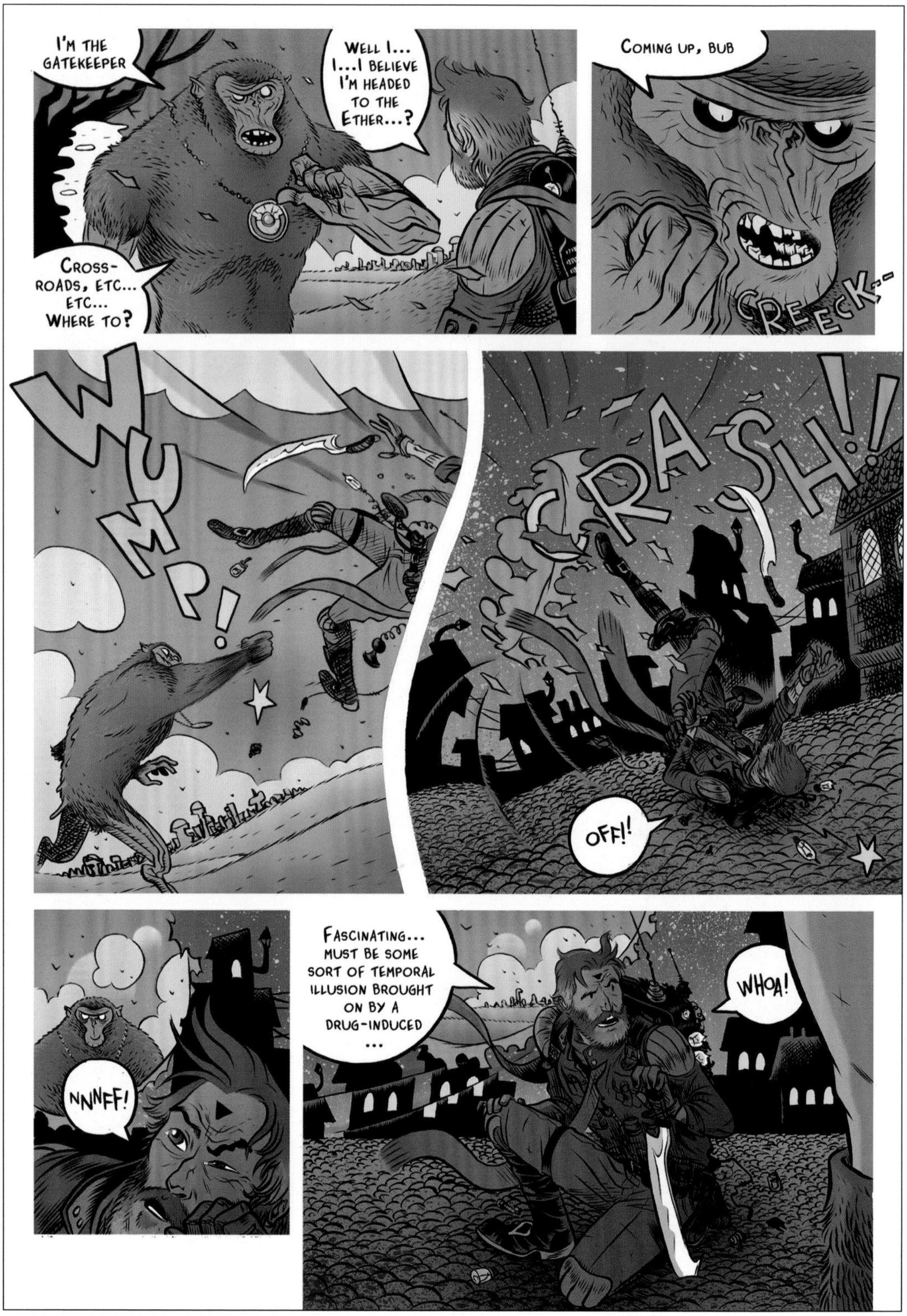
I'M THE GATEKEEPER
CROSS-ROADS, ETC... ETC... WHERE TO?
WELL I... I...I BELIEVE I'M HEADED TO THE ETHER...?
COMING UP, BUB
CREEECK--
WUMP!
CRASH!!
OFF!
NNNFF!
FASCINATING... MUST BE SOME SORT OF TEMPORAL ILLUSION BROUGHT ON BY A DRUG-INDUCED ...
WHOA!

Again, David is using layouts to great effect—playing with the panel gutter in the middle and then shifting the color to darker earth tones to illustrate the change of scene. This kind of storytelling is critical to a story like this that is jumping around from reality to reality and from strange setting to even stranger setting.

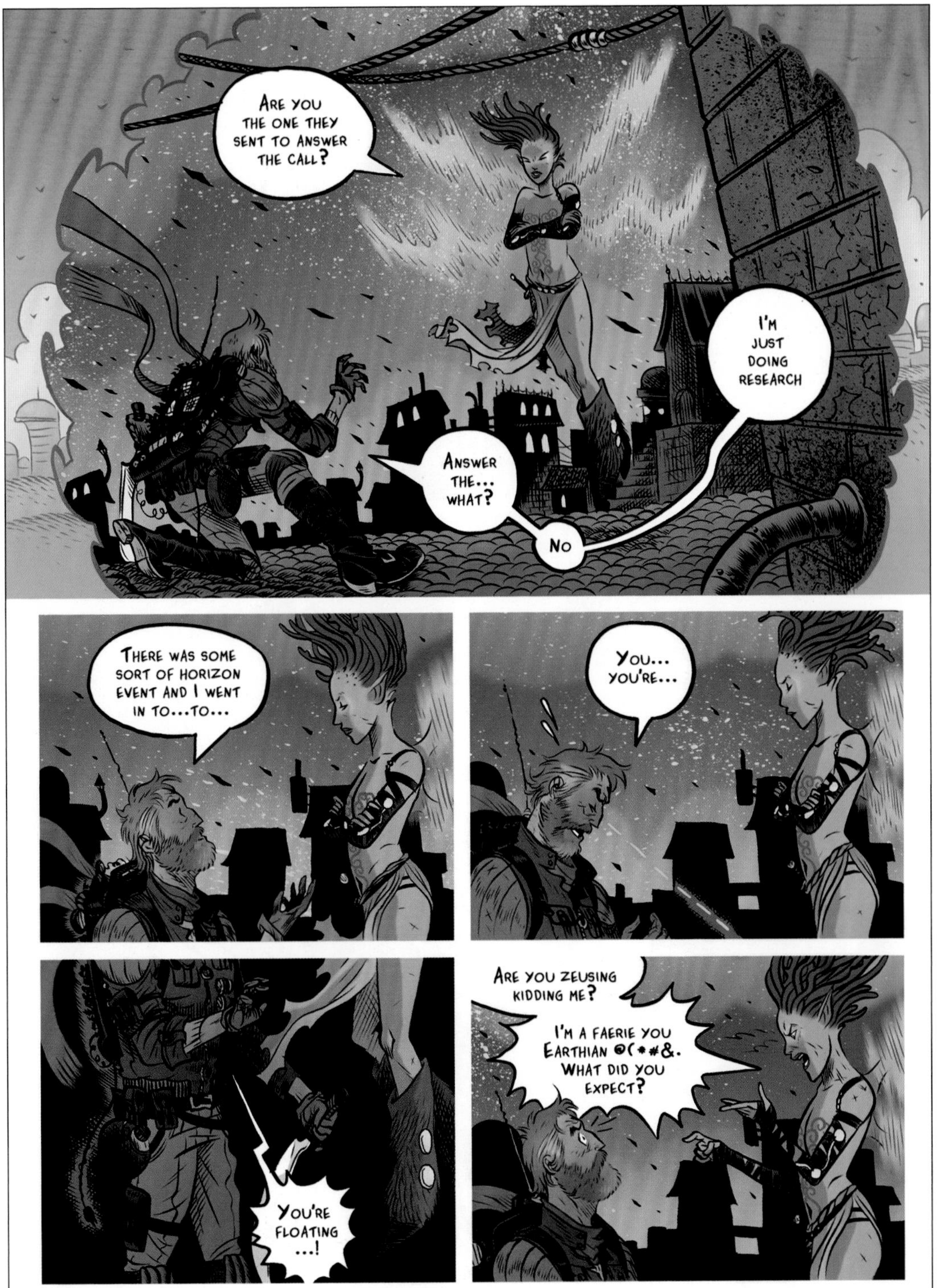

ARE YOU THE ONE THEY SENT TO ANSWER THE CALL?
ANSWER THE... WHAT?
NO
I'M JUST DOING RESEARCH
THERE WAS SOME SORT OF HORIZON EVENT AND I WENT IN TO...TO...
YOU... YOU'RE...
YOU'RE FLOATING ...!
ARE YOU ZEUSING KIDDING ME?
I'M A FAERIE YOU EARTHIAN @(*#&. WHAT DID YOU EXPECT?

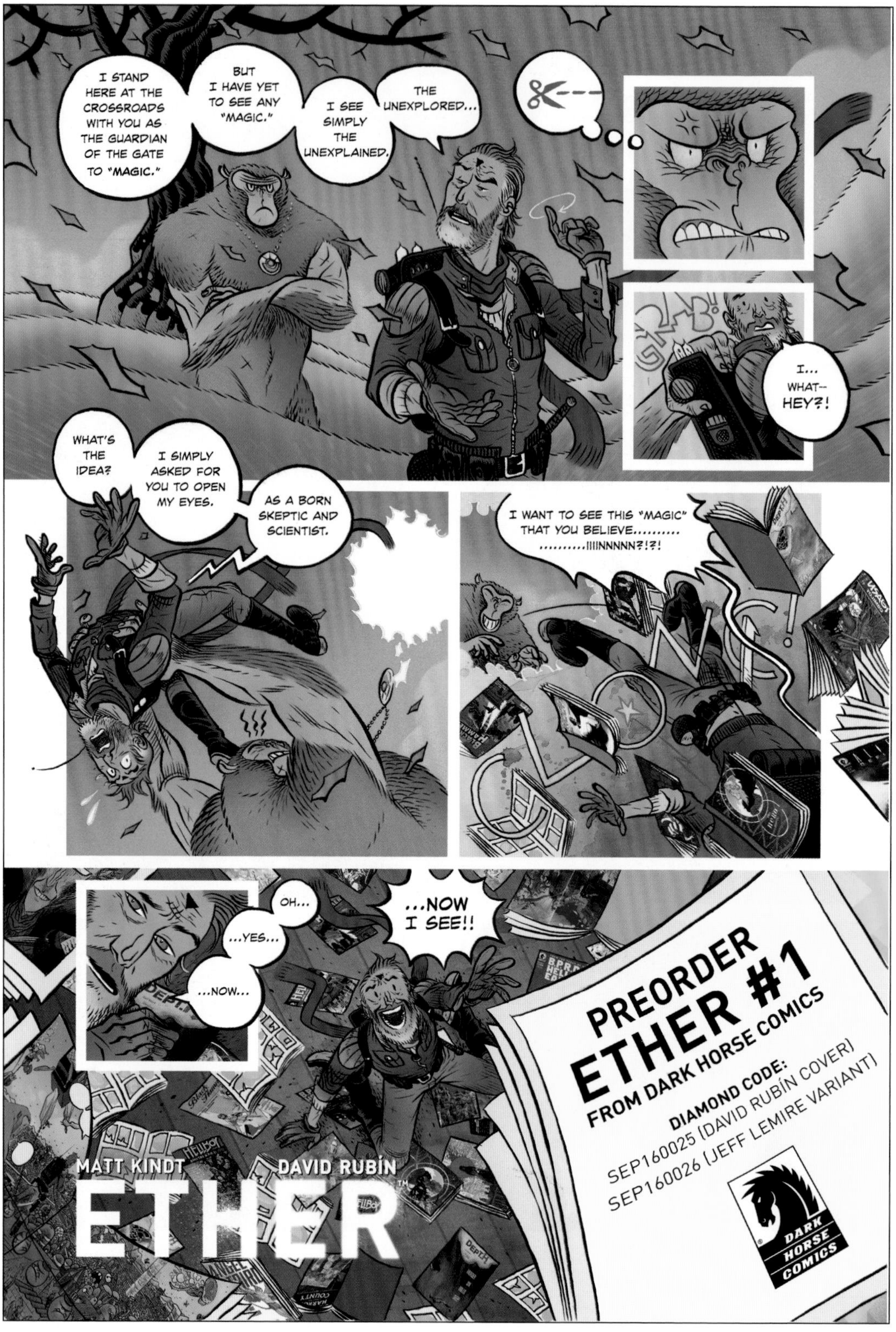
I STAND HERE AT THE CROSSROADS WITH YOU AS THE GUARDIAN OF THE GATE TO "MAGIC."
BUT I HAVE YET TO SEE ANY "MAGIC."
I SEE SIMPLY THE UNEXPLAINED.
THE UNEXPLORED...
I... WHAT-- HEY?!
WHAT'S THE IDEA?
I SIMPLY ASKED FOR YOU TO OPEN MY EYES.
AS A BORN SKEPTIC AND SCIENTIST.
I WANT TO SEE THIS "MAGIC" THAT YOU BELIEVE..........
..........IIIINNNNN?!?!
OH...
...YES...
...NOW...
...NOW I SEE!!
PREORDER
ETHER #1
FROM DARK HORSE COMICS
DIAMOND CODE:
SEP160025 (DAVID RUBÍN COVER)
SEP160026 (JEFF LEMIRE VARIANT)
MATT KINDT
DAVID RUBÍN
ETHER

This is all David. Nothing harder than a one-page story. We did this to promote the book before it was in stores. I absolutely love the "scissors" thought balloon that Glum has here. Glum and Boone scenes are my favorites.

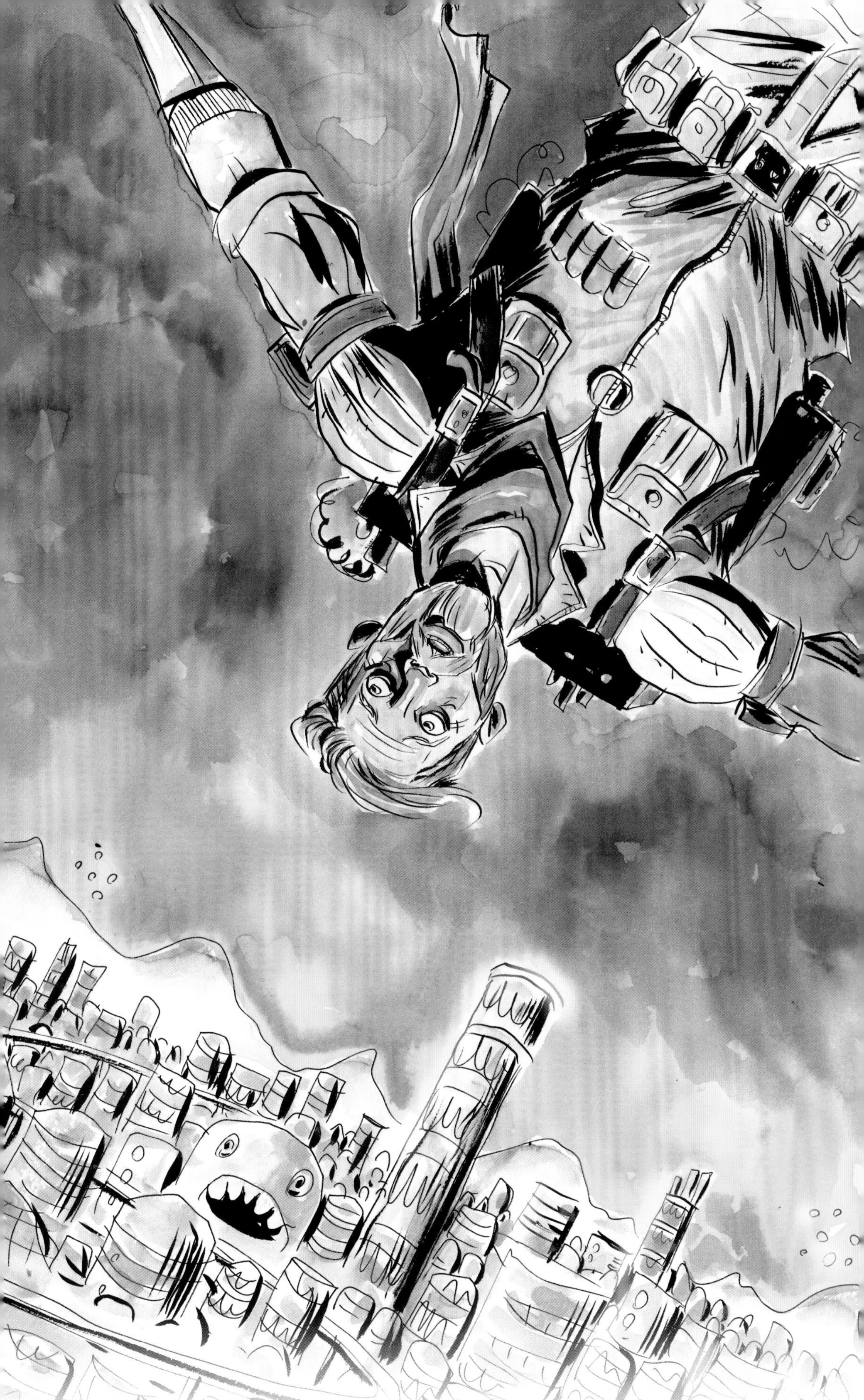

Ether #1 variant cover by **JEFF LEMIRE**

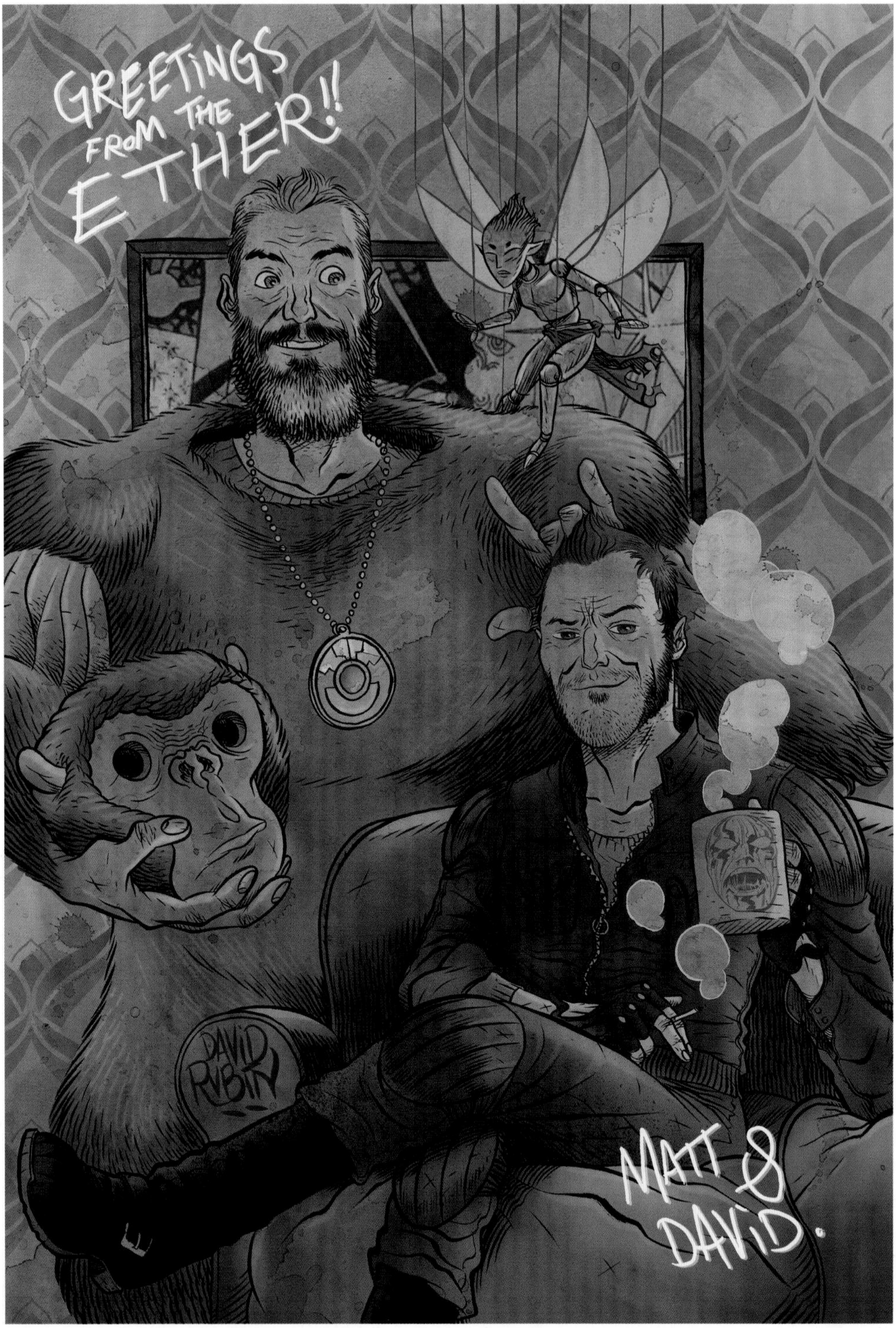
GREETINGS FROM THE ETHER!!
DAVID RUBIN
MATT & DAVID.

MATT KINDT is the *New York Times* best-selling writer and artist of the comics and graphic novels *Dept. H*, *MIND MGMT*, *Revolver*, *3 Story*, *Super Spy*, *2 Sisters*, and *Pistolwhip*, as well as *Justice League of America* (DC), *Spider-Man* (Marvel), and *Unity*, *Ninjak*, *Rai*, and *Divinity* (Valiant). He has been nominated for four Eisner and six Harvey Awards (and won once). His work has been published in French, Spanish, Italian, German, and Korean.

DAVID RUBÍN studied graphic design before entering the world of comics, animation, and illustration. He illustrated a collection of Robert E. Howard tales in *Solomon Kane* and immersed himself in a two-volume retelling of the myth of Hercules in *The Hero*. His latest published works include an adaptation of the epic poem *Beowulf*, two spinoffs of Paul Pope's *Battling Boy*, and *The Fiction* with writer Curt Pires. Along with Marcos Prior, he produced the graphic novel *Grand Hotel Abyss* while also working on *Ether*. He is currently working on chapters of Jeff Lemire's comic book series *Black Hammer*, with an expected release in late 2017.

matt kindt

"I'll read anything Kindt does."—Douglas Wolk, author of *Reading Comics*

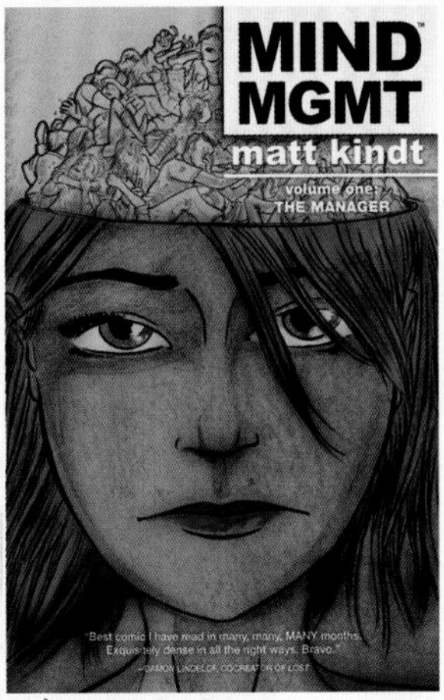

MIND MGMT
matt kindt
volume one: THE MANAGER

MIND MGMT
VOLUME 1: THE MANAGER
ISBN 978-1-59582-797-5
$19.99

VOLUME 2: THE FUTURIST
ISBN 978-1-61655-198-8
$19.99

VOLUME 3: THE HOME MAKER
ISBN 978-1-61655-390-6
$19.99

VOLUME 4: THE MAGICIAN
ISBN 978-1-61655-391-3
$19.99

VOLUME 5: THE ERASER
ISBN 978-1-61655-696-9
$19.99

VOLUME 6: THE IMMORTALS
ISBN 978-1-61655-798-0
$19.99

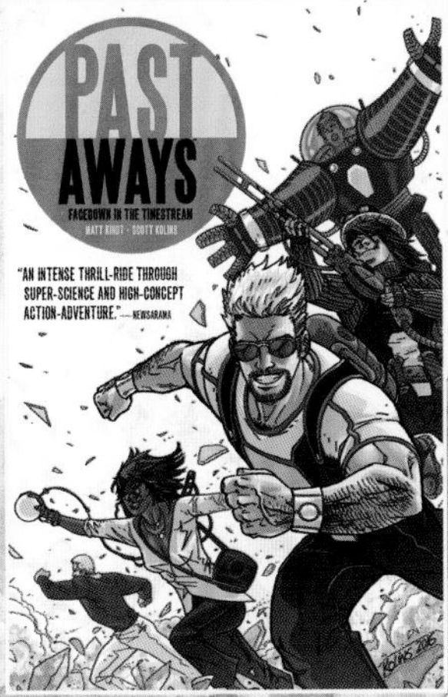

PAST AWAYS
FACEDOWN IN THE TIMESTREAM
MATT KINDT · SCOTT KOLINS
"AN INTENSE THRILL-RIDE THROUGH SUPER-SCIENCE AND HIGH-CONCEPT ACTION-ADVENTURE." —NEWSARAMA

POPPY! AND THE LOST LAGOON
With Brian Hurtt
ISBN 978-1-61655-943-4
$14.99

PAST AWAYS
With Scott Kolins
ISBN 978-1-61655-792-8
$19.99

THE COMPLETE PISTOLWHIP
With Jason Hall
ISBN 978-1-61655-720-1
$27.99

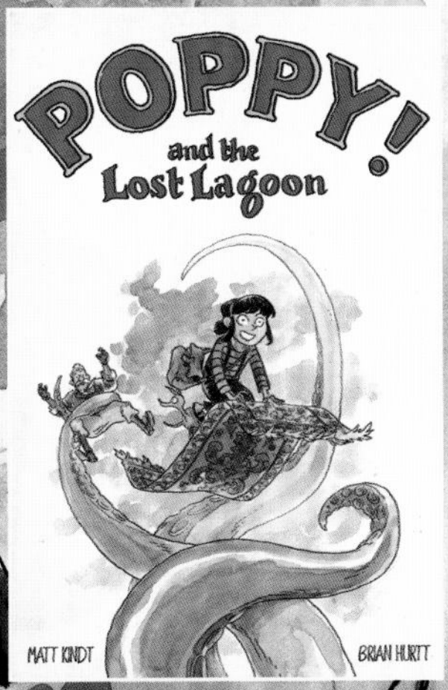

POPPY!
and the Lost Lagoon
MATT KINDT
BRIAN HURTT

3 STORY: THE SECRET HISTORY OF THE GIANT MAN
ISBN 978-1-59582-356-4
$19.99

2 SISTERS
ISBN 978-1-61655-721-8
$27.99

DEPT. H
VOLUME 1: PRESSURE
ISBN 978-1-61655-989-2
$19.99

VOLUME 2: AFTER THE FLOOD
ISBN 978-1-61655-990-8
$19.99

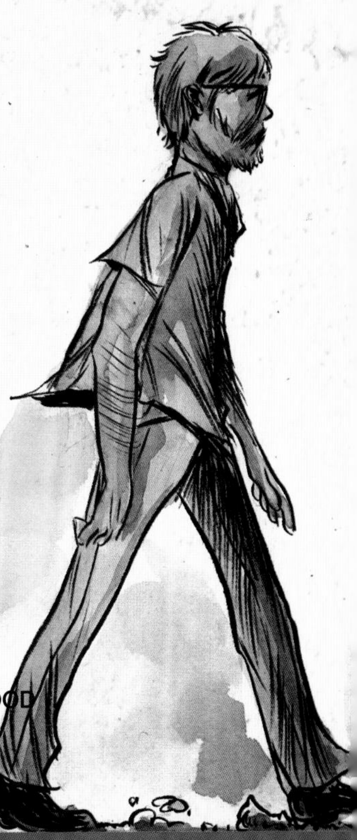

AVAILABLE AT YOUR LOCAL COMICS SHOP OR BOOKSTORE!

To find a comics shop in your area, call 1-888-266-4226. For more information or to order direct visit DarkHorse.com or call 1-800-862-0052 Mon.–Fri. 9 AM to 5 PM Pacific Time.

DARK HORSE BOOKS
DarkHorse.com

Also from **DAVID RUBÍN**!

THE HERO

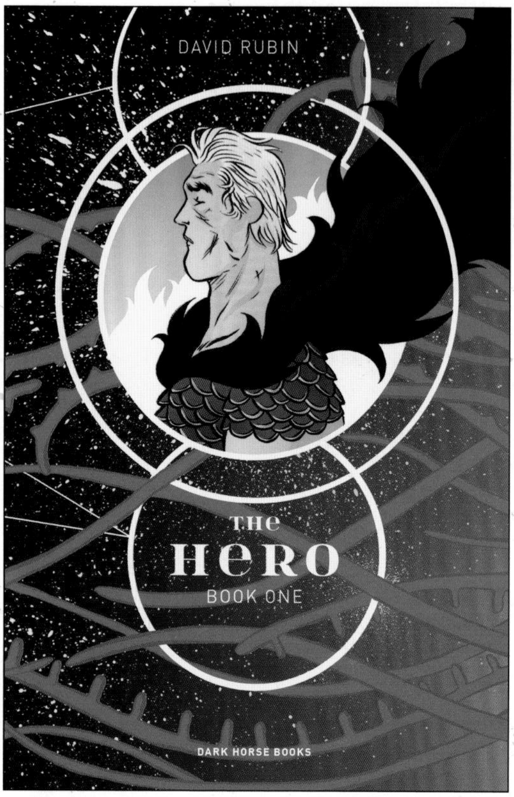
DAVID RUBIN
THE HERO
BOOK ONE
DARK HORSE BOOKS

THE HERO BOOK ONE

$24.99
978-1-61655-670-9

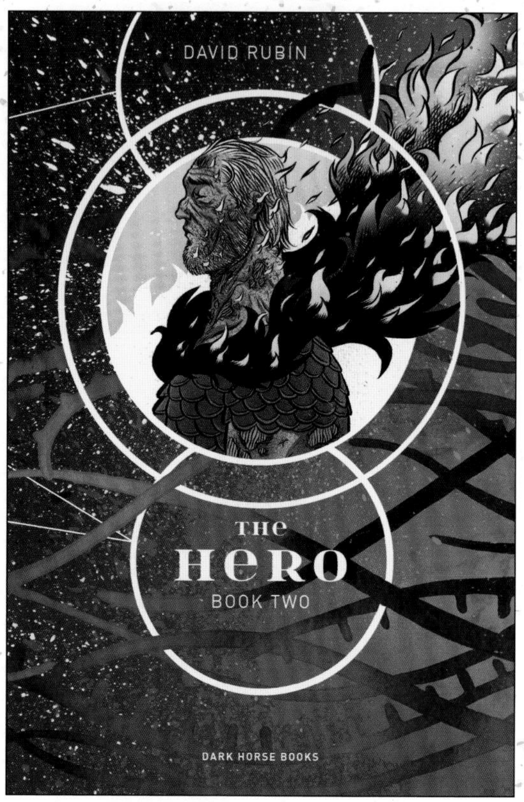
DAVID RUBÍN
THE HERO
BOOK TWO
DARK HORSE BOOKS

THE HERO BOOK TWO

$24.99
978-1-61655-791-1

In ancient Greece the first superhero was born. Heracles, the son of Zeus, came into the world with strength, charm, and a fighting spirit.

The Hero is a modern retelling of the world's greatest champion, and chronicles Heracles's incredible adventures, from his innocent boyhood to his meteoric rise to popularity as he tackles the Twelve Labors.

DARK HORSE BOOKS